Plautus' Poenulus

T0350028

MICHIGAN CLASSICAL COMMENTARIES

Patrick Paul Hogan
  A Student Commentary on Pausanias Book 1

Celia E. Schultz
  A Commentary on Cicero, *De Divinatione I*

Erin K. Moodie
  Plautus' *Poenulus*: A Student Commentary

Plautus' *Poenulus*

A Student Commentary

Erin K. Moodie

University of Michigan Press
Ann Arbor

Copyright © Erin K. Moodie 2015
All rights reserved

This book may not be reproduced, in whole or in part, including illustrations, in any form
(beyond that copying permitted by Sections 107 and 108 of the U.S. Copyright Law and except by
reviewers for the public press), without written permission from the publisher.

Published in the United States of America by the
University of Michigan Press
Manufactured in the United States of America
♾ Printed on acid-free paper

2018   2017   2016   2015   4   3   2   1

A CIP catalog record for this book is available from the British Library.

ISBN 978-0-472-11970-7 (hardcover : alk. paper)
ISBN 978-0-472-03642-4 (paper)

Acknowledgments

This project has benefitted tremendously from the comments, suggestions, and assistance of many people, to whom I wish to express my heartfelt thanks and appreciation. Chief among them are the students and professors who test-drove versions of the commentary and offered suggestions for improving it: Raffaella Dietz, Marvee Espiritu, Nichole Gracik, Alex Grieve, Brad Martin, and Neal Xu at Colgate University; Dave Burns, Max Dietrich, Kate Kiernan, Lauren Miller, Sam O'Donnell, and Andrew Rondeau at Williams College; and Max Goldman and his students at Vanderbilt University: Emily Beugelmans, Gavin Blasdel, Allison Erlinger, Margaret Funkhouser, Blaise Gratton, Eric Mentges, and Edward Nolan. I am grateful too for the metrical expertise of Angelo Mercado and the map-making prowess of Nicholas Rauh. Ellen Bauerle, Susan Cronin, and the editorial staff at the University of Michigan Press have been patient and very helpful, while the Press' anonymous reviewers pointed out my errors and provided invaluable advice regarding further reading and alternative phrasings. Any remaining errors are, alas, my own. Thank you also to Joanne Jan for her research assistance, to colleagues near and far, especially Edan Dekel and Meredith Hoppin at Williams College, to Joseph Farrell for first encouraging me to start, and to family and friends who supported me along the way. I owe the biggest debt of gratitude to Ted, the *sine quō nōn*, who inspired me to get this manuscript off my desk and out the door, and helped me to do so. *Ēcastor, maxumās gratiās tibi agō!*

Contents

Abbreviations

General Abbreviations

1-tr./intr.	First conjugation transitive/intransitive verb
A&G	Allen & Greenough's *New Latin Grammar*
CIL	*Corpus Inscriptionum Latinarum*
f	feminine
fr(r).	fragment(s)
incert.	incertum
K-A	Kassel and Austin's *Poetae Comici Graeci*
m	masculine
MS(S)	manuscript(s)
n	neuter
OCD	*Oxford Classical Dictionary*
OLD	*Oxford Latin Dictionary*
pl	plural

Classical Authors and Works

Apul.	Apuleius	
	Met.	*Metamorphoses*
Ar.	Aristophanes	
	Ach.	*Acharnenses (Acharnians)*
	Av.	*Aves (Birds)*
	Eccl.	*Ecclesiazusae*
	Nub.	*Nubes (Clouds)*
	Pax	*Pax (Peace)*
	Thesm.	*Thesmophoriazusae*
	Vesp.	*Vespae (Wasps)*

Arist.	Aristotle	
	Eth. Eud.	*Eudemian Ethics*
	Poet.	*Poetics*
[Arist.]	Pseudo-Aristotle	
	Pr.	*Problemata*
Caecil.	Caecilius Statius	
	Dem.	*Demandati*
Cato		
	Agr.	*De Agricultura*
Catull.	Catullus	
Cic.	Cicero	
	Att.	*Epistulae ad Atticum*
	Brut.	*Brutus*
	De Or.	*De Oratore*
	Phil.	*Philippicae*
Columella		
	Rust.	*De Re Rustica*
Dem.	Demosthenes	
Din.	Dinarchus	
Donat.	Donatus	
Eub.	Eubulus	
Eur.	Euripides	
	El.	*Electra*
	Med.	*Medea*
Gell.	Aulus Gellius	
	NA	*Noctes Atticae*
Hdt.	Herodotus	
Heliod.	Heliodorus	
	Aeth.	*Aethiopika*
Hom.	Homer	
	Il.	*Iliad*
	Od.	*Odyssey*
Hor.	Horace	
	Epist.	*Epistulae*
	Epod.	*Epodi*
	Sat.	*Satirae* or *Sermones*
Isid.	Isidore of Seville	
	Etym.	*Etymologiae* or *Origines*
Juv.	Juvenal	
Livy		
	Per.	*Periochae*

Men.	Menander	
	Aphr.	*Aphrodisia*
	Asp.	*Aspis*
	Dys.	*Dyskolos*
	Epit.	*Epitrepontes*
	Kith.	*Kitharistes*
	Kol.	*Kolax*
	Mis.	*Misoumenos*
	Pk.	*Perikeiromene*
	Sam.	*Samia*
	Sik.	*Sikyonioi*
Ov.	Ovid	
	Ars Am.	*Ars Amatoria*
	Fast.	*Fasti*
Petron.	Petronius	
	Sat.	*Satyricon*
Plato	Plato	
	Symp.	*Symposium*
Plautus		
	Amph.	*Amphitruo*
	Asin.	*Asinaria*
	Aul.	*Aulularia*
	Bac.	*Bacchides*
	Capt.	*Captiui*
	Cas.	*Casina*
	Cist.	*Cistellaria*
	Curc.	*Curculio*
	Epid.	*Epidicus*
	Men.	*Menaechmi*
	Merc.	*Mercator*
	Mil.	*Miles Gloriosus*
	Most.	*Mostellaria*
	Per.	*Persa*
	Pseud.	*Pseudolus*
	Rud.	*Rudens*
	Sti.	*Stichus*
	Trin.	*Trinummus*
	Truc.	*Truculentus*
	Vid.	*Vidularia*
Plin.	Pliny the Elder	
	HN	*Naturalis Historia*

Polyb.   Polybius
Quint.   Quintilian
          Inst.   *Institutio Oratoria*
Soph.   Sophocles
          Ant.   *Antigone*
          El.   *Electra*
          OT   *Oedipus Tyrannus*
Suet.   Suetonius
          Iul.   *Iulius*
Ter.   Terence
          Ad.   *Adelphoe*
          And.   *Andria*
          Eun.   *Eunuchus*
          Haut.   *Hauton Timoroumenos*
          Hec.   *Hecyra*
          Phor.   *Phormio*
Timocl.   Timocles
          Dion.   *Dionysiazusae*
Theocr.   Theocritus
          Adon.   *Adoniazusae*
Verg.   Vergil
          Aen.   *Aeneid*

Introduction

1. *The Roman Theater*

A. A BRIEF HISTORY OF THE THEATER IN ROME

i. Our Evidence

Residents of Rome during the Republic watched and enjoyed several different types of dramatic performance, and these performances were often integrated into the cultural life of the city. As a popular element of Roman culture, Roman theater became a frequent subject of representation, and thus our evidence comes from both physical objects and textual accounts. The material remains of Roman culture—buildings, mosaics, household items, funerary art—provide us with some information regarding where and how the plays were performed. The manuscripts containing the plays that do survive are of course important evidence as well, since the majority of surviving material comes from the comic poets Plautus and Terence, but so are the texts that contain later authors' observations on Roman drama. Such observations are found, for example, in the work of Roman historians and commentators, or in the *didascaliae*—production notices compiled in the first century BCE and later attached to manuscripts of Plautus and Terence.[1] Plautus' *Poenulus*—the focus of this commentary—belongs to the genre known as the *fābula palliāta* (comedy in Greek dress), which seems to be the only type of play that Plautus wrote. The *fābula palliāta* is the genre for which the greatest quantity of evidence, primarily textual, survives.

---

1. "The origins of the *didascaliae* are uncertain, but Leo's theory is most convincing: they are excerpts of longer *didascaliae*, probably produced by Varro for his *De rebus scaenicis*" [Leo 1883 318] (Moore 2012 9). While the *didascaliae* have not survived for every Plautine comedy, the *didascalia* for his *Stichus* illustrates the type of information they tend to contain: "The *Stichus* of Titus Maccius Plautus. From the Greek *Adelphoe* by Menander. Performed at the Plebeian Games, produced by the Plebeian Aediles Gnaeus Baebius and Gaius Terentius. Titus Publilius Pellio played the melodies. Marcipor the slave of Oppius played the whole thing on Syrian pipes. Gaius Sulpicius and Gaius Aurelius were consuls [200 BCE]."

ii. Scripted versus Nonscripted Genres

Roman dramatic performances could be either scripted or nonscripted, i.e., improvised. Nonscripted genres during the Republic included the mime and Atellan farce, both of which were improvised for each performance, but using stock characters and stock themes. The *fābula palliāta* was one of four scripted genres performed during the Republic: two were tragic and two comic, and the plays were either set in Rome or were set in Greece and based on a Greek model. That the Romans, or at least the playwrights who worked for them, took Greek plays and adapted them for Roman tastes is entirely consistent with their general appropriation and transformation of Greek culture, which intensified during the late third century BCE.[2]

Categories of Scripted Theater (*Fābula*) in Rome

Fābula ("play" or "story")	Comedy	Tragedy
Greek Setting (Usually based on a Greek play)	*Palliāta*: means "in a *pallium*" (a Greek cloak), the plays adapted Greek New Comedies.	*Cothurnāta*: means "in *cothurni*" (platform shoes), the plays adapted Greek tragedies.
Roman/Italian Setting	*Togāta*: means "in a *toga*" (what Roman citizens wore), this genre developed slightly later than the *palliāta*.	*Praetex(tā)ta*: means "in a *toga praetexta*" (what Roman senators wore), the plays portrayed Roman historical subjects.

iii. Theater-Centric Timeline

The following timeline lists the dates of the most famous theatrical events in or related to Rome, along with the major military or political events that helped shape Roman culture.

A Theater-Centric Timeline of Roman History

- 753 BCE: Rome founded, rule by kings begins
- 510–509 BCE: End of regal period, beginning of Republic
- ca. 375–ca. 275 BCE: Lifetime of Alexis, a Greek poet who wrote in the genre we call "Greek New Comedy," and whose play *Karchedonios* served as a model for Plautus' *Poenulus*
- ca. 344/3–292/1 BCE: Lifetime of Menander, another author of Greek New Comedy
- 272 BCE: Fall of Tarentum

---

2. See Wallace-Hadrill 2008.

- 264–241 BCE: First Punic War against Carthage
- 240 BCE: First adaptations of Greek drama in Rome by Livius Andronicus, author of some *palliāta* comedy, but mostly *cothurnāta* tragedy
- ca. 235–ca. 204 BCE: Career of Gn. Naevius, author of *cothurnāta* and *praetexta* tragedy, but mostly *palliāta* comedy, who lived ca. 270–ca. 201 BCE
- 218–201 BCE: Second Punic War
- ca. 205–184 BCE: Career of T. Macc(i)us Plautus, author of *palliāta* comedy (twenty near-complete plays survive), who lived ca. 254–184 BCE
- ca. 204–169 BCE: Career of Q. Ennius, author of mostly *cothurnāta* tragedy, who lived 239–169 BCE
- 194 BCE: Roman senators first sit separately at the theater
- First half of second century BCE: Lifetime of Titinius, author of *togāta* comedy
- 179–168 BCE: Career of Caecilius Statius, author of *palliāta* comedy
- 166–160 BCE: Career of P. Terentius Afer, author of *palliāta* comedy (six complete plays survive), who lived ca.195/185–159 BCE
- mid-second century BCE: Career of M. Pacuvius, who perhaps only wrote tragedy, in any case mostly *cothurnāta*, and lived 220–ca. 130 BCE
- 149–146 BCE: Third Punic War
- 140–86(?) BCE: Career of L. Accius, author of tragedy, mostly *cothurnāta*, and works about drama, who lived 170–ca. 86 BCE
- Second half of second century BCE: Lifetime of L. Afranius, author of *togāta* comedy
- 103 BCE: Death of Turpilius, author of *palliāta* comedy
- 77 BCE: Death of T. Quinctius Atta, author of *togāta* comedy
- 55 BCE: Completion of construction of Pompey's theater in Rome
- 44 BCE: Assassination of Julius Caesar; revival performances of Plautine comedy end
- 31 BCE: Battle of Actium
- 29 BCE: Production date of Varius Rufus' *Thyestes*, a *cothurnāta* tragedy
- Late first century BCE: Livius Andronicus and Terence are still used as school texts; P. Ovidius Naso writes *Medea*, a *cothurnāta* tragedy
- ca. 4 BCE–65 CE: Lifetime of L. Annaeus Seneca the Younger, author of *cothurnāta* tragedy
- Third or fifth century CE: Illustrations of Terentian comedies are drawn that become the source for the illustrations in manuscripts made during the Middle Ages.[3]

---

3. Dutsch 2007 40–41; the dates refer to, respectively, Dodwell (2000 1–21), and Jones and Morey (1930–31 42–45).

- Fourth century CE: Aelius Donatus writes a commentary on Terence; revival performances of Terentian comedy may end.
- ca. 400 CE: Composition of *Querolus, sive Aulularia*, a new type of prose comedy
- 410 CE: Sack of Rome by Visigoths

B. THE *PALLIĀTA* PLAYS: ADAPTATIONS OF GREEK MODELS

i. Greek "New Comedy," Stock Characters, Common Themes, and Adaptation Process

Playwrights like Plautus and Terence, who worked in the *fābula palliāta* genre, based their comedies on Greek plays from the genre we know as New Comedy (as opposed to the "Old Comedy" of Aristophanes and his contemporaries).[4] New Comedy was written and performed in Athens during the fourth–third centuries BCE by poets such as Alexis (ca. 375–ca. 275 BCE), Philemon (368/60–267/63 BCE), Diphilus (ca. 360/50–early third c. BCE), and Menander (ca. 344/3–292/1 BCE). The genre portrayed stock characters sorting through issues of marriage and citizenship in Athens or other Greek cities and colonies, such as Epidamnus or Epidaurus. These stock characters persisted in the Roman versions adapted from the Greek comedies as well and included the following types:

- old men—either harsh or easy-going;
- mercenary soldiers—a manifestation of the mercenaries recruited to fight in the multiple wars waged across the Greek world in the fourth–third centuries BCE, who could become very rich from the plunder they acquired;[5]
- pimps—usually also slave-dealers;
- young men—their love for a young woman, citizen or not, is usually what drives the plot;
- parasites—flattering moochers who make a living by buttering up wealthy men like soldiers;
- wives—many search for lost daughters or attempt to thwart their husbands' pursuit of extra-marital affairs;
- young women—few free young women appear on the comic stage, but some prostitutes and slaves who are the love-objects of the young men are

---

4. I follow Manuwald in my preference for the phrases "Greek model" and "Greek predecessor" to "Greek original," which wrongly "implies that the Greek play is the 'true' and 'real' play and the Latin play is a reproduction at best" (Manuwald 2011 283n3).

5. The stock character survived into the Roman comedies even though the Roman army did not employ mercenaries as the various Greek armies had.

discovered to be citizens during the course of the play and thus eligible for marriage under Athenian law;

- madams and female prostitutes—who can be slaves or free women and either wicked or good-hearted;
- cooks—free men or slaves who are hired to prepare the feasts for the weddings or religious ceremonies;
- male slaves—who can be obedient or disobedient/too clever; and
- female slaves—who are often young.

These stock characters remained popular in the Roman adaptations of Greek New Comedy, as can be seen in lines 35–42 of the prologue from Terence's *Hauton Timorumenos*, where the Prologue-speaker declares, "Observe calmly, and give me the chance to act a calm play as it should be acted—to silence, so that The Running Slave, or The Angry Old Man, or The Hungry Parasite, or, on the other hand, The Shameless Trickster, or The Greedy Pimp, do not always have to be acted by me—an old man—constantly in the loudest voice and with the greatest effort. For my sake, suppose that this cause is just, so that some part of my work may be decreased."[6]

The most common themes found in the *palliāta* comedy and its Greek models include love, recognition, misunderstandings, and deception.[7] In addition, Plautus' comedies tend to emphasize the overturning of social norms, and both Plautus and Terence like to play with the well-known structures, themes, and character-types of the genre; this self-aware play with the genre is known as "metatheater" and is another common theme of their comedy. New Comedies often began with a prologue delivered by an omniscient divinity who provided the necessary background information for the plot and often guaranteed the audience a happy ending. Roman poets occasionally preserved the prologue but often abbreviated it or changed its contents so that the audience was kept in suspense about the happy ending; this is Terence's usual practice, for example.

Plautus himself referred to the adaptation process using the verb *uertere*, "to turn, transform, translate," but also self-deprecatingly referred to the Latin language as "barbarian," employing the same term that Greeks used about all non-Greek languages. Plautus' *Trinummus*, lines 18–20, preserves one of the

---

6. Compare the prologue to Plautus' *Menaechmi*, lines 72–76, which points out both the "stock"ness of the comic characters and the generic nature of the set: "This city is Epidamnus, while this play is being performed: when another play is performed, it will become a different town. In the same way the families are also accustomed to change: now a pimp lives here, now a young man, now an old man, a poor man, a beggar, a king, a parasite, a soothsayer."

7. Recognition means that a character—usually a young woman—is recognized as a citizen and thus becomes eligible for a proper marriage under Athenian law. As McCarthy (2000 161–62) notes, the possibility that this young woman will become a prostitute and therefore lose her opportunity to become a citizen wife creates the tension in plays centering on recognition.

best examples, in which the Prologue-speaker declares, "The name of this play in Greek is *Thesaurus* (*Treasure-box*): Philemon wrote it, Plautus translated it into 'barbarian,' and named it *Trinummus* (*Three-penny Day*)."[8] The *Trinummus'* prologue also reveals that the Latin version of a play did not necessarily employ the same title as its Greek model or even a close translation of it.

ii. Types of Changes Made for Adaptations

The first step in the adaptation process was to choose a model from which to work. Before translating a play into Latin and modifying it to fit Roman performance conventions (both form and context) it was also essential for Roman playwrights to pay attention to what contemporary Roman audiences knew and wanted. The choice of which play to adapt was an important one, and—along with the decision of how to adapt the script itself—shows that Roman playwrights were creative individuals in their own right, in touch with their audiences and the magistrates who bought their scripts.[9]

Plautus, Terence, and the other playwrights of the *fābula palliāta* usually preserved the setting of the Greek model they were adapting, although they could also choose to set the play in a different Greek city.[10] Roman playwrights also seem to have modified the contents of the plays during the adaptation process. We are only able to compare the Roman versions with their Greek models in two cases, but the contrasts are instructive. First, a relatively recent papyrus find has given us some of Menander's *Dis Exapaton* (*The Double-Deceiver*), on which Plautus based his play *Bacchides*.[11] Next, the second-century CE writer Aulus Gellius (at *Noctēs Atticae* 2.23) actually contrasts a scene from Caecilius Statius' *Plocium* with its Greek predecessor *Plokion* (*The Necklace*) by Menander. By comparing the Latin versions with the Greek (and also by considering what the Greek New Comedies and Plautine and Terentian comedies tend to look like), we can tell that the adaptation process usually involved a) increasing the quantity of word-play, verbal jokes, and puns; b) increasing the amount of the play that was accompanied by *tībia* music (see below); c) removing the choral interludes that came between the act divisions—the *fābula palliāta* wasn't

---

8. *huic Graece nomen est Thensauro fabulae:* / *Philemo scripsit, Plautus uortit barbare,* / *nomen Trinummo fecit* . . . Cf. *Asinaria* 10–12: *huic nomen graece Onagost fabulae;* / *Demophilus scripsit, Maccus uortit barbare;* / *Asinariam uolt esse, si per uos licet.* "In Greek, the name for this play is *Donkey-Driver*; Demophilus wrote it, Plautus translated it into barbarian; he wants it to be *The One about Donkeys*, if you allow it." The text is that of Lindsay 1904–5.

9. See Manuwald 2011 284.

10. See note 58 below, e.g.

11. The fragments were first published as Handley 1968, but it has since been re-edited and was officially published as Handley 1997.

divided into acts at all; d) deleting or rearranging lines or scenes as necessary; e) increasing the role of stock characters such as the clever slave; f) adding references to Rome and—ironically—Greece; and g) increasing the quantity of metatheatrical language.[12] Plautus' comedies also feature far more metrical variation than the work of his Greek predecessors does, while Terence's use of meter is more similar to that of Greek New Comedy.

iii. Other Influences: Native Italian and Other Theatrical Traditions

Many of these methods of modification may have been inspired by other theatrical traditions found throughout Italy, such as the mime and Atellan farce. Mime performance (*mīmus*), which consisted of improvised imitation of scenes from daily life by unmasked male and female actors,[13] originated in the Greek world and probably spread from the Greek colonies of southern Italy throughout the peninsula. It also included stock characters: the husband, his cheating wife, the wife's maid, and the wife's lover. Major themes included love and/or adultery; tricksters and deceivers; and a character's change from poor to wealthy. During the early years of the Republic the mime was considered quite lowbrow, but the genre became more literary, i.e., performances became scripted, in the mid-first century BCE.

The Atellan farce (*fābula Atellāna*), so called because it was associated with the town of Atella in southern Italy, also featured stock characters, but different ones from the *fābula palliāta* and Greek New Comedy. It was also improvised—by masked male actors—at every performance, based on the typical characteristics of the stock characters. The stock Atellan characters included the gluttonous Manducus, the foolish Bucco, the clown Maccus, and the old man Pappus. Sometimes these characters were put into funny scenes from daily life similar to the mime, but they were also inserted into well-known myths. Atellan farce was associated with Oscan, an Italic language similar to Latin that was spoken in southern Italy, but was usually performed in Latin in Rome. Like the mime, it had a lowbrow reputation, and it also moved from improvisation to scripted shows in the early first century BCE.

Many of the characteristics of the Atellan farce influenced the *fābula*

---

12. The last three types of modification are mainly true for Plautus. See, e.g., Damen 1992. The prominence of the slave hero in Roman comedy may be due to the increased numbers of freedmen in Plautus' time and their incorporation into the various tribes at Rome (Richlin 2014 208, building off Rawson 1993 229).

13. Marshall (2006 8) notes that inscription *CIL*14.2408 refers to a female leader of a mime troupe and Manuwald (2011 183) notes that Mark Antony had a torrid affair with a mime actress (Cic. *Phil.* 2.58).

palliāta, which often exaggerated the Greek stock characters into more extreme and therefore more humorous forms so they were more similar to their Atellan counterparts. The themes of trickery and deceit from the mime (and its deceptive slave) may have influenced *palliāta* comedy as well.

Theatrical performances at Rome were also likely influenced by the Etruscan people, who lived north of Rome. Although Livy 7.2.3–4 indicates that the origins of dramatic performance in Rome are linked to Etruscan performers, his account may not be completely factual. On the other hand, the theatrical terms *histrio* ("actor"), *lūdius* ("stage actor"), *persōna* ("mask; character"), and *scaena* ("stage") seem to have been Etruscan in origin.[14]

C. THE PLACE: PERFORMANCE CONTEXTS

i. Religious Festivals, Votive Games, and Funerals

Festival "games" (*lūdī*) at Rome could feature dramatic performances of various types (*lūdī scaenicī*, a term used to refer to all of the scripted and unscripted theatrical performances discussed above) or athletic contests of various types (*lūdī circensēs*, a term used to refer to footraces, chariot races, boxing, wrestling, etc.). These festival games were held in three different contexts, each of which had its own name: at a public festival in honor of a deity (*lūdī sollemnēs*), or more rarely, to fulfill a promise made to a god during war or another period of dire need (*lūdī uōtīuī*), or as part of the funeral of a wealthy individual (*lūdī fūnēbrēs*).[15] These *lūdī* were held in various locations around the city of Rome as well as in the Campus Martius just to the northwest of the Capitoline hill. (See the chart below for further information.) For example, we know that the *lūdī Rōmānī* were held in the Roman forum, so lines 470–84 of the Stage-manager's speech in Plautus' *Curculio* hint strongly that the *Curculio* was in fact performed at that festival, since he describes many of the sites in and around that forum:

> Let him who wishes to meet with a perjured man go into the assembly; let him who wishes to meet with a liar and a conceited man seek at the shrine of Cloacina, let him seek rich or prodigal husbands beneath the basilica. In

---

14. Manuwald 2011 24–25. *Ludius* seems to have developed like *ludus* and other derivatives. As Yon noticed, the term *ludus* implies an activity practiced "outside all practical aims," which has no defined goals and is a "free and disinterested" copy or imitation of a real act. Thus dance and theater represents, in a stylized fashion, the everyday events of real life (Yon 1940 393, cited at Zucchelli 1964 25–26, my translation). See Marshall 2006 5–15 for more on the mime, Atellan farce, and other potential influences (both Greek and native Italian) on Roman comedy. Among these potential influences are the Fescennine verses. See, e.g., Hor. *Epist.* 2.1.139–63, where they're suggested as a native quasi-dramatic form.

15. Terence's *Adelphoe*, for example, was first staged at the funeral games in honor of L. Aemilius Paulus in 160 BCE.

the same place will be the older gigolos and those accustomed to bargain; contributors to feasts are in the fish forum. The good and wealthy men walk in the lower forum; the mere boasters are in the middle because of the sewer channel; above the lake are the impudent, the talkative, and the envious, who boldly issue insults at one another for no reason and who possess sufficient cause for a true attack against themselves. Below the old buildings, there are located the men who give and who receive money with interest. Behind the temple of Castor, there are those whom it would be a mistake to trust suddenly. On the Vicus Tuscus, there are the men who sell themselves repeatedly. In the Velabrum [you might find] either a baker or a butcher or a soothsayer or men of the sort who fence goods—or offer them to others when things are fenced.[16]

In Plautus' time, four public religious festivals featured performances of scripted drama (see the chart below).[17] These festivals provided the religious context for dramatic performances, both temporally and in terms of location: performances took place on temporary stages near the temple of the god being honored, either in or around the Roman Forum or in or around the Circus Maximus or the Circus Flaminius in the Campus Martius. Note that the lack of uniform performance venues meant that plays must have been able to be performed on any temporary stage. The connection between religion and theater was one of the main reasons that a permanent performance space wasn't built in Rome until Pompey erected his theater/temple complex in 55 BCE: a permanent theater "would have prevented the holding of performances in front of the temples of the gods of the various festivals or in the Forum at the heart of the community (unless permanent theatres were built in every possible location)."[18] Additionally, there was a political reason for the delay in permanent theaters at Rome: by making the annual construction of theaters depend on the work of the politicians, the Roman elite demonstrated its power and perhaps its control over the arts in Rome.[19] However, it is important to note that Roman comedy—or perhaps any type of drama—was never the main event at these *lūdī*: the circus games probably drew a much larger crowd!

Given that plays were often staged at religious festivals, it is important to mention the concept of *instaurātio*—the repetition of a religious ritual because the previous attempt was interrupted or marred by an error. Historical records

---

16. I follow Taylor 1995 356 in the analysis of this line as referring to fencing stolen property since it offers a wider variety of vices on display. Richlin 2005 105 argues that the line implies male prostitution. The Latin is ambiguous.

17. Mimes were performed at the *lūdī Flōrālēs* though, and some performances likely occurred at the *lūdī Ceriālēs* too.

18. Manuwald 2011 60.

19. See Gruen 1992 209–10.

relate that many religious festivals were repeated during the years when Plautus was active, which suggests that his plays were so popular that the officials, or perhaps even the actors, used *instaurātio* as an excuse to perform the comedies more often.[20]

The following chart summarizes the evidence for the festivals that featured scripted dramatic performance during Plautus' lifetime. That is, it omits the *lūdī Cereālēs* and *Florālēs*, for which there is insufficient evidence for performance of scripted theater in Plautus' time. Note that the Roman calendar was four months out of sync with the solar year and thus our modern Gregorian calendar in the third–second centuries BCE.

Thus, Plautus must have had the opportunity to present his work on at least nine different performance days over the course of three festivals each year. After 194 BCE, his opportunities increased to between eleven and fifteen days over the course of four annual festivals.[21] It is quite unlikely that the professional acting troupes would be able to support themselves with even fifteen performance days each year, so scholars posit that they supplemented their income with private contracts or by traveling to other cities near Rome for performances at other public festivals or market days.[22] Furthermore, it is not clear how many plays were performed at each festival, how many plays were performed on each day devoted to dramatic performances at a festival, whether there were multiple genres performed at each festival, and whether there were any stipulations regarding the relative proportions of each genre performed at a festival.[23]

ii. Temporary Theaters

While the remains of many fine Roman theaters survive around the Mediterranean, all of these stone theaters date to the late Republican and Imperial periods. During Plautus and Terence's time, scripted drama was performed on temporary wooden stages expressly built—and paid for—by the person sponsoring the show. Tacitus describes part of the set-up at *Annals* 14.20: "For before, the games used to be produced with hastily-built tiers and stage built for a short time; or if you should look to even older practices, they report that the people watched while standing since [it was feared that] idleness would last for entire days if one should sit down at the theater." Goldberg has argued convincingly that much of the theatrical audience at the Megalesian

---

20. Taylor 1937 291–98, Beacham 1991 158–59, Duckworth 1994 78. Cf. Livy 31.4.5, and a catalogue of *instaurātiōnēs* at Cohee 1994 466–68.

21. Marshall 2006 17.

22. Taylor 1937 303–4; Richlin 2005 23; Goldberg 2005 65.

23. Manuwald 2011 47.

Festivals That Featured Scripted Dramatic Performance during Plautus' Lifetime

Festival Name	Public Official in Charge	First Theatrical Shows at the Festival in . . .	Festival Scheduled for the Month of . . .	Festival Actually Held in What We Know as . . .	Number of Days of Theatrical Performance	Likely Location of Temporary Theater
lūdī Rōmānī (Roman Games)	curule aedile	240 BCE	September	May[1]	4[2]	Roman Forum or Circus Maximus
lūdī Plēbēiī (Plebeian Games)	plebeian aedile	Probably 220s, annual ca. 216 BCE[3]	November	July	≥ 3	Circus Flaminius (Campus Martius)
lūdī Apollinārēs (Games of Apollo)	urban praetor	212, annual in 208 BCE[4]	July	March	≥ 2	Temple of Apollo, Circus Maximus or Flaminius (Campus Martius)[5]
lūdī Megalēnsēs (Megalesian Games)	curule aedile	194 BCE[6]	April	December	2–6[7]	Temple of Magna Mater (Capitoline Hill)
[*lūdī uōtīuī*] (votive games)	not specified	after a vow in time of need, or at a new temple's dedication	any	any	varied	varied
[*lūdī fūnēbrēs*] (funeral games)	none— family member of deceased	soon after death, or on a significant anniversary	any	any	varied	often in Forum Romanum

1. Marshall 2006 17.

2. A theatrical performance was first staged during the *lūdī Rōmānī* in 240 BCE (Cic. *Brut.*72), but the number of theatrical performances was expanded to last for four days as of 214 BCE (Livy 24.43.7)—Marshall 2006 16.

3. Cf. Livy 23.30.17 and Livy *Per.* 20. Plautus' *Stichus* was performed at the *lūdī plebeiī* in 200 BCE.

4. The games were first established in response to prophesies stating that the Romans would defeat the Carthaginians if they established a festival for Apollo using Greek rites—see Palmer 1997 68 for additional details. Thus a performance of the *Poenulus* at the *lūdī Apollinārēs*—see the note for line 1291—would send some very mixed messages!

5. See Marshall 2006 38 for a discussion of why the Circus Maximus may no longer be the site of the games by Plautus' day.

6. The Megalesian Games were first held in 204 BCE, but in 194 BCE became an annual event and also incorporated theatrical performances for the first time (Livy 29.14.14, 34.54.3)—Marshall 2006 17, where he also notes that Plautus' *Pseudolus* (191 BCE), Terence's *Hecyra* (165 BCE), and probably Plautus' *Trinummus* were all performed at these games.

7. Our evidence is not entirely clear. See Marshall 2006 17.

Games actually sat or stood on the steps of the temple to the Magna Mater, while the stage was erected on the triangular platform in front of temple.[24] Theatrical performances at festivals honoring other deities were also likely to have exploited existing structures to provide seating for the audience. These included the Temple to Apollo in the Campus Martius, even the Comitium in the Roman Forum.[25] It is unclear how elaborate these early stages were, though more complex wooden theaters began to be built in the later Republic. Until the construction of Pompey's theater in 55 BCE, attempts to build permanent stone theaters in Rome were stymied by politicians who warned that a permanent theater would harm Roman morals. However, it is more likely that these politicians were very aware that it was good showmanship and politics to be responsible for the creation of the whole theater, not just the show performed within it, so they tried to maintain control of that aspect of the festivals as well.[26] There were also religious reasons for the annual construction of the performance spaces at religious festivals, as was discussed above. That early Roman dramatic performances employed little more than a stage and some benches or temple steps can perhaps be inferred from the terminology of the theater itself: the frequent reference to the stage (*scaena, proscaenium*) in Plautine comedy, as well as the stage-related terminology for dramatic festivals (*lūdī scaenicī*), "indicates that the Roman theatre developed from the stage as its constituent feature, whereas the Greek term 'theatre' (adopted by the Romans) emphasized the auditorium."[27] The Latin terminology thus focuses on where the actors perform, not on where the audience sits or stands.

Roman comedies like Plautus' require a backdrop with either two or three doors in it, each of which represent the front doors to temples or to the homes of the play's main characters. The *Poenulus* requires only two doors: one for Agorastocles' house and one for Lycus', but if a troupe travelled with a standard three-door backdrop that could be used for any show, then the third door becomes a source of tension for the audience. If it is not used in the opening scene, they wonder, will it ever be?

Finally, we learn from a passage in Terence that plays were not the only type of show at a festival, and in fact the audience might grow distracted or wander off in search of better entertainment. We do not know whether the area for theatrical performance would be distinctly marked off or separated from any other event. In Terence's *Hecyra*, lines 33–41, the Prologue-speaker declares, "When I began to act this play the first time, the boasting of boxers (and the expectation of tightrope walkers in the same spot), the arrival of their

---

24. Goldberg 1998.
25. See Marshall 2006 37–48 on possible performance spaces around Rome.
26. Gruen 1992 209–10.
27. Manuwald 2011 64.

companions, the uproar, the shouting of women made me leave the stage before the play ended. I began to employ my old method of making a fresh trial for this new play: I brought the play back again. I pleased the crowd with the first act; when in the meantime a rumor ran around that gladiators would be shown, the populace rushed together, they made a disturbance, they shouted, they fought over their spots . . . ."

D. THE PEOPLE

i. Poets

The men who adapted Greek models for the Roman stage, or composed new plays on Roman subjects, were a mixed bunch. Given our limited knowledge and our awareness of the weaknesses of the biographies written in the ancient world, however, we can discern a few patterns.[28] Some poets—like Livius Andronicus, Caecilius Statius, and Terence—are said to have been former slaves, or—like Naevius, Ennius, and Plautus—immigrants from northern or southern Italy.[29] They were not Roman citizens (at least to begin with). Regardless of his origin, each playwright who worked in the *palliāta* or *cothurnāta* genres needed to be able to read Greek well in order to adapt a Greek play into Latin. Since Greek was widely spoken in southern Italy due to the long-established Greek colonies there, bilingualism was common among southern Italians. While the theater was not a highly respected medium in Plautus' time, some poets seem to have been connected to elite Roman families, Pacuvius to the family of L. Aemilius Paullus, for example.[30]

ii. Actors

Professional actors—either slaves or free men of the lowest class—performed *fābulae palliātae*. Later legislation labeled all actors *infāmis* ("unspeakable," or "without reputation"), which meant they lacked many of the rights and protections that Roman citizens enjoyed—such as the right to speak in court, vote, hold office, or to remain free from physical punishment. It is likely that

---

28. On the unreliable nature of ancient biography, see, e.g., Lefkowitz 2012.

29. Naevius (ca. 270–ca. 201 BCE) is the first writer of comedy that we know about. He wrote both *cothurnāta* and *praetexta* tragedies (and an epic poem on the First Punic War) but mainly worked in the *palliāta* genre. He increased the amount of music in his plays by converting what were spoken passages in his Greek model into accompanied Latin passages. He also incorporated references to Roman life into the Greek world of his comedies (Manuwald 2011 194–204).

30. See Manuwald 2011 94, 245, e.g. Furthermore, that Terence was compelled to defend himself against accusations that Scipio Aemilianus and Laelius Sapiens had helped write his plays suggests that Terence at least knew both men.

men alone performed in comedy, tragedy, and Atellan farce; we do know that women could perform in mimes.[31] The prologue to Plautus' *Casina* jokes about the low status of actors in Rome—all of them, especially the women, are presumed to be prostitutes as well. At lines 79–86 the Prologue-speaker declares, "I shall return to that foundling girl, whom the slaves seek as a wife with the utmost force; she'll be discovered both free and a virgin, a freeborn daughter of an Athenian, and nobody will do anything naughty with her indeed in this comedy. But, by Hercules, soon, after the play has been finished, if anyone offers silver, she will head off to 'get married' willingly, and won't wait for the auspices!" Despite these promises, the audience will eventually discover that there is no actor playing Casina, who never appears onstage in that comedy!

The acting troupe as a whole was known as a *grex*, or "flock." The troupe was led by a free man—the *actor*—who probably owned some (slave) actors and some equipment and hired the rest.[32] He seems to have both managed and produced the play and to have acted as well, if we can believe Terence's prologues. Line 20 of Terence's *Eunuchus* ("after the *aediles* bought [the play]") indicates that Roman officials could buy scripts directly from playwrights, though perhaps with the assistance of a troupe leader as middleman.[33] This would leave the troupe leader in a strange position: to negotiate, perhaps, with playwrights (of varying status) for the scripts, then to contract with the Roman elite to produce the plays, and then to act in them. Because magistrates entered office on March 15, just a few weeks before the *lūdī Megalēnsēs* in April, and it is unlikely that a magistrate-elect would sign a contract with a troupe before entering office, a troupe could sometimes have only a few weeks to prepare a new play—and might not even have had access to the performance space far in advance of their "opening day."[34] Such a short turnaround time suggests some writing and rehearsal of a play before the contract signing, as well as a high level of professionalism among the actors and musicians in a troupe. Furthermore, the short time span between contract signing and performance may also suggest both that the music of the *cantica* would not have been terribly difficult for the actors to learn and that stock scenes and improvisation were very important for the performers.[35] Furthermore, it is unclear for how long after the initial performance the troupe then had access to the script. It is not clear how the troupe leaders were perceived by magistrates and other Roman

---

31. See note 13 above.

32. As opposed to training actors owned by someone else—cf. Marshall 2006 86–87 on the *tībīcen*. I prefer to use the Latin *actor* to Manuwald's translation *impresario* (2011 81). Cf. Brown 2002 229.

33. Manuwald 2011 81.

34. Marshall 2006 23. They may also have performed plays in Rome that they had already performed elsewhere on tour—see note 22 above.

35. See Marshall 2006 245–79 on improvisation.

elite, given their engagement with and participation in what came to be seen as a very low-status profession. In a culture that privileged agriculture as a source of income over trade and other business enterprises, the professionalism (and cross-dressing!) required in theatrical performances seems incompatible with elite Roman ideals.

Next, each actor in an acting troupe could play multiple roles, or actors could even share a role. Indeed, role-doubling and -sharing meant only three speaking actors were required to perform Greek New Comedies. In contrast, some of the Roman adaptations call for many more speaking characters to be onstage at once. For example, lines 1120–54 and lines 1338–1422 of the *Poenulus* require at least six actors to perform all of the parts. The scenes with the largest number of actors onstage can also indicate the actual size of the acting troupe—which in the case of Plautus' *Pseudolus* could be up to nine men (see lines 133–69).[36] Barsby's analysis of the potential allocation of parts in the *Poenulus* reveals that eight scenes require four or more speaking actors.[37] Barsby notes that the same actor could play both Milphio and Lycus all the way through and hypothesizes that this split also appeared in the *Karchedonios* (*The Carthaginian*), the play's primary Greek model.[38]

iii. Audience

Anyone could watch a play at Rome's publicly funded religious games. Admission was free, and the only limit was the number of seats and/or space for spectators to sit or stand (see the note on 1224). In 194 BCE, places were reserved for Romans of senatorial rank at public games (see Livy 34.54.3–4, 6–8), though most scholars think that the spectators had always been seated roughly according to class.[39] Lines 17–43 of the prologue to Plautus' *Poenulus* suggest how varied the composition of the audience could be; they list male prostitutes, lictors and their magistrates, slaves and freedmen, wet nurses with infants, married women and their husbands, and slave assistants. The same passage also suggests the potentially disruptive atmosphere with which the performers needed to compete, and the relegation of slaves at least to the rear

---

36. Marshall 2006 111. At 113–14 Marshall hypothesizes that a troupe might only have four or five "core" actors and a *tibīcen*, but would hire additional performers for any plays that required more bodies onstage than the troupe had available.

37. Barsby 2004 95–96. This suggests that Plautus has added quite a bit during the adaptation process.

38. Barsby 2004 96.

39. Manuwald (2011 334) argues that this law and the 67 BCE law providing separate reserved seating for equestrians "demonstrate that the authorities had recognized dramatic performances as a vital part of public life, and on the other hand theatre audiences were turned into comprehensive and structured representations of Roman society and could be referred to accordingly."

of the audience. Although dramatic performances could also occur at funeral games (see below), it is unclear how often such games were held and then how many people attended such games, either from within the hosting clan or from other clans.

iv. Producers/Financial Backers

A Roman magistrate, usually an *aedile*, hired the acting troupe to perform a show at one of Rome's festivals. Magistrates received public funds to pay for the *lūdī*, although it is not clear whether magistrates in Plautus' time supplemented these funds with their own money. Competition for public office in Rome was always fierce, given the decrease in available positions as one climbed the *cursus honōrum*,[40] and we know that during the late Republic many politicians were quite willing to spend their own money to ensure that the games they organized were memorable among potential voters.[41] It is not clear whether the practice began as early as Plautus' time, though some believe it had.[42] Furthermore, there is little indication that spending one's money on *lūdī* in general, even on the small portion of the *lūdī* that Roman comedies represented, had much effect on a politician's later career.[43] On the other hand, the prevalence of *instaurātiōnēs* during Plautus' career suggests the repetition of his plays benefitted some party—it is just not clear whether that party was the magistrate or the acting troupe.

Alternatively, the rare opportunities for watching theatrical performances included those at *lūdī uōtīuī* (votive games held to fulfill a vow to a god, and often connected to a military triumph, or connected to the dedication of a new temple) and at private *lūdī fūnēbrēs* (funeral games) held in honor of an important Roman citizen.[44] The surviving family members would hire a troupe

---

40. At the time of Plautus and Terence the *cursus* looked like this: 1a. Quaestor—required (10 positions); 1b. Tribune of the plebs—optional (10 positions); 1c. Aedile—optional (two Curule, two Plebeian); 2. Praetor—required (4 or 6 positions, with the number of positions alternating each year); 3. Consul (2 positions).

41. See Bernstein 2011 231–32, Manuwald 2011 50–51.

42. Manuwald (2011 50) argues that "lavish and magnificent games" were likely still important given "the increase in individual self-presentation from the early second century BCE."

43. Gruen 1992 188–97. Gruen (1992 190) notes that because the voting in Rome's Centuriate Assembly privileged the votes of the wealthier centuries, an *aedile* or *praetor* aimed to sway his peers—the more powerful voters—rather than the entire audience with the success of the production. Both Gruen (1992 190) and Goldberg (1998 13–14) believe that few potential voters would be found in the audience for a Roman comedy in any case, but Gruen argues based on the likely composition of the audience at a low-class form of entertainment, Goldberg on the fact that spectators at an individual performance of a Roman comedy likely numbered below two thousand.

44. Cf. Terence's *Adelphoe* at the funeral games in honor of L. Aemilius Paulus in 160 BCE. For additional examples see Marshall 2006 18.

of actors to perform at the *lūdī fūnēbrēs* for the deceased. Both votive and funeral games resulted from private contracts between a wealthy individual or family and an acting troupe.

E. THE PERFORMANCE

i. Masks

Performers in Roman comedy very likely wore masks, since Greek New Comedy employed masked actors too. There were probably a few types of mask for each of the stock characters, so that even the most distant spectators could identify an actor's role. Although the use of masks might seem to limit the possibilities for creative representation, the angle at which an actor presented his mask to the audience—especially if the mask was asymmetrical—changed its apparent expression, thus enabling an actor to simulate a wide variety of moods.[45] In addition, although gods deliver the prologues for Plautus' *Aulularia* and *Rudens*, the speaker of his other prologues remains unlabeled and undifferentiated. These prologues may have been delivered by an unmasked actor, just as Terence's prologues were delivered by the troupe leader L. Ambivius Turpio. Such a practice would suit the transitional nature of the prologue—neither completely inside or outside the world of the play—and perhaps be slightly more audible to the spectators.[46]

ii. Costumes

Next, as in real life, the characters' costumes were likely to be matched to the gender and status of each character. An acting troupe likely owned its own masks and costumes, some of which could be expensive. Simpler, i.e., easily adaptable, costumes would have been quite convenient, especially if actors needed to share a role—as might happen with a large cast list and a small troupe. Furthermore, Plautus often stages a scene in which one or more characters don an additional "costume" onstage in order to play a new role within a miniature deception known as a "play-within-a-play." In such scenes both the theatrical language—even the unmarked dressing words *uestis* and *ornātus*—and the act of recostuming and/or rehearsing would draw attention to the metatheatrical nature of the enterprise.[47] See, for example, Pseudolus preparing Simia at *Pseud.* 905–54, and Palaestrio preparing Acroteleutium at *Mil.* 906–46, and references to the new "costumes" of Virgo and Sagaristio at *Per.* 158 and 462–64.

---

45. Marshall 2006 134, referring to Wiles 1991 166–67, figs. 5–6.
46. See too the note on line 123.
47. See section 6b below on metatheater.

iii. Music and Movement

The performance was also filled with music: one member of the acting troupe played a *tībia* (a reeded pipe) as accompaniment for many lines, which—depending on the meter—could also have been sung.[48] Dancing, movement, and gesture might also have played a part in the performance, although very little evidence for such actions survives.[49] For example, the medieval manuscripts of Terence's comedies contain drawings of Terentian characters in costume performing various gestures, but it is not clear to what era of performance these pictures refer.[50] However, that actors were associated with "expressive gestures, emphasizing or complementing what was being said" can be inferred from the work of orators in the late Republic and Empire.[51]

F. OUR POET: PLAUTUS

i. Name and "Biography"

Our evidence for Plautus' name, biography, and writings must be treated with caution. His full name, Titus Macc(i)us Plautus, is our first puzzle, as it is too perfect for a comic poet. It is likely a comic fabrication given his own potentially low—we think—status and its joking similarity to the tripartite names of elite Roman citizens and freedmen. To start, Titus is one of fifteen common and rather generic first names used by male citizens in Rome. Next, the name Maccus refers to a stock character of Atellan farce—the clown, in fact—while Maccius, an actual Roman name, means "son of Maccus." And Plautus, another actual Roman name, means something like "flat-foot," which is appropriate for a comic actor—especially the barefoot actors of mime! Thus what looks at a glance like a proper Roman name can actually be translated as "Willy McBozo Greasepaint," "Dickie Clownson Tumbler," "R. Harpoe Clownshoes III (just call me "Dick")," "R. Harpoe Floppé (call me "Dick")," or "Droopy Dick McClown."[52] Such a name must at the very least be a comic pseudonym, but at worst could be a comic fabrication to cover the work of several individuals; no single "Plautus" might ever have existed.[53]

---

48. For more detail, see section 4 below.

49. See Moore 2012 105–34 on dancing in Roman comedy.

50. Arguments have been made for the third century CE (Dodwell 2000 19) and the fifth (Jones and Morey 1930–31 44–45).

51. Manuwald 2011 74; cf. Cic. *De Or.* 2.193; Quint. *Inst.* 11.3.88–89, 181–83.

52. "Willy McBozo Greasepaint"—Lowe 2007 97; "Dickie Clownson Tumbler"—Gratwick 1993 3; "R. Harpoe Clownshoes III (just call me 'Dick')" and "R. Harpoe Floppé (call me 'Dick')"—Richlin 2005 10; "Droopy Dick McClown"—Goldberg 2005 68.

53. Goldberg 2005 68. Cf. Gratwick 1993 3: "On the one hand, for all we know, the person in question might have been too well born to allow his real clan name to be bandied about in

Second, as mentioned above, the biographies written in the ancient world are often unreliable—in fact, biographers often read an author's own works as autobiographical, even if there was no indication that an author wrote in his or her own persona. But Plautus' biographers declare him an Umbrian from Sarsina, who came to Rome, worked in the theater in some way, lost all of his money in bad business deals, and then worked in a mill for some time to recoup his losses. Whether this is true or not, these details reflect what later Romans wanted to believe about Plautus—his biography contains no mention of connections to the upper classes, unlike the biographies of many other playwrights of *comoedia palliāta* such as Caecilius Statius and Terence.[54] Regardless, our sources report that he was born ca. 254 BCE, his first plays were staged around 205, and he died in 184 BCE.

ii. Varro's Role

Compounding the issue of Plautus' name is a third problem: a total of 130 comedies were attributed to Plautus in the centuries after his death. Even for a stage career spanning around twenty years, 130 plays seems rather prolific. The first-century BCE writer Marcus Terentius Varro compiled a list of the twenty-one plays that were widely believed actually to have been written by Plautus. Since twenty-one plays have survived either whole or in large fragments, it is likely that these are the plays "approved" by Varro: they survived because they became the most important, and were therefore copied frequently.[55] A corpus of twenty to thirty plays seems much more reasonable for a single author. Perhaps Plautus' name carried such cachet that others adopted it for their own benefit, as Gratwick and Goldberg believe.[56] What we know about the author of the *Poenulus*—a name and a brief biography—might, therefore, be entirely fictitious. Luckily we know a bit more about the *Poenulus* itself.

---

connection with something so trivial as the comic theatre. On the other, perhaps the names did originate with a particular professional talent, but the troupe with which he was associated could have capitalized on them after his death, bringing out new plays under his name. Worse still, how do we even know that anyone in particular was ever meant at all? What if the name(s) were always just a 'trademark'?"

54. Richlin 2014 211–12.

55. The surviving plays are *Amphitruo, Asinaria, Aulularia, Bacchides, Captiui, Casina, Cistellaria, Curculio, Epidicus, Menaechmi, Mercator, Miles Gloriosus, Mostellaria, Persa, Poenulus, Pseudolus, Rudens, Stichus, Trinummus, Truculentus,* and part of the *Vidularia.* Even the other plays Varro thought were likely to be genuine have been lost, though we do know the names of thirty-four other plays attributed to Plautus, as well as eighty-eight fragments from these plays, and eighty-two fragments from other supposedly Plautine comedies—see Ribbeck 1898 and de Melo 2012 v. 5 for the text of these fragments.

56. See note 53.

2. *The Poenulus in Particular*

A. THE TITLE, THE PLOT, AND THE *POENULUS'* GREEK MODELS

The title of the play as it has been transmitted to us is *Poenulus*, "The Little Punic Man," though line 54 of the prologue may record a different title for the play (see the note on that line). However, *Poenulus* is not the Latin equivalent of the Greek title, Καρχηδόνιος ("The Carthaginian"—see line 53), since the diminutive form and the adjective choice instead carry a more pejorative sense. The Latin adjective for "Carthaginian," *Carthāginiēnsis, -is*, is the "neutral, civic term . . . a version of the Carthaginians' own name for their city, *Qart Hadasht*." In contrast, *Poenus, -a, -um* "Phoenician, Punic" is the "ethnically charged" adjective. Thus, while the non-Carthaginian Milphio and Antamynides use *Poenus* to describe Hanno, all of the Carthaginian characters use the label *Carthāginiēnsis* for themselves.[57]

Set in the Aetolian town of Calydon in west-central Greece,[58] the *Poenulus* focuses on the love of the wealthy young man Agorastocles for the young slave-woman Adelphasium, who is owned by the pimp Lycus and is about to begin her life as a prostitute. Since Lycus refuses to sell Adelphasium to Agorastocles, the young man enlists the help of his clever slave Milphio to trap Lycus in possession of Agorastocles' stolen "property": Collybiscus, the slave overseer of Agorastocles' rural property. While the plot succeeds, it is not guaranteed to deliver Adelphasium to Agorastocles before she enters a life of prostitution. Thus Milphio devises a second scheme to free both Adelphasium and her younger sister Anterastilis (also owned by Lycus) after he learns that both women were actually free-born, kidnapped with their nurse from Carthage many years ago (just as Agorastocles himself had been). In search of a stranger to play the role of the sisters' long-lost father in court,

---

57. Starks 2000 166, 167 and cf. Franko 1994 156. Prag (2006 14n56) reports that "the *Poenulus* is the only play in which the adjective *Carthaginiensis* occurs; *Poenus* is the preferred term otherwise in Plautus." Prag in general provides a useful corrective for later uses of the adjectives: amongst Naevius, Plautus, and Ennius, *Poenus* still seems to apply just to Carthaginians, but after the Third Punic War *Poenus* starts appearing in reference to people from Phoenician colonies other than Carthage, so "all Carthaginians are *Poeni*, but not . . . all *Poeni* are necessarily Carthaginians" (Prag 2006 13–14).

58. It is unclear whether Alexis' *Karchedonios* was also set in Calydon. Rome was at war with the Aetolians, their former allies, until defeating them in 189 BCE, which was likely a year or two before the performance date of the *Poenulus*. Fantham (2004 237) declares that such a back-water town would have been quite "unfamiliar" to an Athenian audience, but de Melo (2012 4) notes that an original Athenian setting is also unfeasible: "[i]n Athens only Athenian citizens could be adopted, so that an important premise of the *Poenulus*, the adoption of Agorastocles by Antidamas, would be impossible to maintain in an Athenian setting. The law of Calydon presumably differed in this respect."

Milphio and Agorastocles meet Hanno, the young women's actual father, who has been traveling around the Mediterranean in search of his daughters. Agorastocles is discovered to be Hanno's first cousin once removed, and the young man successfully negotiates with his relative for Adelphasium's hand in marriage. Hanno is then reunited with his daughters, who are automatically freed from the pimp, and Lycus is threatened with punishment. The *Poenulus* thus combines the themes of trickery and recognition. It is also one of only three Plautine comedies (the *Aulularia* and the *Captiui* are the others) with prologues disclosing part of the play's ending. However, these prologues don't reveal the manner in which the ending takes place, so the plays are still somewhat suspenseful.[59]

The first trick of the *Poenulus* was likely modeled on a Greek New Comedy: Alexis' *Karchedonios (The Carthaginian)*, since the successful entrapment scheme alone would have rendered the pimp liable for twice the cost of the young man's slave (the penalty for theft in Greece). Remnants of this Greek plot can be found at 184 and 1351.[60] In Alexis' play, the large monetary settlement presumably would allow the young man to purchase his beloved and negotiate for her hand in marriage once the arrival of the titular Carthaginian allowed for her recognition as free-born. While short sections of the *Poenulus* parallel fragments from Menander's *Sikyonioi (Men from Sikyon)* and *Misoumenos (The Hated Man)* (lines 1099–1173 and 1296–1318, respectively), it does not seem that either play served as a model for the second trick of Plautus' comedy.[61] In fact, the second trick—whereby Hanno is supposed to pretend to be Adelphasium and Anterastilis' father in order to claim the pair from Lycus as free-born women—seems to be entirely Plautus' invention.[62] Despite being staged in the years following the Second Punic War (see more below), the *Poenulus* portrays Carthaginians in a mostly positive manner[63]—as Alexis' play likely did as well.[64] As usual, the Roman adaptation of the plot expands the role of the clever slave and dispenses with the five-act structure and the chorus in favor of a constant stream of action with additional songs and accompanied speeches by the main characters.

---

59. Duckworth 1994 217.

60. See Lowe 2004.

61. See Arnott 2004, and *pace* Zehnacker 2000 415.

62. de Melo (2012 10–11) summarizes the legal, historical, and theatrical reasons to understand the *Poenulus*' second trick as Plautus' work.

63. The diminutive suffix *-ulus* in Plautus' title, however, may be interpreted pejoratively, as was often the case with the diminutive *Graeculus*.

64. Since Alexis was born in Thurii, a Greek colony in southern Italy, he may have been more likely to invent a Carthaginian main character than playwrights from mainland Greece.

B. THE HISTORICAL CONTEXT

i. Rome, Carthage, and the Second Punic War

During the third–second centuries BCE, the Romans fought a series of three (Punic) wars against the city of Carthage, a Phoenician colony with extensive trade networks and a powerful navy. The first war lasted from 264–241 BCE and resulted in a Roman victory and indemnity payments from Carthage to Rome. However, conflict flared up again in just a few decades, and the Romans and Carthaginians fought the Second Punic War from 218–201 BCE. Again Rome defeated its foe and demanded an indemnity. Soon after the indemnity was paid off, the bellicose Romans (spurred on by M. Porcius "Carthage-must-be-destroyed" Cato) went to war again. The Third Punic War lasted only from 149–146 BCE and ended with the complete destruction of the city and the enslavement of its entire surviving population. But the Third Punic War was still in the future when Plautus was working, and the Second Punic War—and the devastating loss of life that accompanied it—was in much more recent memory.[65]

The talented Carthaginian general Hannibal was responsible for some of Rome's most devastating military losses during the Second Punic War. Before the Romans learned to avoid ambushes, and not to fight in unfavorable settings, they lost three major battles. In the first, around thirty thousand men were killed or captured at the Treb(b)ia River (218 BCE). During the following year, fifteen thousand men were killed and ten thousand captured at Lake Trasimene. And then over forty-eight thousand men were killed and over nineteen thousand captured in the single day's fighting at Cannae (216 BCE).[66] While some captured allied troops were allowed to return to their cities, Roman soldiers were killed or sold into slavery.[67] While such losses would be enormous for a modern nation, the impact on the lower population of the third century BCE was devastating. Many families must have lost at least one man, and the loss

---

65. On the Punic Wars, see Livy (books 21–30) and Polybius (books 1 and 3), as well as Goldsworthy 2000 and Hoyos 2011.

66. The Romans were hardly blameless victims either—Richlin (2006 16) notes several of the army's more unsavory practices: "the Romans themselves commonly practiced decapitation (as in the punishment of deserters); collection of heads for bounty . . . and the taking of heads as trophies (as in the delivery of the head of Hasdrubal to his brother Hannibal)."

67. E.g., Polyb. 3.77.3–7 reports that Hannibal soon released all of the prisoners of war from the Battle of Trebbia who were simply Roman allies. It was common practice in the ancient world to sell prisoners of war into slavery, either immediately following a battle or after the conclusion of the campaign (Thompson 2003 30). In fact, many of the Romans who'd been taken prisoner by the Carthaginians were sold in Greece or on Crete. According to Livy 37.60.3–5, Rome sent a deputation to Crete to try to negotiate for the return of the prisoners in 189 BCE (around the time when the *Poenulus* was probably first performed). Only the city of Gortyn agreed, and the four thousand Romans enslaved there were released (Thompson 2003 28).

of manpower would have severely impaired each family's ability to maintain itself, whether through farming or other occupations. In fact, the loss of so many citizens—and the resulting slower population growth—shaped the next decades of Roman and Italian history.

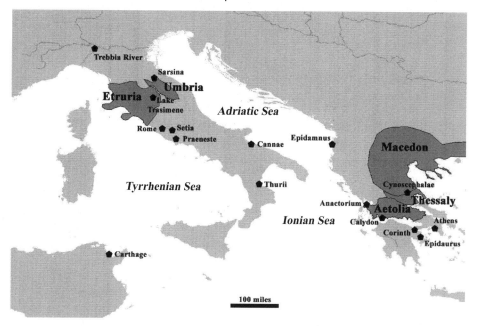

Despite their losses, however, the Romans eventually managed to defeat Hannibal and the Carthaginian army, and the Roman victory brought an influx of Carthaginian slaves, i.e., prisoners of war, into Italy. In fact, the Roman army sold prisoners from towns in Italy, Spain, or Africa into slavery throughout the course of the war. For example, Livy 27.19 states that the Roman general Scipio, after defeating Carthaginian forces in a battle in Spain in 209 BCE, released all of the prisoners of war native to Spain but sold all of the captured African soldiers. In fact, there were several slave revolts in the years following the Second Punic War, one of which was caused by Carthaginian hostages and prisoners (198 BCE in Praeneste and Setia, twenty-five and fifty miles, respectively, from Rome[68]), and another of which may have involved Carthaginian slaves—or pro-Carthaginian people in general—and probably built off of general anti-Roman sentiment (196 BCE in Etruria[69]). It would not be surprising if the influx of Carthaginian slaves inspired a general nervousness regarding the Romans' former enemies, because Roman slaveholders did recognize the danger

---

68. See Livy 32.26.4–18.
69. See Livy 33.36.1–3 and Capozza 1966 162–64, cited at Thompson 2003 252n28.

inherent in high concentrations of slaves from one region. Varro, writing about the practice of large-scale agriculture in early years of the first century CE, for example, advises that clusters of slaves with similar backgrounds should be avoided because the practice could lead to disagreements or unrest.[70]

Though Lancel (1999 183) suggests that many Romans understood the Punic language because of all the Carthaginian slaves seized during the war—and the centuries of trade between the two nations—it is more likely that Greek served as the mutual language of Romans and Carthaginians.[71] In fact, the few Greek terms in the *Poenulus* seem to be mutually comprehensible to the characters, unlike the examples of Punic: Milphio only seems to understand the simplest terms at 961–1038. Additional evidence suggests that at least a few aspects of Carthaginian culture and some language were well known to the Romans before the Second Punic War: types of wood-joinery used in olive-grinding wheels seem to have spread from Carthaginian territory to Roman territory, Punic-style floors appear in Roman territory too, and the *tibiae* used in the performance of sacrifices or theatrical productions—or at least the wood used to make the pipes—probably came from Carthaginian territory at least as early as the introduction of Greek theater in 240 BCE.[72] Finally—although around forty years after the performance date of the *Poenulus*—not only does Cato reveal that African figs could be delivered to Rome within three days of their picking,[73] but even after the Third Punic War the Romans set up a commission to translate the twenty-eight-volume agricultural treatise of the Carthaginian Mago into Latin—and the men on the commission were all "expert in Punic (*periti Punicae*)."[74] Gruen hypothesizes that the portrayal of Carthaginians actually deteriorated after 146 BCE and the end of the Third Punic War since he considers the portrayal of Hanno in the *Poenulus* to be a positive one. Gruen also notes that the association made in the *Poenulus* between Carthaginians

---

70. *Rust.* 1.17.5. Other factors that likely encouraged the slave uprisings in the decades after the Second Punic War include the growth of slave-intensive large-scale farming on *latifundia* (which not only created larger clusters of slaves in one area but also required a different form of supervision—soon afterwards Rome required landowners to employ free men as the overseers for the large estates) and the distribution of public land to veterans, which prevented the slave shepherds from using the area for their flocks (Thompson 2003 252–53). It is not, however, clear how quickly the *latifundia* replaced small farms in Plautus' time.

71. In fact, the series of trade treaties between the two cities starts with one in 508 and extends all the way to 264 BCE (Palmer 1997 12, 20–22, though the entire work is indispensable regarding the long-lived trade relationship between Rome and Carthage). See Starks (2000 170n24) on Greek as the likely common tongue for Romans and Carthaginians, "[c]onsidering the geographical realities of Rome's military involvements with Carthage in heavily Greek Sicily and southern Italy."

72. Palmer 1997 13, 49.

73. Plin. *HN* 15.20.

74. Palmer 1997 46. Gruen (2011 129–30) further notes that the Romans chose to translate this agricultural treatise even after Cato had written on the same subject, and that it went on to influence Varro and Columella.

and bilingualism does not necessarily convey any negative connotation since Romans very much valued knowledge of Greek for its practical benefits; such knowledge provided bilingual Romans with an advantage in encounters with the usually monolingual Greeks.[75]

ii. Calydon and Aetolia

Soon after the Second Punic War, Rome found itself entangled in another, shorter, conflict. Rome went to war with King Philip V of Macedon in 216 BCE, when Philip allied with Hannibal. Rome then allied with the Aetolian League of west-central Greece in 211. Although the Aetolians were compelled to submit to Philip in the peace of 206, the Aetolians again joined Rome in a second war against Macedon starting in 199. After Philip's defeat at Cynoscephalae in 197, the Aetolian League was rewarded with control of part of Thessaly. Annoyed at their small reward—they had wanted control of Thessaly in its entirety, the Aetolians took their revenge by convincing Antiochus III, king of the Seleucids, to "liberate" the Greeks from Roman hegemony. The Roman army therefore made war against Antiochus and his Aetolian allies from 192 until Rome's victory in 189 BCE, soon before the likely performance date of the *Poenulus*. Calydon, the setting of the *Poenulus*, is an Aetolian city located on the Gulf of Corinth. Calydon would have been very unfamiliar to Plautus' Roman audience unless they had served in the Roman campaign, and we do not know of anything specific to the comedy that necessitates such a setting. Calydon is an unusual choice for Plautus—the *Captiui* is the only other Plautine comedy set in Aetolia, and there Plautus does not even name the town. Thus Plautus' decision to set his comedy specifically in Calydon is an interesting one. Fantham thinks Aetolia represents "a kind of lawless Wild West" to Plautus' Roman audience.[76] Starks is actually surprised at Plautus' treatment of the city in the *Poenulus*, given Rome's recent wars against both cities: "in context, Carthage and Calydon are treated as if they are typically random settings of New Comedy in Greek cities of no particular significance." He thinks that the audience in Rome would have had "at best, mixed feelings about them."[77]

C. THE DATING CONTROVERSY

Scholars attempting to date the *Poenulus* must rely on the internal evidence of the play, since no *didascaliae* (production notices) survive. However, a date between 189 and 187 BCE is most likely for several reasons. First, Rome drove

---

75. Gruen 2011 129.
76. Fantham 2004 237.
77. Starks 2000 166.

King Antiochus III of the Seleucids (mentioned on 694) out of Greece in 191–190 and demanded that his Aetolian allies (perhaps compare *Aetōlī cīuēs* on 621) surrender in a war that ended in 189. Second, Adelphasium and Anterastilis may allude to the repeal of the Oppian sumptuary law in 195 BCE during their discussion of personal adornment at 210–407.[78] Third, Welsh argues that lines 200–2 make a joke on the name of the popular villain Ballio from Plautus' *Pseudolus* of 191 BCE. The *Poenulus* is therefore likely to have been staged soon afterwards, so that the joke would be recognizable for the audience.[79] Finally, Rome and Carthage signed a peace treaty in 189 BCE, which rendered Carthage technically Rome's ally at that time.[80] Further, Carthage had rebuilt its economy significantly after a decade or so of peace. Hanno may refer to the resurrection of the Carthaginian economy in lines 1018–20, where he talks about his own grain harvest, notes Starks, who further observes that Carthage was wealthy enough by 191 BCE to offer Rome's army free grain, some ships to help fight Antiochus, and multiple payments of their indemnity.[81] Note that a date between 189 and 187 BCE falls toward the end of Plautus' career, when perhaps audiences had become more attuned to the conventions of the genre.[82]

D. ITS AFTERLIFE

The *Poenulus* has not been the most popular choice for postclassical revival performances,[83] nor has it inspired many later authors or artists. Along with Plautus' *Mostellaria* and *Rudens*, however, it did serve as a model for the first Italian comedy: Ludovico Ariosto's *La Cassaria* of 1508.[84]

3. Plautus' Latin

A. ARCHAIC FORMS AND SYNTAX

Spelling in the manuscripts of Plautus is inconsistent: the Ambrosian palimpsest (which dates from the fifth century CE) employs the spelling conventions of the

---

78. See Johnston 1980 150–53.

79. Welsh 2009 97.

80. de Melo 2012 13.

81. Starks 2000 182–83, referring to Livy 36.4.5–9. For discussions of the *Poenulus'* date see Duckworth 1994 55, Henderson 1994 28, Starks 2000 182–83, Zehnacker 2000 430, Woytek 2004 136, Welsh 2009 97n17, de Melo 2012 13–14.

82. Slater (1992 133) doubts that Plautus' audiences would have been very knowledgeable about the *palliata* genre, calling them "at best second-generation theatre-goers." Although he questions any close connection between theater and religious festivals since dramatic performances could be part of funerary celebrations too, the existence of multiple performance contexts (and reperformance) would allow spectators to learn the genre's conventions more quickly than the Roman festival schedule might suggest.

83. Though see Jeppesen 2013 241–315 on a potential revival in 181 BCE.

84. Duckworth 1994 399.

late first century BCE, not those of Plautus' time. The Palatine manuscripts, which derive from a later copy of the plays, tend to use even further "modernized" spellings.[85]

However, the preclassical/early/archaic Latin of Plautus' time used different spelling, syntax, and pronunciation from classical Latin. Below is a brief list of the most common divergences you will see in this text. All are mentioned in the commentary proper, though the most frequent alternative spellings may not be noted more than twice. For more detail, see de Melo 2011 and Hammond et al. 1963 49–57.

Spelling, Constructions, and Word Order:

- Short *o* often appears instead of a short *e* (e.g., *uester*, *uertō*, etc., were written as *uoster*, *uortō*—cf. 396).
- Long *ī* is often spelled *ei* (in the *Poenulus* only at 414, 534, 1187).
- *Qu* often replaces initial *c* in conjunctions and pronouns like *quom/cum* and *quoi/cui* (cf. 9, 27).
- Early Latin prefers the short forms *perīclum* and *hercle* to *perīculum* and *hercule* (cf. 878, 910).
- The emphatic suffixes *-te* and *-met* mark colloquial speech (cf. 91, 251, 1381).
- Plautus also likes adding the demonstrative enclitic *-c(e)* to *hīc* and *ille* to make the forms even more emphatic (cf. 551, 1121).[86]
- Hyperbaton (inversion of normal word order) is very common in Plautus (cf. 602)—so much so that it may be "stylistically unmarked."[87]
- Weak (unstressed) connective elements (e.g., *autem*) and pronouns (e.g., *ego*) normally appear second in their clauses: this is known as Wackernagel's Law (cf. 882).[88]

Noun and Adjective Forms and Constructions:

- The nominative singular ending for nouns in the second declension is *-os* (with a short *o*) not *-us*, after consonantal *u*. Similarly, the accusative singular in *-om* often appears as well (cf. 181).
- An alternative nominative masculine singular *ipsus* for *ipse* appears (cf. 708).

---

85. For more, see de Melo 2011 322–24.

86. Because the resulting demonstratives are especially emphatic, it seems likely that actors would have employed some sort of gesture to accompany them. For example, *hōsce* on 715 refers to some gold coins, so the actor may have raised the bag containing them. Even though the manuscripts of Roman comedy lack any sort of stage directions, we can still deduce some stage action from the Latin text.

87. de Melo 2011 329.

88. de Melo 2011 328.

- A disyllabic first-declension genitive singular in -*āī* appears (cf. 51).
- Fourth-declension genitive singulars in -*ī* appear (cf. 95).
- The archaic genitive plural in -*um* can be used for the second declension (cf. 254, 1062).
- Partitive genitives frequently appear with neuter pronouns (cf. 1089).
- *Similis* takes the genitive (cf. 613).
- *Is, ea, id* features a dative plural in *īs* (cf. 1190) and may also be combined with the exclamation *ecce* to become more emphatically demonstrative (cf. 203).
- The ablative singular of personal pronouns appears as *med* and *ted*—both of which are adopted as accusative singular too (cf. 301).
- Superlative adjectives may end in -*umus* not -*imus* (cf. 749, 1176a).
- Plautus also uses the possessive adjective *quoius, quoia, quoium*, meaning "whose" (cf. 274).
- This text employs the alternative accusative plural ending -*īs* for third-declension i-stem nouns and adjectives (cf. 107). The accusative singular ending -*im* often appears for i-stem nouns as well (cf. 1019, 1025).

Verb Forms and Constructions:

- Plautus is fond of frequentative verbs (cf. 397).[89]
- Second person singular indicative passives ending in -*re* appear (cf. 359).
- Medio-passive present infinitives ending in -*ier* instead of -*ī* appear— often because they're more suited to the meter than an infinitive ending in -*ārī* (cf. 265).[90]
- The present subjunctive of *sum* has an additional set of disyllabic forms: *siem, siēs, siet*, etc. (cf. 276). The -*ie*- is a remnant of the earlier Indo-European optative.[91]
- The imperfect *esset* is often replaced with *foret*, etc. (cf. 262).
- Fourth-conjugation imperfects ending in -*ībam, -ībās*, etc., and futures ending in -*ībō, -ībis*, etc., appear (cf. 462, 509).
- Futures built off an -*s*- stem also appear, such as *ausim* and *faxō* (cf. 149, 162), though the stem is also used for future perfect indicatives and perfect subjunctives.
- The future perfect active indicative and perfect subjunctive often employ sigmatic stems with -*ss*- instead of -*uer*- (cf. 553).
- Plautus likes syncopated (contracted) forms of the perfect and pluperfect

---

89. Augoustakis 2009 3.
90. de Melo 2011 327.
91. Hammond et al. 1963 56.

indicative—especially if the stem ends in -x and the ending contains the letter s (cf. 422).[92]

- The use of *fuī* instead of *sum* in the perfect passive indicative was also common in Plautus (cf. 1347).
- The third-person plural perfect active ending -*ēre* is rare; it only appears in comedy in "contexts where the register is elevated" (cf. 84, 86).[93]
- *Amābō, obsecrō,* and *quaesō* are often used parenthetically as "please"; *crēdō* and *opīnor* are often used parenthetically as "I think" (cf. 240, 1016).
- The *a* of *aiō* is often scanned long, though never in *ait; ais* and *ait* can be either disyllabic or monosyllabic through synizesis (cf. 343).
- *Fīō* usually has a long *ī* except in the form *fit* (cf. 611).
- *Nē* followed by a present imperative means "stop doing X" (cf. 261).[94]
- The future imperatives ending in -*to* (second and third person singular—cf. 346), -*tote* (second person plural—cf. 600), and -*nto* (third person plural—cf. 1281) are common as well.
- The present subjunctive of *perdere* employs -*uit* and -*uint* for the third person (cf. 610, 739).
- Prohibitions employing *nē* and perfect subjunctives are also common (cf. 553).[95]
- *Cum* clauses never use subjunctives: "in Plautus and Terence the subjunctive could only occur because of attraction of mood."[96]

B. COLLOQUIALISMS, SLANG, AND WORDPLAY

Plautus' comedies feature a mixture of everyday language, slang, and Greek (as is appropriate for the typical slave characters and their friends and associates), as well as more sophisticated phrases associated with tragedy (the last of which are often used for parodic purposes). Prologues also tend to use language of a slightly higher register.[97] In Roman comedy, Greek is not associated with learned individuals but with slaves. Colloquialisms found in Plautus include diminutives, use of *suus* instead of *eius*, the use of *uterque* with a plural verb, the use of the phrases "*bene facis*," "*equidem crēdō*," and "*iste quidem*" and the like.[98] Pleonasm (the use of more words than necessary) is common in Roman

---

92. Hammond et al. 1963 54.
93. de Melo 2011 328.
94. de Melo 2011 330.
95. de Melo 2011 331.
96. de Melo 2011 330.
97. de Melo 2010 85.
98. See the following works: de Melo 2010 72 (*suus*), de Melo 2011 334–35 (*uterque*), Halla-aho and Kruschwitz 2010 148 (*bene facis*), Harrison 2010 274 (*equidem crēdō*), Harrison 2010 277 (*iste quidem*).

comedy and is often colloquial, but not necessarily so, as it is also found frequently in religious language.[99] Many studies show how the use of Latin may vary according to the speaker's gender, age, and class. Some of the patterns that emerge from these studies include the propensity for female characters in Plautus to use more diminutives than male characters, to be more polite and employ *miser* and its relatives more frequently, and to avoid Greek words and constructions.[100] The speeches of old men, on the other hand, are often more repetitive, pleonastic, and "long-winded."[101] Finally, slave characters are much more likely to use loan-words from Greek, or switch into Greek, when speaking with other slaves.[102]

In general, early Latin tends to employ sound effects—whether from alliteration, assonance and consonance, anaphora, paranomasia, etc.—in order to raise the level of discourse above the colloquial.[103] This tendency is especially strong in comedy. The arrangement of words in a phrase or speech is also important, so "anadiplosis,[104] tricolon, climax, polysyndeton" also appear, as do plays with the multiple meanings and resonances of individual words (resulting in "antithesis, zeugma, metonymy, literal interpretation of common phrases, puns, etymological jingles").[105] Plautus in particular is also known for inventing new terms (neologisms) but also tends to play on the multiple meanings of Latin words—see, e.g., Milphio's puns and overly literal interpretations of Latin terms throughout the play. Plautine style thus includes "hyperbolic comparisons, nonce-formations, bizarre identifications, riddles, military imagery in inappropriate contexts, jokes exploiting formulae and concepts of Roman law as well as comparisons with figures from myth."[106] This barrage of wordplay, so characteristic of Plautus, is often referred to as "verbal fireworks."

C. GREEK AND PUNIC

Many Plautine comedies employ Greek terms, either as untranslated slang or in a somewhat Latinized form. For example, Plautus takes Greek adjectives and adverbs and sticks Latin adjectival and adverbial endings on them, e.g.,

---

99. Gaertner 2010 250.

100. See, respectively, Dutsch 2008, Adams 1984, Karakasis 2005. See Clackson 2011 "Social Dialects" for an overview of Latin dialects in general.

101. Clackson 2011 "Social Dialects" 512. See Maltby 1979 and Karakasis 2005 for more on the speech-patterns of old men.

102. See, respectively, Maltby 1995 and Adams 2003. The context-dependent language switch is known as "code-switching."

103. Manuwald 2011 325.

104. The repetition of a key word from one clause at the start of the next clause.

105. Manuwald 2011 325–26.

106. Manuwald 2011 228.

with *basilicus* and *basilicē* (577). And, as Fontaine 2010 has shown, many of Plautus' jokes require knowledge of Greek. The *Poenulus* is unique in its inclusion of Punic words—and entire speeches in Punic—as well. But as Babič 2003 demonstrates, Plautus treats these two languages very differently. In conversations involving Greek both characters understand both Greek and Latin, and the Greek words are rare and their meaning is not necessarily clear to the audience, so any incidental comic effect depends upon the knowledge of individual spectators. On the other hand, in conversations involving Punic there is no linguistic contact between the two speakers—no actual communication can occur since only one of them understands Punic. Babič thus argues that Punic only appears in the play for entertainment purposes.[107] Even if some spectators did understand Punic (see section 2.b.i above), that would simply allow the same kind of incidental humor as knowledge of Greek would.

4. Music and Meter

A. MUSIC

i. *Tībia* and *tībīcen*

Music in Roman comedy came from the actors, who sang during portions of the play, and the *tībia*, a wooden pipe with a reed mouthpiece like the modern-day oboe. The *tībia* was played by a *tībīcen*, who, according to the *didascaliae*, was a slave likely owned by the troupe.[108] The *tībīcen* was extremely important to the success of a play and must have been a valued member of the troupe (especially since the production notices recount his name and not those of the actors!). It is not clear where the *tībīcen* stood to perform, whether onstage, off to one side, or directly in front of the stage, but he accompanied—in some way—all parts of the play that were not in iambic senarii, the "spoken" meter.[109] (A more technical discussion of meter in Roman comedy follows in sections 4b–d.) It is unclear whether the *tībia* produced a drone or a specific tune that harmonized or played in unison with the actor, but there seem to have been several types of *tībiae*, each of which produced a different sound.[110] The actor,

---

107. Babič 2003 29.

108. Marshall 2006 86–87. That *tībīcinēs* were slaves, as many actors probably were, does not tell us much about their treatment. While slaves were literally owned by their masters, there was no uniform slave "underclass," since slavery was a civil status not a social class (Richlin 2014 204). Indeed—slaves could have very different experiences both during and before slavery (think of all the Greek slaves hired as tutors for wealthy Roman families), and performed many different duties across Italy.

109. These passages are labeled as *deuerbia* in the manuscripts.

110. The *didascaliae* for Plautus' *Stichus* preserves the name of the *tībīcen* and his owner, and also reports on the type of *tībia* he played: ". . . Marcipor the slave of Oppius [played] the whole

in turn, seems to have sung—perhaps like the recitative sections of opera—when the verses were written in all other meters (both trochaic septenarii and during all polymetric *cantica*). Different meters were associated with different types of scene and types of characters in the *fabūla palliāta*—see sections d–f for additional details. Overall, however, almost all unaccompanied (*deuerbia*) passages are those explaining or describing plans or providing necessary information, while the sung *cantica* and accompanied passages are usually there as "performance for its own sake."[111] As Moore describes it, "[t]he areas where information predominates over emotion tend to be unaccompanied."[112] Interested readers are urged to consult Moore 2012, which addresses these issues at great length.

ii. Music in the *Poenulus*

However, *Poenulus* is Plautus' "least musical play": an enormous 59 percent of the extant verses are unaccompanied iambic senarii.[113] We cannot use the comedy's lack of music to help determine the date of composition either: early plays are by no means less likely to be heavily musical than late ones—only the polymetric and stichic *cantica* become more prevalent over time, not accompanied speech in general.[114] Furthermore, the composition of the acting troupe meant to perform a specific play had nothing to do with the proportion (or type of) music incorporated into the play.[115] The *Poenulus'* high proportion of unaccompanied lines partially results from interpolation, since the iambic senarius was the easiest type of line to compose, and actors or directors of later performances did introduce interpolations into Plautus' plays before official versions of the scripts were produced. Indeed, in any comedy, iambic senarii comprise the majority of the verses "that we can with reasonable certainty identify as post-Plautine"—see, for example, lines 1355–71, which close the first ending of the *Poenulus*.[116]

---

thing on Syrian pipes." Cf. the *didascaliae* for Terence's *Hauton Timorumenos*, which report, in part, "Flaccus, the slave of Claudius, played the melodies (*modōs fēcit Flaccus Claudī*). It was performed with the uneven pipes and then with two right-handed pipes." As Moore (2012 155) notes, the phrase *modōs fēcit* "implies that the author of the *didascaliae* . . . viewed the *tibicen*/composer as creating rhythms as well as melodies."

111. Moore 2004 144. This includes the deceptions, metatheatrical passages, etc.—most of the sections that Plautus added or expanded during the adaptation process.

112. Moore 2004 150.

113. Moore 2004 139. *Trinummus*, with 52 percent of its iambic senarii unaccompanied, is the second least musical play, while *Epidicus* lies at the opposite end of the spectrum—only 21 percent of its verses are unaccompanied (Moore 2004 139n1).

114. Moore 2004 140–41.

115. Moore 2004 141.

116. Moore 2004 140.

But Moore argues that Plautus also intentionally restricted the amount of music in the *Poenulus*, in order to draw attention to (or not to distract from) "its great amount of verbal humor and its heavy reliance on visual effects."[117] First, the *Poenulus* contains more puns and jokes than other plays.[118] Furthermore, the visual effects are striking in the sisters' entrance/dressing scene, the advocates' entrance scene, the entrance of Collybiscus disguised as a soldier, the entrance of Hanno and his Carthaginian slaves, the recognition scene between the sisters and Hanno, and during Antamynides' rant against Hanno. Music actually starts up for or accompanies all of these scenes except for Hanno's entrance and Antamynides' outburst.[119] Although Hanno's entrance in iambic senarii would not normally be accompanied by the *tibia*, Franko wonders whether any "unusual, Punic-sounding music" might have marked the character's entrance.[120] However, Hanno's use of regular Latin meters (apart from his prose Punic at 930–49) suggests that he was treated like any other *senex* figure in Roman comedy.

B. METER

All Latin meter is based on the alternation of long (¯) and short (˘) syllables.[121] (The number of syllables in a word is determined by the number of vowels or dipthongs in it, absent any elision.) Long syllables should be understood as taking twice as long to pronounce as short syllables (e.g., a half note vs. a quarter note in modern musical notation). Syllables start and end with consonants if possible, so syllables should be separated either before a single consonant or between two consonants. A syllable is long because its vowel is either long by nature—i.e., a diphthong or anything featuring a macron—or because the vowel is long by position—i.e., appearing before two consonants. Thus long syllables end in a long vowel, a diphthong, or a consonant. A short syllable is short because its vowel is short, i.e., it has no reason to be long; short syllables therefore end in a short vowel. Notable exceptions to the above include the following:[122]

---

117. Moore 2004 142.

118. Moore 2004 142.

119. Moore 2004 143.

120. Franko 1996 430n9, where he adds, "[f]or the use of music to enhance the alterity of foreign characters see Hall, *Inventing the Barbarian* 129–32."

121. This introduction to Plautine meter is informed by Moore 2012, to which interested readers are referred. Also recommended: Halporn et al. 1994, Questa 2007.

122. See, e.g., #1–6: Allen and Greenough 2006 (A&G) 603, 629; #3: de Melo 2011 323; #7: Questa 1967 9–10, cited at Christenson 2000 58n187; #8: Augoustakis 2009 5.

1) Do not divide syllables between two consonants if the two consonants are a mute [b, c, d, g, k, p, q, t] followed by a liquid [l, r], in which case they are grouped together at the start of a syllable.

2) The letters *x* and *z* count as double consonants since they represent the *ks* and *ds* sounds, respectively.

3) Final *-s* is very weak in early Latin, so sometimes doesn't count towards creating a long syllable if it follows a short vowel and precedes a consonant. This text therefore replaces any weak final *-s* with an apostrophe. E.g., *magi'* (*magis*) and *priu'* (*prius*).

4) Similarly, final *-e* after a consonant isn't always long enough to count for scansion since it was often rushed over when pronounced. This text therefore uses an apostrophe to abbreviate any such words, e.g., *ind'* (*inde*).

5) *H* doesn't count as a consonant and the combination *qu* counts as a single consonant.

6) The consonant clusters consisting of a mute [b, c, d, g, k, p, q, t] or fricative [f] followed by a liquid [l, r] or nasal [m, n] sometimes lengthen preceding vowels, but don't always do so.

7) Vowel length in early Latin sometimes differs from vowel length in classical Latin: the long vowels of the verb stems do not shorten before final *-t*, for example, and the endings *-ar*, *-er*, *-or*, and *-al* usually scan as long vowels.

8) A mute [b, c, d, g, k, p, q, t] plus a liquid [l, r] or the combination *st-* or *sc-* at the start of a word need not lengthen a vowel at the end of the preceding word.

C. IMPORTANT METRICAL TERMS

The following terms appear in this commentary.

Elision: The mixing of a vowel or diphthong at the end of a word (or vowel sound from the nasal final *-m*) with the initial vowel/diphthong/*h-* at the start of the next word. While we do not know how the Romans handled elisions, modern readers usually drop the final syllable entirely when pronouncing the phrase.

Caesura: The pause (near the middle of a line in Plautus) that occurs when a word ends in the middle of a foot. It is represented here by a double forward slash (//).

Catalectic: An adjective referring to a line of poetry in a particular meter that has lost its final syllable(s).

Crasis: The combining through elision of two commonly connected words that would not otherwise be combined. E.g., *sīs* from *sī uīs* (225), or with the interrogative enclitic *-ne* the examples *audīn* (*audīsne*, 405), *uidēn* (*uidēsne*, 314), *pergin* (*pergisne*, 433), *uīn* (*uīsne*, 161), *satin* (*satisne*, 171), etc.

Diaeresis: A natural pause (near the middle of a line in Plautus) occurring when the end of a foot coincides with the end of a word. You can represent a diaeresis with a double colon (::), though it's less important to differentiate between diaereses and caesurae in comedy since the two types of pauses are functionally equivalent for iambo-trochaic meters.[123]

Enclisis: The addition of *quidem, quis,* or *quid* to the end of a long monosyllable sometimes shortens that syllable, e.g., *sĭquidem* on 1045.

Hiatus: The yawning "gap" that occurs between vowels (or final -*m* or initial *h-*) that would otherwise be elided. It is quite common in Plautus and is marked in the text by a vertical line (|) between the two words. Hiatus occurs frequently at caesurae, diaereses, when there is a change in speaker, or for emotional effect, e.g. *Sciō.| Oculōs* on 191.

Iambic shortening (breuis breuians): The shortening of a long syllable 1) after a short syllable in a two-syllable word (e.g., *tĭbĭ* on 602), 2) in monosyllabic words or in the first syllable of words immediately following monosyllabic words (e.g., *ĕst* on 52), 3) in a longer word when the long syllable is preceded by a short syllable and is followed by an accented syllable (e.g., *uolŭptātī* on 1205), 4) at the start of *ille* and *iste* (e.g., *ĭstam* on 1078). Iambic shortening occurs frequently, but not in every place it is possible.

Ictus: The beat of a line of poetry. Since the putative ictus doesn't always coincide with the natural word accents in Plautus' iambo-trochaic meters, its existence in Plautine comedy is a matter of much debate. It is therefore not a part of our discussion here.

Prodelision (aphaeresis): when the *e-* of *es* or *est* is swallowed by the preceding syllable. The syllable usually ends in -*us*, -*um*, or -*e*, but even final -*a* and -*is* can trigger prodelision.[124] This text shows prodelision of the most confusing instances, using apostrophes to mark where -*us* or -*a* elides with *es* so it will not be confused with the normal nominative -*us* or accusative -*ās* (cf. *factūru's* on 167) and printing the elided form of all places where a word ending in -*is* or -*us* elides with *est* (cf. *sordist* on 315). Prodelision following -*um*, -*e*, and -*a* is simply a slight modification of usual elision practice. Thus *opus est* on 311 is written and pronounced *opust*, while *parātum est* on 9 is pronounced *parātumst* but still written *parātum est*.

Prosodic hiatus: Hiatus accompanied by the shortening of the long vowel or diphthong at the end of a word (or followed by final -*m*) when the next word starts with a vowel or *h-* (e.g., *tŭ | huic*, 395).

Synizesis (synaeresis): When two vowels or a vowel and a diphthong are

---

123. Fortson 2008 27.

124. This is not necessarily true in later Latin: "prodelision in comedy can take place more freely than in Classical poetry. Vowel-less forms of *es* 'you are' and *est* 'he is' can be attached to words ending in -*us* etc., which is no longer allowed later on" (de Melo 2011 324).

combined into a single syllable. Synizesis frequently occurs with forms of *meus*, *tuus*, and *suus*; forms of *is, ea, id*; forms of *deus*; and genitive singular forms of relative and demonstrative pronouns (e.g., *huius* on 83) (Christenson 2000 61). Where synizesis, iambic shortening, or prosodic hiatus is necessary for a word or phrase to fit the meter, synizesis is often considered the simplest explanation (Barsby 1999 296, Christenson 2000 61).

D. IAMBIC SENARII

In iambic senarii (Ia6), the unaccompanied, spoken meter, lines consist of six (hence *senarii*) iambic feet. This meter tends to be used in passages containing information that the audience must learn; either because a letter is being read or an oath is being sworn, the specific words spoken are important.[125] Note that passages of iambic senarii "tend to be simpler in style and language than those in other metres."[126] While iambs technically consist of short syllables followed by long syllables, as in ˘ ¯, in practice there was a lot of flexibility with any long and short syllables in Latin, so it is better to consider the iamb as XL, where X (an *anceps*, "two-headed" or "doubtful," syllable) can represent either one or two "beats" in the form of a single short syllable ˘, two short syllables ˘ ˘, or as a single long syllable ¯. The L syllable <u>must</u> be long, on the other hand, so L represents either two short syllables ˘ ˘ (a "resolution") or a single long syllable ¯. A line of iambic senarii can simply be represented by five XL pairs in a row, followed by the very regular two-syllable sixth foot: SQ, where S is always one short syllable and Q is either short or long and always just a single syllable. Iambic senarii thus can be represented as XL XL X//L XL XL SQ, where the double slash "//" represents the caesura.[127] You can see the scansion of two relatively complex lines below, where / marks foot boundaries, () marks elision and prodelision, {} marks synizesis and diphthongs, and | marks hiatus.

---

125. Moore 2012 175.

126. Manuwald 2011 326.

127. While it's possible to represent these meters using metrical symbols alone, I find Moore's letter-based system easier to remember. This is a podic (by feet) analysis, but analysis by metra (where a metron = two feet) allows more nuanced analysis of the play in terms of where resolution and hiatus tend to occur. See, e.g., Gratwick 1993 40–63, Barsby 1999 290–304. According to their method, a metron can be represented as a four-syllable unit ABCD, where A and C are the *ancipita* (the X of our method) and B and D are the *longa* (the L of our method), and resolutions and short syllables are represented by lower-case letters so a line of iambic senarii = ABCDA//BCDABcD and a line of trochaic septenarii = BCDABCDA//BCDABcD. As Goldberg (2013 38–39) notes, however, any such metrical analysis obscures the fact that any line on the comic stage that wasn't in iambic senarii was sung, and knowing the rhythm of the line tells us absolutely nothing about what it actually sounded like in performance or how the music of the actor and *tībīcen* interacted!

line 2: īnd' mĭhĭ/ prīncĭpĭ/ŭm // căpĭ/(am), ēx {eā} / trăg{oē}/dĭā.
line 83: sĕd īl/lī pā/trŭō/ | {huiūs}, quī/ uīuĭt/ sĕnēx,

E. TROCHAIC SEPTENARII

Trochaic septenarii (Tr7) tend to move the plot along and show lively emotion.[128] Since trochaic septenarii are based around the trochee (‾ ˘) instead of the iamb, a line of this meter can be represented as LX LX LX LX // LX LX L SQ, where the long syllables, *anceps* syllables, and disyllabic final syllable are composed of the same elements as above. (Note that there are actually seven-and-a-half feet in this line, though the term *septenarii* implies only seven.) In fact, a comparison with the iambic senarius pattern above shows that a trochaic septenarius pattern is simply LXL followed by the pattern for the iambic senarius—both meters end a line in exactly the same way. Here is the scansion for two relatively complex lines of trochaic septenarii:

859: d(i) ōmnēs/ {deaē}qu(e) ă/mēnt. Quēm/n(am) hŏmĭnēm?// Nēc tē/ nēc mē,/ Mīl/phĭō:
876: tăcĭtās/ tĭbĭ rēs/ sīstām/ quām quōd// dīctūm (e)st/ mūt{aē}/ mŭlĭ/ĕrī.

F. EXPLANATION OF OTHER METERS FOUND IN THE *POENULUS*

Anapests: A sequence of anapests (An) can feel fast, "exuberant," and/or out of control, especially since iambic shortening is frequent with anapests.[129] An anapest (˘ ˘ ‾) may be represented as LL, therefore the anapestic tetrameter as LL LL LL LQ.

Bacchiacs: Bacchiacs (Ba) are associated with slow speeds and/or solemnity.[130] A bacchiac foot can be represented by ˘ ‾ ‾, though the "resolution" of long syllables into two short syllables is frequent, and the short syllable can also—if rarely—be replaced with a single long or two short syllables as well. This sequence of three longs in a row (LLL) is known as a molossus. A bacchiac foot can therefore be represented as XLL. A bacchiac colon is just two *ancipita* (XX) coming either before or after a bacchiac foot (XLL), where at least one of the *ancipita* must be long.

Cretics: Cretics (Cr) are associated with slowness, but with a "rhythmic 'bounce.'"[131] The cretic foot (‾ ˘ ‾) can also be represented as LQL. A cretic

---

128. Moore 2012 173.
129. Moore 2012 201.
130. Moore 2012 197–99.
131. Moore 2012 192.

colon is just two *ancipita* (XX) coming either before or after a cretic foot (LQL), where at least one of the *ancipita* must be long.

Iambic octonarii: Associated with slaves carrying messages,[132] these lines employ iambs as above, but a longer sequence thereof: XL XL XL XL X/L XL XL SQ.

Iambic septenarii: Associated with people in love,[133] with the pattern XL XL XL SQ / XL XL XL Q.

Ithyphallicus: Three trochees in a row: ‾ ˘ ‾ ˘ ‾ ˘ (LXLXLX).

Reizian Verse: Showing "closure and transition."[134] Four iambs (XLXLXLXL) then XLXLX.

G. LIST OF METERS APPEARING IN THE *POENULUS*

(Here I follow Lindsay 1905, with Questa's modifications at 210–60 and 1174–1200.)

Argumentum: Iambic senarii (Ia6)

Prologue: Ia6

129–209: Ia6

210–60: Bacchiac quaternarii (Ba4)

> (but 230 = Ba2 and Bacchiac Colon [BaC]; 231 = Ba3; 231a = Tr4 catalectic [cat.]; 232 = An7; 238 = Reizian Verse; 239 = Ia7; 244 = Ba2 and BaC; 245 = BaC; 245a-246 = Ba3; 247 = Ba2; 251 = An4cat. and An4; 253 = Ba1 and Ia2; 254 = Cr3; 254a = Ithyphallicus; 258 = Ba and BaC; 260 = Ba3)

261–409: Trochaic septenarii (Tr7)

410–503: Ia6

504–614: Tr7

> (but 609 has no meter)

615–816: Ia6

817–20: Iambic octonarii (Ia8)

821–22: Iambic septenarii (Ia7)

823–929: Tr7

930–1173: Ia6

1174–1200: Anapestic tetrameter (An4)

---

132. Moore 2012 183.
133. Moore 2012 185.
134. Moore 2012 204.

(but 1174–5 = An8; 1177 = Cr2 and Cretic Colon; 1178 = An8; 1183a = An2; 1183b = An4cat.; 1184–6 = An7; 1187–90 = An8; 1191a = An4cat.; 1191b-2 = Reizian Verse; 1192a-4 = Ia8; 1195 = Ia6; 1196 = Ia4; 1196a = Ia6; 1197 = An4cat.; 1197a-98a = Ia4; 1199 = Ia7; 1200 = An4 and Reizian Verse)

1201–25: Tr7
1226–73: Ia7
1274–1303: Tr7
1304–97: Ia6
1398–1422: Tr7

5. The Manuscript Tradition/Stemma

A. THE MANUSCRIPT TRADITION

A lot of time and space lie between Plautus' original *Poenulus* script and the copy of the play you are reading, and there are many reasons to doubt whether everything that survives was what Plautus wrote, not to mention whether we have every bit of what he wrote. The first issue is that there is no evidence that Plautus actually wrote down his plays before they were performed; in contrast, the verb *scrībere* appears in all of Terence's prologues. Thus Marshall suggests that much of each play resulted from improvisation on stock themes and scenes, and that the texts we have derive from much-edited transcriptions of particular performances.[135] While the metrical complexity of Plautus' Latin precludes the possibility that the plays were completely improvised, it does seem clear from lines 5–22 of the *Casina* that Plautus' comedies were performed long after his death, and that the plays were modified during revivals. It is not always clear to what extent these performers, or even the original actors or Plautus himself, modified the text for later performances, but some plays do seem to contain multiple versions of a scene. These multiples could arise from the incorporation of performance doublets into the scripts as time went on and acting troupes made copies of their own version of the play.[136] On the other hand, every repetitive passage in the text should not be interpreted as a sign of later or non-Plautine additions, because some repetition of information is necessary to ensure that the entire audience in a makeshift theatrical space hears all information relevant to the plot, especially if the surrounding festival entertainments are noisy or

---

135. Marshall 2006 256–79.
136. Marshall 2006 provides a long list of doublets from 266–72.

distracting. Repetition can also occur simply because it's funny![137] Although there is no external evidence for a reperformance of the *Poenulus*, at least some of the repetition (the manuscripts contain multiple versions of the play's ending) must have arisen in later revivals of the play, when modifications were made to the script and then were introduced into Plautus' text when copies were made for other actors or producers.[138]

Next, during the late second century BCE, Roman scholars started studying the plays. Since 130 plays had been attributed to Plautus by this time, scholars tried to determine which were genuine. Although many different scholars weighed in on the question, Varro likely determined which twenty-one comedies would eventually survive (see Gellius *Noctēs Atticae* 3.3).

The texts of Plautus' comedies survive in two different strands, or branches, of manuscripts: the Palatine branch, the earliest examples of which date to the tenth–eleventh centuries, and the fifth-century Ambrosian palimpsest (Milan G 82 *sup.*).[139] Of the Palatine family, B (Palatinus Vaticanus 1615, tenth–eleventh century) is the most reliable, but the initial P is used to label the text (likely from the eighth–tenth century[140]) that must have served as the source for B, C (Palatinus Heidelbergensis 1613, tenth–eleventh century), and D (Vaticanus 3870, tenth–eleventh century), given the agreement between all three texts for most plays. Manuscript B is also helpful because of the corrections written upon it.[141] The work of ancient scholars and grammarians such as Nonius Marcellus (fourth century) can also help us correct some errors in the manuscripts.

As discussed above in 3a, these manuscripts do not always employ consistent spellings: some archaic forms have been "corrected" to a later spelling. On the other hand, Plautus wrote in a time when the "proper" spelling of Latin

---

137. See Henderson (1994 47–48): "Inertia rules this famishing play . . . Stunts delay exits, delay staggers E V E R Y T H I N G; repetition and repetitiousness rule, even become, the script." He cites the following examples: five appearances of "Let's went, sister" from 263–406, cf. 1210–12; the repetition of "what's enough" at 238–39, 297–99, 317, 1204–5; Milphio's epithets at 365–400; the advocates' slow pace at 506–42, then re-rehearsal with Collybiscus at 547–66, 583–604, 721–43; Agorastocles keeps addressing the departing sisters at 406–9 and then is ordered to leave eight times (424–43). Furthermore, other characters also delay their departures: see Antamynides at 491–92, Agorastocles at 607–8, Collybiscus at 801–9, Syncerastus at 916; finally, we find multiple greetings at 851–63 too.

138. For more on the process of textual transmission, especially details about the manuscripts, see Tarrant 1983.

139. Sometime during the eighth or ninth century, a scribe erased the original Plautine manuscript and reused some of it for a copy of the books of Kings and Chronicles from the Old Testament. However, the Ambrosian text is incomplete for two reasons: first, because the scribe did not reuse these manuscript pages in their original order or even use the entire manuscript, and second, because the acid used to render the underlying ink legible in the nineteenth century also damaged the pages.

140. Gratwick 1993 34.

141. Tarrant 1983 305.

terms was changing, so he may not have been entirely consistent in his spelling either.[142] Although the attribution of speeches to specific characters in Roman comedy can be difficult due to the unclear and imprecise labeling of speakers in some manuscripts,[143] the attribution of speeches in the *Poenulus* is relatively certain (other than line 977).

B. THE TEXT

This text is based on Leo's 1906 edition, but with some modifications based on the editions of Lindsay (1905), Maurach (1988), and de Melo (2012), plus the work of Questa (1995) and Welsh (2007).

6. Approaches to Roman Comedy

A. PERFORMANCE CRITICISM

Aside from considering the historical context of the *Poenulus*, it is also profitable to consider what a performance of the play would look like. Although the original performance context of this comedy is unknown (both in terms of its festival setting and thus the location of the stage), we can still consider what the interaction between actors and audience would look like, especially in the scenes during which the characters reveal their knowledge of the audience's presence (such as the advocates at 550–54). Other aspects of performance criticism that can illuminate a play include the timing and location of entrances and exits, or the treatment of space: what happens inside, and what happens outside, for example. It can also be helpful to consider how many actors it would take to stage the comedy and whether or not the acting troupe would share roles or play multiple roles. The musicality of a play—and the location of the *tībīcen*—might also influence the audience's reactions to a performance. Because Carthaginian characters appear in the *Poenulus*, we can also consider what their masks and costumes may have looked like: while Hanno's clothes are described, those of his attendants are not, for example. Finally, while we do not know whether the masks of the Carthaginian characters were different

---

142. Christenson 2000 76.

143. As Gratwick (1993 37) explains, "Speakers were indicated in A [the Ambrosian palimpsest] by single letters in red ink which has disappeared. Presumably this was done 'algebraically', A B Γ Δ . . . , in order of appearance, a standard convention attested elsewhere in the *traditio*, for obviously single-letter initials would be useless in this play [*Menaechmi*, but true for many others as well]. Consequently change of speaker is now only marked within lines by a gap (#) and at line-beginning not at all. In P the names abbreviated to three letters were used; this arrangement survives in degenerate form in B and more sporadically in D, the spaces generally gone and the *notae* added above."

from the standard masks used by a Roman troupe, it is important to consider how unique or standard masks for these characters would affect the audience's responses.

B. METATHEATER AND PRETENSE DISRUPTION

Plautus' comedies often express awareness of themselves as comedies performed before a live audience. The term "metatheater" is used to describe these moments of self-awareness. Niall Slater was the first to popularize the term—and the approach—for Roman comedy.[144] As he describes it, metatheater is "theatrically self-conscious theatre, i.e., theatre that demonstrates an awareness of its own theatricality," its status as a performance by actors in front of an audience.[145] As modern examples, both *30 Rock* and *Community* employed metatheatrical humor as they self-consciously played with the conventions of the television sitcom.[146] In the world of Roman comedy, metatheater can consist of direct address to the audience (with the use of the word *spectātōrēs*, second-person verbs, etc.); awareness of the audience or of being an actor in a play (*spectātōrēs*, etc.); reference to the theater in general (*cōmoedia, tragoedia*, etc.); the use of semi-theatrical language (*auctor, fābula, lūdus, pars, poēta, simulāre, spectāre, sȳcophanta*); reference to costumes and costuming (*exornāre, ornāmentum, ornātus, uestis*, etc.); a play-within-a-play deception and rehearsals for it (which are often marked by the language of teaching and learning lines—*docēre*, etc.); paratragedy and implicit reference to theatrical convention; and general language of deception (*dolus, fallācia, īnsidiae, lūdere*, etc.).[147]

One of the potential effects of metatheater is "pretense disruption," when the actors break through the fourth wall between themselves and the audience (compare Ferris Bueller's speeches directly to the camera in *Ferris Bueller's Day Off*,[148] or similar moments in *Malcolm in the Middle*,[149] *How I Met Your Mother*,[150] and many Woody Allen films[151]). Like Gregory Dobrov, I prefer the

---

144. The term originally comes from Abel 1963.

145. Slater 1985 14.

146. Fey, Tina & Klein, Marci & Michaels, Lorne (Producers). 2006. *30 Rock* (Television series). New York: NBC; Aust, Jake (Producer). 2009. *Community* (Television series). New York: NBC.

147. For more details, see Barsby 2001, Moodie 2007, Muecke 1986, Sharrock 2009, Slater 1985 and 2002.

148. Chinich, Michael (Producer) & Hughes, John (Director). 1986. *Ferris Bueller's Day Off* (Motion picture). United States: Paramount Pictures.

149. Glouberman, Michael (Producer). 2000. *Malcolm in the Middle* (Television series). Los Angeles: Fox.

150. Bays, Carter & Fryman, Pamela & Thomas, Craig (Producers). 2005. *How I Met Your Mother* (Television series). New York: CBS.

151. E.g., Greenhut, Robert (Producer) & Allen, Woody (Director). 1977. *Annie Hall* (Motion picture). United States: United Artists. Comedy tends to be disruptive in many ways: "The comic

term "dramatic pretense" for the "uninterrupted concentration of the fictitious personages of the play on their fictitious situation," rather than the phrase "dramatic illusion," since nobody is actually ever deceived by the illusion of reality presented onstage.[152] The fourth-century grammarian Evanthius (*De Fabula* 3.8) notes that Plautus ruptures the dramatic pretense often, whereas Terence never does.

Metatheatrical themes (costumes, role-playing, a play-within-a-play deception) take center stage in many Plautine comedies. Indeed, the *Poenulus* can be grouped with other so-called metatheatrical deception plays: *Captiui, Casina, Miles Gloriosus, Persa, Pseudolus.*[153] See especially Maurice 2004 on metatheater in the *Poenulus*.

---

script is primarily a place where law, solemn oath, house, mood are there for breaking" (Henderson 1994 48).

152. Dobrov 2001 12. The quotation is from Dover 1972 56.

153. González Vázquez 2001 803.

Text

PERSONAE

AGORASTOCLES: adulescens
MILPHIO: seruos
ADELPHASIVM: uirgo
ANTERASTILIS: uirgo
LYCVS: leno
ANTAMYNIDES: miles
ADVOCATI
COLLYBISCVS: uilicus
SYNCERASTVS: seruos
HANNO: Poenus
GIDDENIS: nutrix
PVER

ARGVMENTVM

Puer septuennis surripitur Carthagine.
Osor mulierum emptum adoptat hunc senex
Et facit heredem. <deinde> eius cognatae duae
Nutrixque earum raptae. mercatur Lycus,
Vexatque amantem. at ille cum auro uilicum
Lenoni obtrudit, itaque eum furto | alligat.
Venit Hanno Poenus, gnatum hunc fratris repperit
Suasque adgnoscit quas perdiderat filias.

Prologus   Achillem Aristarchi mihi commentari lubet:
ind' mihi principium capiam, ex ea tragoedia.
"sileteque et tacete atque animum aduortite,

audire iubet uos imperator" . . . histricus,
bonoque ut animo sedeant in subselliis, 5
et qui esurientes et qui saturi uenerint:
qui edistis, multo fecistis sapientius,
qui non edistis, saturi fite fabulis;
nam quoi paratum est quod edit, nostra gratia
nimia est stultitia sessum impransum incedere. 10
"exsurge, praeco, fac populo audientiam."
iam dudum exspecto, si tuom officium scias:
exerce uocem, quam per uiuisque et clues.
nam nisi clamabis, tacitum te obrepet fames.
age nunc reside, duplicem ut mercedem feras. 15
bonum facesse, edicta ut seruetis mea.
scortum exoletum ne quis in proscaenio
sedeat, neu lictor uerbum aut uirgae muttiant,
neu dissignator praeter os obambulet
neu sessum ducat, dum histrio in scaena siet. 20
diu qui domi otiosi dormierunt, decet
animo aequo nunc stent, uel dormire temperent.
serui ne opsideant, liberis ut sit locus,
uel aes pro capite dent; si id facere non queunt,
domum abeant, uitent ancipiti infortunio, 25
ne et hic uarientur uirgis et loris domi,
si minu' curassint, quom | eri reueniant domum.
nutrices pueros infantis minutulos
domi ut procurent neu quae spectatum adferat,
ne et ipsae sitiant et pueri pereant fame 30
neue esurientes hic quasi haedi obuagiant.
matronae tacitae spectent, tacitae rideant,
canora hic uoce sua tinnire temperent,
domum sermones fabulandi conferant,
ne et hic uiris sint et domi molestiae. 35
quodque ad ludorum curatores attinet,
ne palma detur quoiquam artifici iniuria
neue ambitionis causa extrudantur foras,
quo deteriores anteponantur bonis.
et hoc quoque etiam, quod paene oblitus fui: 40
dum ludi fiunt, in popinam, pedisequi,
inruptionem facite; nunc dum occasio est,
nunc dum scriblitae | aestuant, occurrite.
haec quae imperata sunt pro imperio histrico,

bonum hercle factum pro se quisque ut meminerit. 45
ad argumentum nunc uicissatim uolo
remigrare, ut aeque mecum sitis gnarures.
eius nunc regiones, limites, confinia
determinabo: ei rei ego finitor factus sum.
sed nisi molestum est, nomen dare uobis uolo 50
comoediai; sin odio est, dicam tamen,
siquidem licebit per illos quibus est in manu.
Καρχηδόνιος uocatur haec comoedia,
latine Plautus patruus pultiphagonides.
nomen iam habetis. nunc rationes ceteras 55
accipite; nam argumentum hoc hic censebitur:
locus argumento est suom sibi proscaenium,
uos iuratores estis. quaeso, operam date.
Carthaginienses fratres patrueles duo
fuere, summo genere et summis ditiis; 60
eorum alter uiuit, alter est emortuos.
propterea apud uos dico confidentius,
quia mihi pollictor dixit qui eum pollinxerat.
sed illi seni qui mortuost, <ei> filius,
unicu' qui fuerat, ab diuitiis a patre 65
puer septuennis surripitur Carthagine,
sexennio priu' quidem quam moritur pater.
quoniam periisse sibi uidet gnatum unicum,
conicitur ipse in morbum ex aegritudine:
facit illum heredem fratrem patruelem suom, 70
ipse abit ad Acheruntem sine uiatico.
ill' qui surripuit puerum Calydonem auehit,
uendit eum domino hic diuiti quoidam seni,
cupienti liberorum, osori mulierum.
emit hospitalem is filium imprudens senex 75
puerum illum eumque adoptat sibi pro filio
eumque heredem fecit, quom ipse obiit diem.
is illic adulescens habitat in illisce aedibus.
reuortor rursus denuo Carthaginem:
si quid mandare uoltis aut curarier, 80
argentum nisi qui dederit, nugas egerit;
uerum qui dederit, magi' maiores [nugas] egerit.
sed illi patruo | huius, qui uiuit senex,
Carthaginiensi duae fuere filiae,
altera quinquennis, altera quadrimula; 85

cum nutrice una periere a Magaribus.
eas qui surripuit, in Anactorium deuehit,
uendit eas omnis, et nutricem et uirgines,
praesenti argento | homini, si leno est homo,
quantum hominum terra sustinet sacerrumo.   90
uosmet nunc facite coniecturam ceterum,
quid id sit hominis, quoi Lyco nomen siet.
is ex Anactorio, ubi prius habitauerat,
huc commigrauit in Calydonem | hau diu,
sui quaesti causa. is in illis habitat aedibus.   95
earum hic adulescens alteram efflictim perit,
suam sibi cognatam, imprudens, neque scit quae siet
neque eam umquam tetigit, ita eum leno macerat:
neque quicquam cum | ea fecit etiamnum stupri
neque duxit umquam, neque ille uoluit mittere: 100
quia amare cernit, tangere hominem uolt bolo.
illam minorem in concubinatum sibi
uolt emere miles quidam qui illam deperit.
sed pater illarum Poenus postquam eas perdidit,
mari te<rraque> | usquequaque quaeritat.   105
ubi quamque in urbem | est ingressus, ilico
omnis meretrices, ubi quisque habitant, inuenit;
dat aurum, ducit noctem, rogitat postibi
und' sit, quoiatis, captane an surrupta sit,
quo genere gnata, qui parentes fuerint.   110
ita docte atque astu filias quaerit suas.
et is omnis linguas scit, sed dissimulat sciens
se scire: Poenus plane est. quid uerbis opust?
is heri huc in portum naui uenit uesperi,
pater harunc; idem huic patruos adulescentulo est.   115
iamne hoc tenetis? si tenetis, ducite . . .
caue dirumpatis, quaeso, sinite transigi!
ehem, paene oblitus sum relicuom dicere.
ille qui adoptauit hunc sibi pro filio,
is illi Poeno | huius patruo hospes fuit.   120
is hodie huc ueniet reperietque hic filias
et hunc sui fratris filium, ut quidem didici ego.
ego ibo, ornabor; uos aequo animo noscite.
[hic qui hodie ueniet, reperiet suas filias
et hunc sui fratris filium. dehinc ceterum   125
ualete, adeste. ibo, alius nunc fieri uolo.]

quod restat, restant alii qui faciant palam.
ualete atque adiuuate, ut uos seruet Salus.

Agorastocles Saepe ego res multas tibi mandaui, Milphio,
dubias, egenas, inopiosas consili,   130
quas tu sapienter, docte et cordate et cate
mihi reddidisti | opiparas opera tua.
quibu' pro bene factis fateor deberi tibi
et libertatem et multas gratas gratias.
Milphio Scitum est, per tempus si obuiam est, uerbum uetus.   135
nam tuae blanditiae mihi sunt, quod dici solet,
gerrae germanae, αἱ δὲ κολλῦραι λύραι.
nunc mihi blandidicus es: heri in tergo meo
tris facile corios contriuisti bubulos.
Agor. Amans per amorem si quid feci[t], Milphio,   140
ignoscere id te mi aequom est. **Mil.** Haud uidi magis.
em, nunc ego amore pereo. sine te uerberem,
item ut tu mihi fecisti, ob nullam noxiam:
post id locorum tu mihi amanti ignoscito.
Agor. Si tibi lubido est aut uoluptati, sino: 145
suspende, uinci, uerbera; auctor sum, sino.
Mil. Si auctoritatem postea defugeris,
ubi dissolutus tu sies, ego pendeam.
Agor. Egone istuc ausim facere, praesertim tibi?
quin si feriri uideo te, extemplo dolet.   150
Mil. Mihi quidem hercle. **Agor.** Immo mihi. **Mil.** Istuc mauelim.
sed quid nunc tibi uis? **Agor.** Quor ego apud te mentiar?
amo immodeste. **Mil.** Meae istuc scapulae sentiunt.
Agor. At ego hanc uicinam dico Adelphasium meam,
lenonis huius meretricem maiusculam.   155
Mil. Iam pridem equidem istuc ex te audiui. **Agor.** Differor
cupidine eius. sed lenone istoc Lyco,
illius domino, non lutum est lutulentius.
Mil. Vin tu illi nequam dare nunc? **Agor.** Cupio. **Mil.** Em me dato.
Agor. Abi dierectus. **Mil.** Dic mihi uero serio: 160
uin dare malum illi? **Agor.** Cupio. **Mil.** Em, eundem me dato:
utrumque faxo habebit, et nequam et malum.
Agor. Iocare. **Mil.** Vin tu illam hodie sine [damno et] dispendio
tuo tuam libertam facere? **Agor.** Cupio, Milphio.
Mil. Ego faciam ut facias. sunt tibi intus aurei   165
trecenti nummi Philippi? **Agor.** Sescenti quoque.

Mil. Sati' sunt trecenti. **Agor**. Quid iis facturu's? **Mil**. Tace.
totum lenonem tibi cum tota familia
dabo hodie dono. **Agor**. Qui id facturu's? **Mil**. Iam scies.
tuos Collybiscus nunc in urbe est uilicus;   170
eum hic non nouit leno. satin intellegis?
Agor. Intellego hercle, sed quo euadas nescio.
Mil. Non scis? **Agor**. Non hercle. | **Mil**. At ego iam faxo scies.
ei dabitur aurum, ut ad lenonem deferat
dicatque se peregrinum esse, ex alio oppido: 175
se amare uelle atque opsequi | animo suo;
locum sibi uelle liberum praeberier,
ubi nequam faciat clam, ne quis sit arbiter.
leno ad se accipiet auri cupidus ilico:
celabit hominem et aurum. **Agor**. Consilium placet.   180
Mil. Rogato seruos ueneritne ad eum tuos.
ill' me censebit quaeri: continuo tibi
negabit. quid tu? dubitas quin extempulo
dupli tibi auri et hominis fur leno siet?
neque id unde efficiat habet: ubi in ius uenerit,   185
addicet praetor familiam totam tibi.
ita decipiemus fouea lenonem Lycum.
Agor. Placct consilium. **Mil**. Immo etiam, ubi expoliuero,
magis hoc tum demum dices: nunc etiam rude est.
Agor. Ego in aedem Veneris eo, nisi quid uis, Milphio.   190
Aphrodisia hodie sunt. **Mil**. Scio. | **Agor**. Oculos uolo
meos delectare munditiis meretriciis.
Mil. Hoc primum agamus quod consilium cepimus.
abeamus intro, ut Collybiscum uilicum
hanc perdoceamus ut ferat fallaciam.   195
Agor. Quamquam Cupido in corde uorsatur, tamen
tibi auscultabo.— **Mil**. Faciam ut facto gaudeas.
inest amoris macula huic homini in pectore,
sine damno magno quae elui ne utiquam potest.
itaque hic scelestus est homo leno Lycus,   200
quoi iam infortuni intenta ballista est probe,
quam ego haud multo post mittam e ballistario.
sed Adelphasium eccam exit atque Anterastilis.
haec est prior, quae meum erum dementem facit.
sed euocabo. heus, i foras, Agorastocles,   205
si uis uidere ludos iucundissumos.
Agor. Quid istuc tumulti est, Milphio? | **Mil**. Em amores tuos,

si uis spectare. **Agor.** O multa tibi di dent bona,
quom hoc mi optulisti tam lepidum spectaculum.

Adelphasium Negoti sibi qui uolet uim parare,   210
nauem et mulierem, haec <sibi> duo comparato.
nam nullae magis res duae plus negoti
habent, forte si occeperis exornare,
[neque umquam satis hae duae res ornantur]
neque eis ulla ornandi satis satietas est.   215
atque haec, ut loquor, nunc domo docta dico.
nam nos usque ab aurora ad hoc quod diei est,
[postquam aurora inluxit, numquam concessamus]
ex industria ambae numquam concessamus
lauari aut fricari aut tergeri aut ornari,   220
poliri expoliri, pingi fingi; et una
binae singulis quae datae ancillae nobis,
eae nos lauando eluendo operam dederunt,
aggerundaque aqua sunt uiri duo defessi.
apage sis, negoti quantum in muliere una est!   225
sed uero duae, sat scio, maxumo uni
poplo cuilubet plus satis dare potis sunt,
quae noctes diesque omni in aetate semper
ornantur, lauantur, tergentur, poliuntur.
postremo modus muliebris nullus est: 230
neque umquam lauando et fricando
scimus facere neniam.   231a
nam quae lauta est nisi perculta | est, meo quidem animo quasi inluta est.
Anterastilis Miror equidem, soror, te istaec sic fabulari,
quae tam callida et docta sis et faceta.
nam quom sedulo munditer nos habemus,   235
uix aegreque amatorculos inuenimus.
Ad. Ita est. uerum hoc unum tamen cogitato:
modus omnibus rebus, soror, optumus est habitu.
nimia omnia nimium exhibent negoti hominibus ex se.
Ant. Soror, cogita, amabo, | item nos perhiberi   240
quam si salsa muriatica esse autumantur:
sine omni lepore | et sine suauitate
nisi multa aqua usque et diu macerantur,
olent, salsa sunt, tangere ut non uelis.
item nos sumus.   245
eius seminis mulieres sunt: 245a

insulsae admodum atque inuenustae
sine munditia et sumptu.
Mil. Coqua est haec quidem, Agorastocles, ut ego opinor:
scit muriatica ut maceret. **Agor**. Quid molestu's?
Ad. Soror, parce, amabo: sat est istuc alios   250
dicere nobis, ne nosmet in nostra etiam uitia loquamur.
Ant. Quiesco. **Ad**. Ergo amo te. sed hoc nunc responde
mihi: sunt hic omnia,
quae ad deum pacem oportet ades-
se? **Ant**. Omnia accuraui.   254a
Agor. Diem pulchrum et celebrem et uenustatis plenum,   255
dignum Venere pol, quoi sunt Aphrodisia hodie.
Mil. Ecquid gratiae, quom huc foras te euocaui?
iam num me decet donari
cado uini ueteris? dic dare. nil respondes?
lingua huic excidit, ut ego opinor.   260
quid hic, malum, astans opstipuisti? **Agor**. Sine amem, ne opturba ac tace.
Mil. Taceo. **Agor**. Si tacuisses, iam istuc "taceo" non gnatum foret.
Ant. Eamus, mea soror. **Ad**. Eho amabo, quid illo nunc properas? **Ant**. Rogas?
quia erus nos apud aedem Veneris mantat. **Ad**. Maneat pol. mane:
turba est nunc apud aram. an te ibi uis inter istas uorsarier   265
prosedas, pistorum amicas, reliquias alicarias,
miseras schoeno delibutas seruolicolas sordidas,
quae tibi olant stabulum statumque, sellam et sessibulum merum,
quas adeo hau quisquam umquam liber tetigit neque duxit domum,
seruolorum sordidulorum scorta diobolaria?   270
Mil. I in malam crucem. tun audes etiam seruos spernere,
propudium? quasi bella sit, quasi eampse reges ductitent,
monstrum mulieris, tantilla tanta uerba funditat,
quoius ego nebulai cyatho septem noctes non emam.
Agor. Di immortales omnipotentes, quid est apud uos pulchrius? 275
quid habetis qui mage immortalis uos credam esse quam ego siem,
qui haec tanta oculis bona concipio? nam Venus non est Venus:
hanc equidem Venerem uenerabor, me ut amet posthac propitia.
Milphio, heus, ubi es? **Mil**. Adsum apud te, eccum. | **Agor**. At ego elixus sis
uolo.
Mil. Enim uero, ere, facis delicias. **Agor**. De tequidem haec didici omnia. 280
Mil. Etiamne ut ames eam quam numquam tetigeris? **Agor**. Nihil id quidem
est:
deos quoque edepol et amo et metuo, quibu' tamen apstineo manus.
Ant. Eu ecastor, quom ornatum aspicio nostrum ambarum, paenitet

exornatae ut simus. **Ad**. Immo uero sane commode;
nam pro erili et nostro quaestu sati' bene ornatae sumus.   285
non enim potis est quaestus fieri, ni sumptus sequitur, scio,
et tamen quaestus non consistet, si eum sumptus superat, soror.
eo illud satiust, satis quod habitu, <haud satis est quod> plus quam sat est.
Agor. Ita me di ament, ut illa me amet malim quam di, Milphio.
nam illa mulier lapidem silicem subigere ut se amet potest.   290
Mil. Pol id quidem hau mentire, nam tu es lapide silice stultior,
qui hanc ames. **Agor**. At uide sis, cum illac numquam limaui caput.
Mil. Curram igitur aliquo ad piscinam aut ad lacum, limum petam.
Agor. Quid eo opust? **Mil**. Ego dicam: ut illi et tibi limem caput.
Agor. I in malam rem. **Mil**. Ibi sum equidem. **Agor**. Perdis. **Mil**. Taceo.   295
    Agor. At perpetuo uolo.
Mil. Enim uero, ere, meo me lacessis ludo et delicias facis.
Ant. Sati' nunc lepide ornatam credo, soror, te tibi uiderier;
sed ubi exempla conferentur meretricum aliarum, ibi tibi
erit cordolium, si quam ornatam melius forte aspexeris.
Ad. Inuidia in me numquam innata est neque malitia, mea soror.   300
bono med esse ingenio ornatam quam auro multo mauolo:
aurum, id fortuna inuenitur, natura ingenium bonum.
[bonam ego quam beatam me esse nimio dici mauolo.]
meretricem pudorem gerere magi' decet quam purpuram:
[magi'que meretricem pudorem quam aurum gerere condecet.]   305
pulchrum ornatum turpes mores peius caeno conlinunt,
lepidi mores turpem ornatum facile factis comprobant.
Agor. Eho tu, uin tu facinus facere lepidum et festiuom? **Mil**. Volo.
Agor. Potesne mi auscultare? **Mil**. Possum. **Agor**. Abi domum ac suspende te.
Mil. Quam ob rem? **Agor**. Quia iam numquam audibis uerba tot   310
    tam suauia.
quid tibi opust uixisse? ausculta mihi modo ac suspende te.
Mil. Siquidem tu es mecum futurus pro uua passa pensilis.
Agor. At ego amo hanc. **Mil**. At ego esse et bibere. | **Ad**. Eho tu, quid ais? **Ant**.
    Quid rogas?
Ad. Viden tu? pleni oculi sorderum qui | erant, iam splendent mihi.
Ant. Immo etiam medio oculo paullum sordist. **Ad**. Cedo sis deteram.   315
Agor. Vt quidem tu huius oculos inlutis manibus tractes aut teras?
Ant. Nimia nos socordia hodie tenuit. **Ad**. Qua de re, opsecro?
Ant. Quia non iam dudum ante lucem ad aedem Veneris uenimus,
primae ut inferremus ignem in aram. **Ad**. Aha, non facto est opus:
quae | habent nocturna ora, noctu sacruficatum ire occupant.   320
priu' quam Venus expergiscatur, priu' deproperant sedulo

sacruficare; nam uigilante Venere si ueniant eae,
ita sunt turpes, credo ecastor Venerem ipsam e fano fugent.
Agor. Milphio. **Mil**. Edepol Milphionem miserum. quid nunc uis tibi?
Agor. Opsecro hercle, ut mulsa loquitur. **Mil**. Nil nisi laterculos,   325
sesumam papaueremque, triticum et frictas nuces.
Agor. Ecquid amare uideor? **Mil**. Damnum, quod Mercurius minime amat.
Agor. Namque edepol lucrum | <ullum> amare nullum amatorem addecet.
Ant. Eamus, mea germana. | **Ad**. Age sis, ut lubet. **Ant**. Sequere hac. **Ad**.
   Sequor.
Mil. Eunt hae. **Agor**. Quid si adeamus? **Mil**. Adeas. **Agor**. Primum   330
   prima salua sis,
et secunda tu [in] secundo salue in pretio; tertia
salue extra pretium. **Ancilla**. Tum pol ego et oleum et operam perdidi.
Agor. Quo te agis? **Ad**. Egone? in aedem Veneris. **Agor**. Quid eo? **Ad**. Vt
   Venerem propitiem.
Agor. Eho, an irata est? propitia hercle est. uel ego pro illa spondeo.
quid tu ais? **Ad**. Quid mihi molestu's, opsecro? **Agor**. Aha, tam saeuiter.   335
Ad. Mitte, amabo. **Agor**. Quid festinas? turba nunc illi est. **Ad**. Scio.
sunt illi aliae quas spectare ego, et me spectari uolo.
Agor. Qui lubet spectare turpis, pulchram spectandam dare?
Ad. Quia apud aedem Veneris hodie est mercatus meretricius:
eo conucniunt mercatores, ibi ego me ostendi uolo.   340
Agor. Inuendibili merci oportet ultro emptorem adducere:
proba mers facile emptorem reperit, tam etsi in aptruso sita est.
quid ais tu? quando illi apud me mecum palpas et λαλεῖς?
Ad. Quo die Orcus Acherunte mortuos amiserit.
Agor. Sunt mihi intus nescio quot nummi aurei lymphatici.   345
Ad. Deferto ad me, faxo actutum constiterit lymphaticum.
Mil. Bellula hercle. **Agor**. I dierecte in maxumam malam crucem.
Mil. Quam magis aspecto, tam magis est nimbata et nugae merae.
Ad. Segrega sermonem. taedet. **Agor**. Age, sustolle hoc amiculum.
Ad. Pura sum, comperce amabo me attrectare, Agorastocles.   350
Agor. Quid agam nunc? **Ad**. Si sapias, curam hanc facere compendi potes.
Agor. Quid? ego non te curem? quid ais, Milphio? **Mil**. Ecce odium meum.
quid me uis? **Ag**. Quor mi haec irata est? **Mil**. Quor haec irata est tibi?
cur ego id curem? Nam qui istaec magi' mea est curatio?
Agor. Iam hercle tu periisti, nisi illam mihi tam tranquillam facis   355
quam mare olim est, quom | ibi alcedo pullos educit suos.
Mil. Quid faciam? **Agor**. Exora, blandire, expalpa. **Mil**. Faciam sedulo.
sed uide sis, ne tu oratorem hunc pugnis pectas postea.
Agor. Non faciam. **Ad**. Non aequos in me es, sed morare et male facis.

bene promittis multa ex multis: omnia in cassum cadunt.   360
liberare iurauisti me haud semel, sed centiens:
dum te exspecto, neque ego usquam aliam mihi paraui copiam
neque istuc usquam apparet; ita nunc seruio nihilo minus.
i, soror. apscede tu a me. **Agor**. Perii. ecquid agis, Milphio?
Mil. Mea uoluptas, mea delicia, mea uita, mea amoenitas,   365
meus ocellus, meum labellum, mea salus, meum sauium,
meum mel, meum cor, mea colustra, meu' molliculus caseus . . .
Agor. Mene ego illaec patiar praesente dici? discrucior miser,
nisi ego illum iubeo quadrigis cursim ad carnuficem rapi.
Mil . . . . noli, amabo, suscensere ero meo, causa mea.   370
ego faxo, si non irata es, ninnium pro te dabit
atque te faciet ut sis ciuis Attica atque libera.
quin adire sini'? quin tibi qui bene uolunt, bene uis item?
si ante quid mentitust, nunciam dehinc erit uerax tibi.
sine te exorem, sine prehendam auriculis, sine dem sauium.   375
Ad. Apscede hinc sis, sycophanta par ero. **Mil**. At scin quo modo?
iam hercle ego faciam ploratillum, nisi te facio propitiam,
atque hic ne me uerberetillum faciat, nisi te propitio,
male formido: noui ego huius mores morosi malos.
quam ob rem amabo, mea uoluptas, sine te hoc exorarier.   380
Agor. Non ego homo trioboli sum, nisi ego illi mastigiae
exturbo oculos atque dentes. em uoluptatem tibi!
em mel! em cor! em labellum! | em salutem, em sauium!
Mil. Impias, ere, te: oratorem uerberas. **Agor**. Iam istoc magis:
[etiam ocellum addam et labellum et linguam. **Mil**. Ecquid facies modi?   385
Agor.] sicine ego te orare iussi? **Mil**. Quo modo ergo orem? **Agor**. Rogas?
sic enim diceres, sceleste: huius uoluptas, te opsecro,
huius mel, huius cor, huius labellum, huius lingua, huius sauium,
huius delicia, huius salus amoena, huius festiuitas:
huiu' colustra, | huius dulciculus caseus, mastigia,   390
[huius cor, huius studium, huius sauium, mastigia]   390a
omnia illa, quae dicebas tua, esse ea memorares mea.
Mil. Opsecro hercle te, uoluptas huius atque odium meum,
huius amica mammeata, mea inimica et maleuola,
oculus huius, lippitudo mea, mel huius, fel meum,
ut tu | huic irata ne sis aut, si id fieri non potest,   395
capias restim ac te suspendas cum ero et uostra familia.
nam mihi iam uideo propter te uictitandum sorbilo,
itaque iam quasi ostreatum tergum ulceribus gestito
propter amorem uostrum. **Ad**. Amabo, men prohibere postulas

ne te uerberet magi' quam ne mendax me aduorsum siet?   400
Ant. Aliquid huic responde, amabo, commode, ne incommodus
nobis sit. nam detinet nos de nostro negotio.
Ad. Verum. etiam tibi hanc amittam noxiam unam, Agorastocles.
non sum irata. **Agor**. Non es? **Ad**. Non sum. **Agor**. Da ergo, ut credam,
  sauium.
Ad. Mox dabo, quom ab re diuina rediero. **Agor**. I ergo strenue.   405
Ad. Sequere me, soror. **Agor**. Atque audin? **Ad**. Etiam? **Agor**. Veneri dicito
multam meis uerbis salutem. **Ad**. Dicam. **Ag**. Atque hoc audi. **Ad**. Quid est?—
Agor. Paucis uerbis rem diuinam facito. atque audin? respice.
respexit. idem edepol Venerem credo facturam tibi.
quid nunc mi es auctor, Milphio? **Mil**. Vt me uerberes   410
atque auctionem facias: nam impunissume
tibi quidem hercle uendere hasce aedis licet.
Agor. Quid iam? **Mil**. Maiorem partem in ore habitas meo.
Agor. Supersede istis uerbis. **Mil**. Quid nunc ueis tibi?
Agor. Trecentos Philippos Collybisco uilico   415
dedi dudum, priu' quam me euocauisti foras.
nunc opsecro te, Milphio, hanc per dexteram
perque hanc sororem laeuam perque oculos tuos
perqu' meos amores perque Adelphasium meam
perque tuam libertatem . . . **Mil**. Em nunc nihil opsecras.   420
Agor. . . . mi Milphidisce, mea commoditas, mea salus,
fac quod facturum te esse promisti mihi,
ut ego hunc lenonem perdam. **Mil**. Perfacile id quidem est.
i, adduce testis tecum; ego intus interim
iam et ornamentis meis et sycophantiis   425
tuom exornabo uilicum. propera atque abi.
Agor. Fugio. **Mil**. Meum est istuc magis officium quam tuom.
Agor. Egone egone, si istuc lepide ecfexis . . . **Mil**. I modo.
Agor . . . . ut non ego te hodie . . . **Mil**. Abi modo. **Agor** . . . . emittam manu . . .
Mil. I modo. **Ag** . . . . non hercle meream . . . **Mil**. Oh . . . **Ag** . . . . uah! . . . **Mil**.
  Abi modo.   430
Agor . . . . quantum Acherunte est mortuorum . . . **Mil**. Etiamne abis?
Agor . . . . neque quantum aquai est in mari . . . | **Mil**. Abiturun es?
Agor . . . . neque nubes omnes quantumst . . . **Mil**. Pergin pergere?
Agor . . . . neque stellae in caelo . . . **Mil**. Pergin auris tundere?
Agor . . . . neque hoc neque illud neque . . . enim uero serio . . .   435
neque . . . hercle uero . . . quid opust uerbis? quippini?
quod uno uerbo . . . dicere hic quiduis licet . . .
neque . . . hercle uero serio, scin quo modo?

ita me di amabunt . . . uin bona dicam fide,
quod hic inter nos liceat, ita me Iuppiter . . .   440
scin quam uidetur? credin quod ego fabuler?
Mil. Si nequeo facere ut abeas, egomet abiero;
nam isti quidem hercle orationi | Oedipo
opust coniectore, qui Sphingi interpres fuit.—
Agor. Illic hinc iratus abiit. nunc mihi cautio est,   445
ne meamet culpa meo amori obiexim moram.
ibo atque arcessam testis, quando Amor iubet
me oboedientem | esse seruo liberum.—

Lycus Di illum infelicent omnes, qui post hunc diem
leno ullam Veneri umquam immolarit hostiam   450
quiue ullum turis granum sacruficauerit.
nam ego hodie infelix dis meis iratissumis
sex immolaui | agnos, nec potui tamen
propitiam Venerem facere uti | esset mihi.
quoniam litare nequeo, | abii illim ilico   455
iratus, uotui | exta prosicarier;
[neque ea poricere uolui, quoniam non bona   456a
haruspex dixit; deam esse indignam credidi.]   456b
eo pacto auarae Veneri pulchre adii manum.
quando id quod sat erat satis habere noluit,
ego pausam feci. sic ago, sic me decet.
ego faxo posthac di deaeque ceteri   460
contentiores mage erunt atque auidi minus,
quom scibunt Veneri ut adierit leno manum.
condigne haruspex, non homo trioboli,
omnibus in extis aibat portendi mihi
malum damnumque et deos esse iratos mihi.   465
quid ei diuini aut humani aequom est credere?
mina mihi argenti dono postilla data est.
sed quaeso, ubinam illic restitit miles modo,
qui hanc mihi donauit, quem ego uocaui ad prandium?
sed eccum incedit. **Antamynides** Ita ut occepi dicere,   470
lenulle, de | illa pugna Pentetronica,
quom sexaginta milia hominum uno die
uolaticorum manibus occidi meis.
Lyc. Volaticorum | hominum? | **Antam.** Ita dico quidem.
Lyc. An, opsecro, usquam sunt homines uolatici?   475
Antam. Fuere. uerum ego interfeci. **Lyc.** Quo modo

potuisti? **Antam**. Dicam. uiscum legioni dedi
fundasque; eo praesternebant folia farferi.
Lyc. Quoi rei? **Antam**. Ad fundas uiscus ne adhaeresceret.
Lyc. Perge. optume hercle periuras. quid postea?   480
Antam. In fundas uisci indebant grandiculos globos,
in illos uolantis iussi funditarier.
quid multa uerba? quemquem uisco offenderant,
tam crebri ad terram | accidebant quam pira.   484–85
ut quisque acciderat, eum necabam | ilico
per cerebrum pinna sua sibi, quasi turturem.
Lyc. Si hercle istuc umquam factum est, tum me Iuppiter
faciat ut semper sacruficem nec umquam litem.
Antam. An mi haec non credis? **Lyc**. Credo, ut mi aequom est credier.   490
age eamus intro. **Antam**. Dum exta referuntur, uolo
narrare tibi etiam unam pugnam. **Lyc**. Nil moror.
Antam. Ausculta. **Lyc**. Non hercle auscultabo. **Antam**. Quo modo?
colaphis quidem hercle tuom iam dilidam caput,
nisi aut auscultas aut is in malam crucem.   495
Lyc. Malam crucem ibo potius. **Antam**. Certumne est tibi?
Lyc. Certum. **Antam**. Tum tu igitur die bono Aphrodisiis
addice tuam mihi meretricem minusculam.
Lyc. Ita res diuina mihi fuit: res serias
omnis extollo ex hoc die in alium diem.   500
Antam. Profestos festos habeam decretum est mihi.
Nunc hinc eamus intro. **Lyc**. Sequere hac me.— **Antam**. Sequor.
in hunc diem iam tuos sum mercennarius.—

Agorastocles Ita me di | ament, tardo amico nihil est quicquam nequius,
praesertim homini amanti, qui quidquid agit properat omnia.   505
sicut ego hos duco aduocatos, homines spissigradissumos,
tardiores quam corbitae sunt in tranquillo mari.
atque equidem hercle dedita opera amicos fugitaui senes:
scibam aetate tardiores, metui meo amori moram.
nequiquam hos procos mi elegi loripedes, tardissumos.   510
quin si ituri hodie estis, ite, aut ite hinc in malam crucem.
sicine oportet ire amicos homini amanti operam datum?
nam iste quidem gradus succretust cribro pollinario,
nisi cum pedicis condidicistis istoc grassari gradu.
Aduocati Heus tu, quamquam nos uidemur tibi plebeii et pauperes,   515
si nec recte dicis nobis, diues de summo loco,
diuitem audacter solemus mactare infortunio.

nec tibi nos obnoxii [sumus] istuc, quid tu ames aut oderis:
quom argentum pro capite dedimus, nostrum dedimus, non tuom;
liberos nos esse oportet. nos te nihili pendimus,   520
ne tuo nos amori seruos [tuos] esse addictos censeas.
liberos homines per urbem modico magi' par est gradu
ire, seruoli esse duco festinantem currere.
praesertim in re populi placida atque interfectis hostibus
non decet tumultuari. sed si properabas magis,   525
pridie nos te aduocatos huc duxisse oportuit.
ne tu opinere, haud quisquam hodie nostrum curret per uias,
neque nos populus pro cerritis insectabit lapidibus.
Agor. At si ad prandium me in aedem uos dixissem ducere,
uinceretis ceruom cursu uel gralatorem gradu;   530
nunc uos quia mihi aduocatos dixi et testis ducere,
podagrosi estis ac uicistis cocleam tarditudine.
Adu. An uero non iusta causa est, quor curratur celeriter
ubi bibas, edas de alieno quantum ueis usque ad fatim,
quod tu inuitus numquam reddas domino, de quoio ederis?   535
sed tamen cum eo cum quiqui, quamquam sumu' pauperculi,
est domi quod edimus, ne nos tam contemptim conteras.
quidquid est pauxillulum illuc, nostrum id omne, non tuom est,
neque nos quemquam flagitamus neque nos quisquam flagitat.
tua causa nemo nostrorum est suos rupturus ramites.   540
Agor. Nimis iracundi estis: equidem haec uobis dixi per iocum.
Adu. Per iocum itidem dictum habeto quae nos tibi respondimus.
Agor. Opsecro hercle, operam celocem hanc mihi, ne corbitam date;
attrepidate saltem, nam uos adproperare haud postulo.
Adu. Si quid tu placide otioseque agere uis, operam damus;   545
si properas, cursores meliust te aduocatos ducere.
Agor. Scitis rem, narraui uobis quod uostra opera mi opu' siet,
de lenone hoc, qui me amantem ludificatur tam diu,
ei paratae ut sint insidiae de auro et de seruo meo.
Adu. Omnia istaec scimus iam nos, si hi spectatores sciant;   550
horunc hic nunc causa haec agitur spectatorum fabula:
hos te satius est docere, ut, quando agas, quid agas sciant.
nos tu ne curassis: scimus rem omnem, quippe omnes simul
didicimus tecum una, ut respondere possemus tibi.
Agor. Ita profecto est. sed agite igitur, ut sciam uos scire rem,   555
expedite [et] mihi quae uobis dudum dixi dicite.
Adu. Itane? temptas an sciamus? non meminisse nos ratu's,
quo modo trecentos Philippos Collybisco uilico

dederis, quos deferret huc ad lenonem inimicum tuom,
isqu' se ut assimularet peregrinum [esse] aliunde ex alio oppido? 560
ubi | is detulerit, tu eo quaesitum seruom aduenies tuom
cum pecunia. **Agor.** Meministis memoriter, seruasti' me.
Adu. Ill' negabit: Milphionem quaeri censebit tuom;
id duplicabit omne furtum. leno addicetur tibi.
ad eam rem nos esse testis uis tibi. **Agor.** Teneti' rem? 565
Adu. Vix quidem hercle, | ita pauxilla est, digitulis primoribus.
Agor. Hoc cito et cursim est agendum. propera iam quantum potest.
Adu. Bene uale igitur. te aduocatos meliust celeris ducere;
tardi sumu' nos. **Agor.** Optume itis, pessume hercle dicitis.
quin etiam deciderint uobis femina in talos uelim. 570
Adu. At edepol nos tibi | in lumbos linguam atque oculos in solum.
Agor. Heia, hau uostrum est iracundos esse, quod dixi ioco.
Adu. Nec tuom quidem est amicis per iocum iniuste loqui.
Agor. Mittite istaec. quid uelim uos, scitis. **Adu.** Callemus probe:
lenonem ut periurum perdas, id studes. **Agor.** Teneti' rem. 575
euge, opportune egrediuntur Milphio una et uilicus.
basilice exornatus incedit et fabre ad fallaciam.

Mil. Iam tenes praecepta in corde? **Collybiscus** Pulchre. **Mil.** Vide sis calleas.
Coll. Quid opust uerbis? callum aprugnum callere aeque non sinam.
Mil. Fac modo ut condocta tibi sint dicta ad hanc fallaciam. 580
Coll. Quin edepol condoctior sum quam tragoedi aut comici.
Mil. Probus homo est. **Agor.** Adeamus propius. **Mil.** Adsunt testes? **Agor.** Tot
    quidem.
Mil. Non potuisti adducere homines magis ad hanc rem idoneos.
nam istorum nullus nefastust: comitiales sunt meri;
ibi habitant, ibi eos conspicias quam praetorem saepius. 585
hodie iuris coctiores non sunt qui litis creant,
quam hi sunt, qui si non est quicum litigent, litis emunt.
Adu. Di te perdant. **Mil.** Vos quidem hercle . . . cum | eo cum quiqui tamen
et bene et benigne facitis, quom | ero amanti operam datis.
sed isti iam sciunt, negoti quid sit? **Agor.** Omne in ordine. 590
Mil. Tum uos animum aduortite igitur. hunc uos lenonem Lycum
nouistis? **Adu.** Facile. **Coll.** At pol ego eum, qua sit facie, nescio.
eum mihi uolo demonstretis hominem. **Adu.** Nos curabimus.
sati' praeceptum est. **Agor.** Hic trecentos nummos numeratos habet.
Adu. Ergo nos inspicere oportet istuc aurum, Agorastocles, 595
ut sciamus quid dicamus mox pro testimonio.

Coll. Agite, inspicite. **Adu**. Aurum est profecto hoc, spectatores, comicum:
macerato hoc pingues fiunt auro in barbaria boues;
uerum ad hanc rem agundam Philippum est: ita nos adsimulabimus.
Coll. Sed ita adsimulatote quasi ego sim peregrinus. **Adu**. Scilicet,   600
et quidem quasi tu nobiscum adueniens hodie oraueris,
liberum ut commostraremus tibi locum et uoluptarium,
ubi ames, potes, pergraecere. **Coll**. Eu, edepol mortales malos!
Agor. Ego enim docui. **Mil**. Quis te porro? **Coll**. Agite intro abite,
    Agorastocles,
ne hic uos mecum conspicetur leno neu fallaciae   605
praepedimentum obiciatur. **Adu**. Hic homo sapienter sapit.
facite quod iubet. **Agor**. Abeamus. sed uos . . . **Adu**. Sati' dictum est. abi.
Agor. Abeo. **Adu**. Quaeso, di immortales, quin abis? **Agor**. Abeo.— **Adu**.
    Sapis.
Coll. St!
tace. **Adu**. Quid est? **Coll**. Fores hae fecerunt magnum flagitium modo.   609a
Adu. Quid <id> est flagiti? **Coll**. Crepuerunt clare. **Adu**. Di te perduint.   610
pone nos recede. **Coll**. Fiat. **Adu**. Nos priores ibimus.
Coll. Faciunt scurrae quod consuerunt: pone sese homines locant.
Adu. Illic homo est, qui egreditur, leno. **Coll**. Bonus est, nam similis mali est.
iam nunc ego illi egredienti sanguinem exsugam procul.

Lycus Iam ego istuc reuortar, miles: conuiuas uolo   615
reperire nobis commodos, qui una sient;
interibi attulerint exta, atque eadem mulieres
iam ab re diuina credo apparebunt domi.
sed quid huc tantum hominum incedunt? ecquidnam adferunt?
et ill' chlamydatus quisnam est, qui sequitur procul?   620
Adu. Aetoli ciues te salutamus, Lyce,
quamquam hanc salutem ferimus inuiti tibi et
quamquam bene uolumus leniter lenonibus.   622a
Lyc. Fortunati omnes sitis, quod certo scio
nec fore nec Fortunam id situram fieri.
Adu. Istic est thensaurus stultis in lingua situs,   625
ut quaestui habeant male loqui melioribus.
Lyc. Viam qui nescit, qua deueniat ad mare,
eum oportet amnem quaerere comitem sibi.
ego male loquendi uobis nesciui uiam:
nunc uos mihi amnes estis; uos certum est sequi: 630
si bene dicetis, uostra ripa uos sequar,
si male dicetis, uostro gradiar limite.

Adu. Malo bene facere tantundem est periculum
quantum bono male facere. **Lyc**. Qui uero? **Adu**. Scies.
malo si quid bene facias, [id] beneficium interit;   635
bono si quid male facias, aetatem expetit.
Lyc. Facete dictum. sed quid istuc ad me attinet?
Adu. Quia nos honoris tui causa ad te uenimus,
quamquam bene uolumus leniter lenonibus.
Lyc. Si quid boni adportatis, habeo gratiam.   640
Adu. Boni de nostro tibi nec ferimus nec damus
neque pollicemur, neque adeo uolumus datum.
Lyc. Credo hercle uobis: ita uostra est benignitas.
sed quid nunc uoltis? **Adu**. Hunc chlamydatum quem uides,
ei Mars iratust. **Coll**. Capiti uostro istuc quidem!   645
Adu. Nunc hunc, Lyce, ad te diripiundum adducimus.
Coll. Cum praeda hic hodie incedet uenator domum:
canes compellunt in plagas lepide lupum.
Lyc. Quis hic est? **Adu**. Nescimus nos quidem istum qui siet;
nisi dudum mane ut ad portum processimus,   650
atque istum e naui exeuntem oneraria
uidemus. adiit ad nos extemplo exiens;
salutat, respondemus. **Coll**. Mortalis malos!
ut ingrediuntur docte in sycophantiam!
Lyc. Quid deinde? **Adu**. Sermonem ibi nobiscum copulat.   655
ait se peregrinum esse huius ignarum oppidi;
locum sibi uelle liberum praeberier,
ubi nequam faciat. nos hominem ad te adduximus.
tu, si te di amant, agere tuam rem occasio est.
Lyc. Itane? **Adu**. Ille est cupiens, aurum habet. **Lyc**. Praeda haec mea est. 660
Adu. Potare, amare uolt. **Lyc**. Locum lepidum dabo.
Adu. At enim hic clam furtim | esse uolt, ne quis sciat
neue arbiter sit. nam hic latro in Sparta fuit,
ut quidem ipse nobis dixit, apud regem Attalum;
ind' huc aufugit, quoniam capitur oppidum.   665
Coll. Nimi' lepide de latrone, de Sparta optume.
Lyc. Di deaeque uobis multa bona dent, quom mihi
et bene praecipitis et bonam praedam datis.
Adu. Immo ut ipse nobis dixit, quo accures magis,
trecentos nummos Philippos portat praesidi.   670
Lyc. Rex sum, si ego illum hodie ad me hominem adlexero.
Adu. Quin hic quidem tuos est. **Lyc**. Opsecro hercle hortamini,
ut deuortatur ad me in hospitium optumum.

Adu. Neque nos hortari neque dehortari decet
hominem peregrinum: tuam rem tu | ages, si sapis.   675
nos tibi palumbem ad aream usque adduximus:
nunc te illum meliust capere, si captum esse uis.
Coll. Iamne itis? quid quod uobis mandaui, hospites?
Adu. Cum illoc te meliust tuam rem, | adulescens, loqui:
illic est ad istas res probus, quas quaeritas.   680
Coll. Videre equidem uos uellem, quom huic aurum darem.
Adu. Illinc procul nos istuc inspectabimus.
Coll. Bonam dedistis mihi operam. **Lyc.** It ad me lucrum.
Coll. Illud quidem quorsum asinus caedit calcibus.
Lyc. Blande hominem compellabo. | hospes hospitem   685
salutat. saluom te aduenire gaudeo.
Coll. Multa tibi di dent bona, quom me saluom esse uis.
Lyc. Hospitium te aiunt quaeritare. **Coll.** Quaerito.
Lyc. Ita illi dixerunt, qui hinc a me abierunt modo,
te quaeritare a muscis. **Coll.** Minime gentium.   690
Lyc. Quid ita? **Coll.** Quia <a> muscis si mi hospitium quaererem,
adueniens irem in carcerem recta uia.
ego id quaero hospitium, ubi ego curer mollius,
quam regi Antiocho | oculi curari solent.
Lyc. Edepol ne tibi illud possum festiuom dare,   695
siquidem potes esse te pati in lepido loco,
in lecto lepide strato lepidam mulierem
complexum contrectare . . . | **Coll.** Is, leno, uiam.
Lyc . . . . ubi tu Leucadio, Lesbio, Thasio, Chio,
uetustate uino edentulo aetatem inriges;   700
ibi ego te replebo usque unguentum geumatis,
quid multa uerba? faciam, ubi tu laueris,
ibi ut balneator faciat unguentariam.
sed haec latrocinantur, quae ego dixi, omnia.
Coll. Quid ita? **Lyc.** Quia aurum poscunt praesentarium.   705
Coll. Quin hercle accipere tu non mauis quam ego dare.
Adu. Quid si euocemus huc foras Agorastoclem,
ut ipsus testis sit sibi certissumus?
heus tu, qui furem captas, egredere ocius,
ut tute inspectes aurum lenoni dari.   710

Agorastocles Quid est? quid uoltis, testes? **Adu.** Specta ad dexteram.
tuo' seruos aurum | ipsi lenoni dabit.
Coll. Age, accipe hoc sis: hic sunt numerati aurei

trecenti nummi qui uocantur Philippei.
hinc me procura; propere hosce apsumi uolo.　　　　715
Lyc. Edepol fecisti prodigum promum tibi.
age, eamus intro. Coll. Te sequor. Lyc. Age, age, ambula,
ibi, quae reliqua, alia fabulabimur.
Coll. Eadem narrabo tibi res Spartiaticas.
Lyc. Quin sequere me ergo.— Coll. Abduc intro. addictum tenes.—　　　720
Agor. Quid nunc, mi auctores estis? Adu. Vt frugi sies.
Agor. Quid si animus esse non sinit? Adu. Esto ut sinit.
Agor. Vidistis, leno quom aurum accepit? Adu. Vidimus.
Agor. Eum uos meum esse seruom scitis? Adu. Sciuimus.
Agor. Rem aduersus populi saepe leges? Adu. Sciuimus.　　　725
Agor. Em istaec uolo ergo uos commeminisse omnia,
mox quom ad praetorem | usus ueniet. Adu. Meminimus.
Agor. Quid si recenti re aedis pultem? Adu. Censeo.
Agor. Si pultem, non recludet? Adu. Panem frangito.
Agor. Si exierit leno, quid tum? hominem interrogem,　　　730
meu' seruos ad eum ueneritne? Adu. Quippini?
Agor. Cum auri ducentis nummis Philippis? Adu. Quippini?
Agor. Ibi extemplo leno errabit. Adu. Qua de re? Agor. Rogas?
quia centum nummis minu' dicetur. Adu. Bene putas.
Agor. Alium censebit quaeritari. Adu. Scilicet.　　　735
Agor. Extemplo denegabit. Adu. Iuratus quidem.
Agor. Homo furti sese adstringet. Adu. Hau dubium id quidem est.
Agor. Quantumquantum ad eum erit delatum. Adu. Quippini?
Agor. Diespiter uos perduit! Adu. Te quippini?
Agor. Ibo et pultabo ianuam. | Adu. Ita, quippini?　　　740
Agor. Tacendi tempus est, nam crepuerunt fores.
foras egredier uideo lenonem Lycum.
adeste quaeso. Adu. Quippini? <sine> si uoles
operire capita, ne nos leno nouerit,
qui illi malae rei tantae fuimus inlices.　　　745

Lycus Suspendant omnes nunciam se haruspices,
quam ego illis posthac quod loquantur creduam,
qui in re diuina dudum dicebant mihi
malum damnumque maxumum portendier:
is explicaui meam rem postilla lucro.　　　750
Agor. Saluos sis, leno. Lyc. Di te ament, Agorastocles.
Agor. Magi' me benigne nunc salutas quam antidhac.

Lyc. Tranquillitas euenit, quasi naui in mari:
utquomque est uentus, exim uelum uortitur.
Agor. Valeant apud te quos uolo atque haud te uolo.   755
Lyc. Valent ut postulatum est, uerum non tibi.
Agor. Mitte ad me, si audes, hodie Adelphasium tuam,
die festo celebri nobilique Aphrodisiis.
Lyc. Calidum prandisti prandium hodie? dic mihi.
Agor. Quid iam? **Lyc**. Quia os nunc frigefactas, quom rogas.   760
Agor. Hoc age sis, leno. seruom esse audiui meum
apud te. **Lyc**. Apud me? numquam factum reperies.
Agor. Mentire. nam ad te uenit aurumque attulit.
ita mihi renuntiatum est, quibus credo satis.
Lyc. Malus es, captatum me aduenis cum testibus.   765
tuorum apud me nemo est nec quicquam tui.
Agor. Mementote illud, aduocati. **Adu**. Meminimus.
Lyc. Hahahae! iam teneo quid sit, perspexi modo.
hi qui illum dudum conciliauerunt mihi
peregrinum Spartanum, id nunc his cerebrum uritur,   770
me esse hos trecentos Philippos facturum lucri.
nunc hunc inimicum quia esse sciuerunt mihi,
eum adlegarunt, suom qui seruom diceret
cum auro esse apud me; composita est fallacia,
ut eo me priuent atque inter se diuidant.   775
lupo agnum eripere postulant. nugas agunt.
Agor. Negasne apud te esse aurum nec seruom meum?
Lyc. Nego. et negando, si quid refert, aruio.
Adu. Periisti, leno. nam iste est huius uilicus
quem tibi nos esse Spartiatam diximus,   780
qui ad te trecentos Philippeos modo detulit.
idque in istoc adeo | aurum inest marsuppio.
Lyc. Vae uostrae aetati. | **Adu**. Id quidem <in> mundo est tuae.
Agor. Age omitte actutum, furcifer, marsuppium:
manufesto fur es. mihi quaeso hercle operam date,   785
dum me uideatis seruom ab hoc abducere.—
Lyc. Nunc pol ego perii certo, haud arbitrario.
consulto hoc factum est, mihi ut insidiae fierent.
sed quid ego dubito fugere hinc in malam crucem,
priu' quam hinc optorto collo ad praetorem trahor?   790
eheu, quom ego habui | hariolos haruspices;
qui si quid bene promittunt, perspisso euenit,
id quod mali promittunt, praesentarium est.

nunc ibo, amicos consulam, quo me modo
suspendere aequom censeant potissumum.—   795

Agorastocles Age tu progredere, ut [testes] uideant te ire istinc foras.
estne hic meu' seruos? **Collybiscus** Sum hercle uero, Agorastocles.
Agor. Quid nunc, sceleste leno? **Adu.** Quicum litigas
apscessit. **Agor.** Vtinam hinc abierit malam crucem!
Adu. Ita nos uelle aequom est. **Agor.** Cras subscribam homini dicam.   800
Coll. Numquid me? **Agor.** Apscedas, sumas ornatum tuom.
Coll. Non sum nequiquam miles factus; paululum
praedae intus feci: dum lenonis familia
dormitat, extis sum satur factus probe.
apscedam hinc intro. **Agor.** Factum a uobis comiter.   805
bonam dedistis, aduocati, operam mihi.
cras mane, quaeso, in comitio estote obuiam.
tu sequere me intro. uos ualete.— **Adu.** Et tu uale.
iniuriam illic insignite postulat:
nostro seruire nos sibi censet cibo.   810
uerum ita sunt <morati> isti nostri diuites:
si quid bene facias, leuior pluma est gratia,
si quid peccatum est, plumbeas iras gerunt.
domos abeamus nostras, sultis, nunciam,
quando id, quoi rei operam dedimus, impetrauimus,   815
ut perderemus corruptorem ciuium.—

Milphio Exspecto quo pacto meae techinae processurae sient.
studeo hunc lenonem perdere, qui meum erum miserum macerat,
is me autem porro uerberat, incursat pugnis, calcibus:
seruire amanti miseria est, praesertim qui quod amat caret.   820
attat! e fano recipere uideo se Syncerastum,
lenonis seruom; quid habeat sermonis auscultabo.
Syncerastus Sati' spectatum est, deos atque homines eius neclegere gratiam,
quoi homini erus est consimilis uelut ego habeo hunc huius modi.
neque periurior neque peior alter usquam est gentium,   825
quam | erus meus est, neque tam luteus neque tam caeno conlitus.
ita me di ament, uel in lautumiis uel in pistrino mauelim
agere aetatem praepeditus latere forti ferreo,
quam apud lenonem hunc seruitutem colere. quid illuc est genus!
quae illic hominum corruptelae fiunt! di uostram fidem!   830
quoduis genus ibi hominum uideas, quasi Acheruntem ueneris,
equitem, peditem, libertinum, furem an fugitiuom uelis,
uerberatum, uinctum, addictum: qui habet quod det, <ut>ut homo est,

omnia genera recipiuntur; itaque in totis aedibus
tenebrae, latebrae, bibitur, estur quasi in popina, | hau secus.   835
ibi tu uideas litteratas fictiles epistulas,
pice signatas, nomina insunt cubitum longis litteris:
ita uinariorum habemus nostrae dilectum domi.
Mil. Omnia edepol mira sunt, nisi erus hunc heredem facit,
nam id quidem, illi, uti meditatur, uerba faciet mortuo.   840
et adire lubet hominem et autem nimis eum ausculto lubens.
Sync. Haec quom hic uideo fieri, crucior: pretiis emptos maxumis,
apud nos expeculiatos seruos fieri suis eris.
sed ad postremum nihil apparet: male partum male disperit.
Mil. Proinde habet orationem, quasi ipse sit frugi bonae,   845
qui ipsus hercle ignauiorem potis est facere Ignauiam.
Sync. Nunc domum haec ab aede Veneris refero uasa, ubi hostiis
eru' nequiuit propitiare Venerem suo festo die.
Mil. Lepidam Venerem! **Sync.** Nam meretrices nostrae primis hostiis
Venerem placauere extemplo. **Mil.** O lepidam Venerem denuo!   850
Sync. Nunc domum ibo. **Mil.** Heus, Synceraste. **Sync.** Syncerastum qui uocat?
Mil. Tuos amicus. **Sync.** Haud amice faci', qui cum onere offers moram.
Mil. At ob hanc moram tibi reddam operam ubi uoles, ubi iusseris.
habe rem pactam. **Sync.** Si futurum est, do tibi operam hanc. **Mil.** Quo modo?
Sync. Vt enim ubi mihi uapulandum sit, tu corium sufferas.   855
apage, nescio quid uiri sis. **Mil.** Malu' sum. **Sync.** Tibi sis. **Mil.** Te uolo.
Sync. At onus urget. **Mil.** At tu appone et respice ad me. **Sync.** Fecero,
quamquam haud otium est. **Mil.** Saluos sis, Synceraste. **Sync.** O Milphio,
di omnes deaeque ament . . . **Mil.** Quemnam hominem? **Sync** . . . . nec te nec
   me, Milphio:
neque erum meum adeo. **Mil.** Quem | ament igitur? **Sync.** Aliquem   860
   id dignus qui siet.
nam nostrorum nemo dignust. **Mil.** Lepide loquere. **Sync.** Me decet.
Mil. Quid agis? **Sync.** Facio quod manufesti moechi | hau ferme solent.
Mil. Quid id est? **Sync.** Refero uasa salua. **Mil.** Di te et tuom erum perduint.
Sync. Me non perdent; illum ut perdant facere possum, si uelim,
meum erum ut perdant, ni mihi metuam, Milphio. **Mil.** Quid id est? cedo.   865
Sync. Malus es? **Mil.** Malu' sum. **Sync.** Male mihi est. **Mil.** Memora<dum>,
   num esse aliter decet?
quid est quod male sit tibi, quoi domi sit quod edis quod ames adfatim,
neque triobolum ullum amicae das et ductas gratiis?
Sync. Diespiter me sic amabit . . . **Mil.** Vt quidem edepol dignus es.
Sync . . . . ut ego hanc familiam interire cupio. **Mil.** Adde operam, si cupis.   870
Sync. Sine pennis uolare hau facile est: meae alae pennas non habent.
Mil. Nolito edepol deuellisse: iam his duobus mensibus

uolucres tibi erunt tuae | hirquinae. | **Sync**. I in malam rem! **Mil**. I tu atque
erus.
Sync. Verum. enim qui homo eum norit, norit. cito homo peruorti potest.
Mil. Quid iam? **Sync**. Quasi tu tacitum habere quicquam poti' sis. 875
Mil. Rectius
tacitas tibi res sistam quam quod dictum est mutae mulieri.
Sync. Animum inducam facile ut tibi istuc credam, ni te nouerim.
Mil. Crede audacter meo periclo. **Sync**. Male credam, et credam tamen.
Mil. Scin tu erum tuom meo ero esse inimicum capitalem? **Sync**. Scio.
Mil. Propter amorem? **Sync**. Omnem operam perdis. **Mil**. Quid iam? 880
Sync. Quia doctum doces.
Mil. Quid ergo dubitas quin lubenter tuo ero meu', quod possiet
facere, faciat male, eius merito? tum autem si quid tu adiuuas,
eo facilius facere poterit. **Sync**. At ego hoc metuo, Milphio.
Mil. Quid est quod metuas? **Sync**. Dum | ero insidias paritem, ne me
perduim.
si eru' meus me esse elocutum quoiquam mortali sciat, 885
continuo is me ex Syncerasto Crurifragium fecerit.
Mil. Numquam edepol mortalis quisquam fiet e me certior,
nisi ero meo | uni indicasso, atque ei quoque ut ne enuntiet
id esse facinus ex ted ortum. **Sync**. Male credam, et credam tamen.
sed hoc tu tecum tacitum habeto. **Mil**. Fide non melius creditur. 890
loquere (locus occasioque est) libere: hic soli sumus.
Sync. Eru' si tuo' uolt facere frugem, meum erum perdet. **Mil**. Qui id potest?
Sync. Facile. **Mil**. Fac ergo id "facile" noscam ego, ut ille possit noscere.
Sync. Quia Adelphasium, quam | erus deamat tuos, ingenua est. **Mil**. Quo
modo?
Sync. Eodem quo soror illius altera Anterastilis. 895
Mil. Cedo qui id credam. **Sync**. Quia illas emit in Anactorio paruolas
de praedone Siculo. **Mil**. Quanti? **Sync**. Duodeuiginti minis,
duas illas et Giddenenem nutricem earum tertiam.
et ille qui eas uendebat dixit se furtiuas uendere:
ingenuas Carthagine aibat esse. **Mil**. Di uostram fidem, 900
nimium lepidum memoras facinus! nam eru' meus Agorastocles
ibidem gnatust, ind' surptus fere sexennis, postibi
qui eum surrupuit huc deuexit meoque ero | eum hic uendidit.
is in diuitias homo adoptauit hunc, quom diem obiit suom.
Sync. Omnia memoras quo id facilius fiat: manu eas adserat 905
suas populeris liberali causa. **Mil**. Tacitu' tace modo.
Sync. Profecto ad incitas lenonem rediget, si eas abduxerit.
Mil. Quin priu' disperibit faxo quam unam calcem ciuerit.

ita paratum est. **Sync.** Ita di faxint, ne apud lenonem hunc seruiam.
Mil. Hercle qui meus conlibertus faxo eris, si di uolent. 910
Sync. Ita di faxint! numquid aliud me morare, Milphio?
Mil. Valeas beneque ut tibi sit. **Sync.** Pol istuc tibi et tuost ero in manu.
uale et haec cura clanculum ut sint dicta. **Mil.** Non dictum est. uale.
Sync. At enim nihil est, nisi dum calet hoc agitur. **Mil.** Lepidu's quom mones.
et ita hoc fiet. **Sync.** Proba materies data est, si probum adhibes fabrum. 915
Mil. Potin ut taceas? **Sync.** Taceo atque abeo.— **Mil.** Mihi commoditatem
    creas.
illic hinc abiit. di immortales meum erum seruatum uolunt
et hunc disperditum lenonem: tantum eum instat exiti.
satine priu' quam unum est iniectum telum, iam instat alterum?
ibo intro, haec ut meo ero memorem. nam huc si ante aedes euocem, 920
quae audiuistis modo, nunc si eadem | hic iterum iterem, inscitia est.
[ero] uni potius ero odio intus, quam hic sim uobis omnibus.—
[di immortales, quanta clades, quanta aduentat calamitas
hodie ad hunc lenonem! sed ego nunc est quom me commoror.
ita negotium institutum est, non datur cessatio; 925
nam | et hoc docte consulendum, quod modo concreditum est,
et illud autem inseruiendum est consilium uernaculum.
remora si sit, qui malam rem mihi det merito fecerit.
nunc intro ibo: dum erus adueniat a foro, opperiar domi.—]

Hanno *Yth alonim ualonuth sicorathi symacom syth* 930
chy mlachthi in ythmum ysthyalm ych-ibarcu mysehi
li pho caneth yth bynuthi uad edin byn ui
bymarob syllohom alonim uybymysyrthohom
byth limmoth ynnocho thuulech-antidamas chon
ys sidobrim chi fel yth chyl is chon chen liful 935
yth binim ys dybur ch-innocho-tnu agorastocles
yth emanethi hy chirs aelichot sith nasot
bynu yid chi-lluch gubulim lasibithim
bodi aly thera ynnynu yslym mon cho-th iusim
Ythalonimualoniuthsicorathisthymhimihymacomsyth 940
combaepumamitalmetlotiambeat
iulecantheconaalonimbalumbar dechor
bats . . . . hunesobinesubicsillimbalim
esseantidamossonalemueduberteket
donobun . huneccilthumucommucroluful 945
altanimauosduberithemhuarcharistolem
sittesedanecnasotersahelicot

alemusdubertimurmucopsuistiti
aoccaaneclictorbodesiussilimlimmimcolus
deos deasque ueneror qui hanc urbem colunt,   950
ut (quod de mea re huc ueni) rite uenerim,
measque hic ut gnatas et mei fratris filium
reperire me siritis, di uostram fidem.
[quae mihi surruptae sunt et fratris filium.]
sed hic mihi antehac hospes Antidamas fuit;   955
eum fecisse aiunt, sibi quod faciundum fuit.
eius filium esse hic praedicant Agorastoclem:
ad eum hospitalem hanc tesseram mecum fero;
is in hisce habitare monstratust regionibus.
hos percontabor qui hinc egrediuntur foras.   960

Agorastocles Ain tu tibi dixe Syncerastum, Milphio,
eas esse ingenuas ambas surrupticias
Carthaginiensis? **Milphio** Aio, et, si frugi esse uis,
eas liberali iam adseres causa manu.
nam tuom flagitium est tuas te popularis pati   965
seruire ante oculos, domi quae fuerint liberae.
Han. Pro di immortales, opsecro uostram fidem,
quam orationem hanc aures dulcem deuorant!
creta est profecto | horunc hominum oratio,
ut mi apsterserunt omnem sorditudinem!)   970
Agor. Si ad eam rem testis habeam, faciam quod iubes.
Mil. Quid tu mihi testis? quin tu insistis fortiter?
aliqua Fortuna fuerit adiutrix tibi.
Agor. Incipere multo est quam impetrare facilius.
Mil. Sed quae illaec auis est, quae huc cum tunicis aduenit?   975
numnam in balineis circumductust pallio?
Agor. Facies quidem edepol Punica est. **Mil**. Gugga est homo.
seruos quidem edepol ueteres antiquosque habet.
Agor. Qui scis? **Mil**. Viden homines sarcinatos consequi?
atque ut <ego> opino[r] digitos in manibus non habent.   980
Agor. Quid iam? **Mil**. Quia incedunt cum anulatis auribus.
Han. Adibo <ego> hosce atque appellabo Punice.
si respondebunt, Punice pergam loqui;
si non, tum ad horum mores linguam uortero.
Mil. Quid ais tu? | ecquid commeministi Punice?   985
Agor. Nihil edepol. nam qui scire potui, dic mihi,
qui illim sexennis perierim Carthagine?

Han. Pro di immortales, plurumi | ad illum modum
periere pueri liberi Carthagine.
Mil. Quid ais tu? **Agor**. Quid uis? **Mil**. Vin appellem hunc Punice?   990
Agor. An scis? **Mil**. Nullus me est hodie Poenus Poenior.
Agor. Adi atque appella quid uelit, quid uenerit,
qui sit, quoiatis, unde sit: ne parseris.
Mil. *Auo.* quoiates estis aut quo ex oppido?
Han. *Anno byn mytthymballe udradait annech.*   995
Agor. Quid ait? **Mil**. Hannonem se esse ait Carthagine,
Carthaginiensis Mytthumbalis filium.
Han. *Auo.* **Mil**. Salutat. **Han**. *Donni.* **Mil**. Doni uolt tibi
dare hic nescio quid. audin pollicitarier?
Agor. Saluta hunc rursus Punice uerbis meis.   1000
Mil. *Auo donni* inquit hic tibi uerbis suis.
Han. *Me har bocca.* **Mil**. Istuc tibi sit potius quam mihi.
Agor. Quid ait? **Mil**. Miseram esse praedicat buccam sibi.
fortasse medicos nos esse arbitrarier.
Agor. Si <ita> est, nega esse; nolo ego errare hospitem.   1005
Mil. Audin tu? **Han**. *Rufeyn nyccho issam.* **Agor**. Sic uolo
profecto uera cuncta huic expedirier.
roga numquid opu' sit. **Mil**. Tu qui zonam non habes,
quid in hanc uenistis urbem | aut quid quaeritis?
Han. *Muphursa.* **Agor**. Quid ait? **Han**. *Miuulec hianna.* **Agor**. Quid   1010
    uenit?
Mil. Non audis? mures Africanos praedicat
in pompam ludis dare se uelle aedilibus.
Han. *Lech lachanna niliminiichto!* **Agor**. Quid nunc ait?
Mil. Ligulas, canalis ait se aduexisse et nuces:
nunc orat, operam ut des sibi, ut ea ueneant.   1015
Agor. Mercator, credo, est. **Han**. *Assam.* | **Mil**. Aruinam quidem.
Han. *Palu mirga detha.* **Agor**. Milphio, quid nunc ait?
Mil. Palas uendundas sibi ait et mergas datas,
ad messim credo, nisi quid tu | aliud sapis.
[ut hortum fodiat atque ut frumentum metat.]   1020
Agor. Quid istuc ad me? **Mil**. Certiorem te esse uolt,
ne quid clam furtim se accepisse censeas.
Han. *Mufonnim siccoratim.* **Mil**. Hem, caue sis feceris
quod hic te orat. **Agor**. Quid ait aut quid orat? expedi.
Mil. Sub cratim ut iubeas se supponi atque eo   1025
lapides imponi multos, ut sese neces.
Han. *Gunebbal samem lyryla.* **Agor**. Narra, quid est?
quid ait? **Mil**. Non hercle nunc quidem quicquam scio.

Han. At ut scias, nunc dehinc latine iam loquar.

seruom hercle te esse oportet et nequam et malum,   1030

hominem peregrinum atque aduenam qui inrideas.

Mil. At hercle te hominem et sycophantam et subdolum,

qui huc aduenisti nos captatum, migdilix,

bisulci lingua quasi proserpens bestia.

Agor. Maledicta hinc aufer, linguam compescas face.   1035

maledicere huic tu temperabis, si sapis.

meis consanguineis nolo te iniuste loqui.

Carthagini ego sum gnatus, ut tu sis sciens.

Han. O mi popularis, salue. **Agor**. Et tu edepol, quisquis es.

et si quid opus est, quaeso, dic atque impera   1040

popularitatis causa. | **Han**. Habeo gratiam.

[uerum ego hic hospitium | habeo: Antidamae filium

quaero (commostra si nouisti) Agorastoclem.]

sed ecquem adulescentem tu hic nouisti Agorastoclem?

Agor. Siquidem Antidamai quaeris adoptaticium,   1045

ego sum ipsus quem tu quaeris. **Han**. Hem, quid ego audio?

Agor. Antidamae gnatum me | esse. **Han**. Si ita est, tesseram

conferre si uis hospitalem, eccam attuli.

Agor. Agedum huc ostende. est par probe. nam habeo domi.

Han. O mi hospes, salue multum! nam mihi tuo' pater   1050

patritus certo | hospes Antidamas fuit.

haec mi hospitalis tessera cum illo fuit.

Agor. Ergo hic apud me hospitium tibi praebebitur.

nam haud repudio hospitium neque Carthaginem,

und' sum oriundus. **Han**. Di dent tibi omnis quae uelis.   1055

quid ais? qui potuit fieri, ut Carthagini

gnatus sis? hic autem habuisti Aetolum patrem.

Agor. Surruptus sum illim. hic me Antidamas hospes tuos

emit, et is me sibi adoptauit filium.

Han. Demarcho item ipse fuit adoptaticius.   1060

sed mitto de illoc, ad te redeo. dic mihi,

ecquid meministi tuom parentum nomina,

patris atque matris? **Agor**. Memini. **Han**. Memoradum mihi,

si noui forte aut si sunt cognati mihi.

Agor. Ampsigura mater mihi fuit, Iahon pater.   1065

Han. Patrem atque matrem uiuerent uellem tibi.

Agor. An mortui sunt? **Han**. Factum, quod <ego> aegre tuli.

nam mihi sobrina Ampsigura tua mater fuit;

pater tuos, is erat frater patruelis meus,

et is me heredem fecit, quom suom obiit diem, 1070
quo me priuatum | aegre patior mortuo.
sed si | ita est, ut tu sis Iahonis filius,
signum esse oportet in manu laeua tibi,
ludenti puero quod memordit simia.
ostende. <**Agor.**> inspice iam. | **Han.** Aperi, si audes . . . atque adest! 1075
Agor. Mi patrue, salue. | **Han.** Et tu salue, Agorastocles.
iterum mihi gnatus uideor, quom te repperi.
Mil. Pol istam rem uobis bene euenisse gaudeo.
sed te moneri num neuis? **Han.** Sane uolo.
Mil. Paterna oportet filio reddi bona. 1080
aequom est habere hunc bona quae possedit pater.
Han. Haud postulo aliter: restituentur omnia;
suam sibi rem saluam sistam, si illo aduenerit.
Mil. Facito sis reddas, etsi hic habitabit, tamen.
Han. Quin mea quoque iste habebit, si quid me fuat. 1085
Mil. Festiuom facinus uenit mi in mentem modo.
Han. Quid id est? **Mil.** Tua opus est opera. **Han.** Dic mihi quid lubet:
profecto uteris, ut uoles, operam meam.
quid est negoti? **Mil.** Potin tu fieri subdolus?
Han. Inimico possum, amico est insipientia. 1090
Mil. Inimicus hercle est huius. **Han.** Male faxim lubens.
Mil. Amat ab lenone hic. **Han.** Facere sapienter puto.
Mil. Leno hic habitat uicinus. **Han.** Male faxim lubens.
Mil. Ei duae puellae sunt meretrices seruolae
sorores: earum hic alteram efflictim perit, 1095
neque eam incestauit umquam. **Han.** Acerba amatio est.
Mil. Hunc leno ludificatur. **Han.** Suom quaestum colit.
Mil. Hic illi malam rem dare uolt. **Han.** Frugi est, si id facit.
Mil. Nunc hoc consilium capio et hanc fabricam apparo,
ut te allegemus, filias dicas tuas 1100
surruptasque esse paruolas Carthagine,
manu liberali causa | ambas adseras,
quasi filiae tuae sint ambae. intellegis?
Han. Intellego hercle. nam mihi item gnatae duae
cum nutrice una surruptae sunt paruolae. 1105
Mil. Lepide hercle adsimulas. iam in principio id mihi placet.
Han. Pol magi' quam uellem. **Mil.** Eu! | hercle mortalem catum,
malum crudumque, et callidum et subdolum!
ut adflet, quo illud gestu faciat facilius.
me quoque dolis iam superat architectonem. 1110

Han. Sed earum nutrix qua sit facie, mi expedi.
Mil. Statura hau magna, corpore aquilo est. **Han**. Ipsa ea est.
Mil. Specie uenusta, | ore atque oculis pernigris.
Han. Formam quidem hercle uerbis depinxti probe.
Mil. Vin eam uidere? **Han**. Filias malo meas. 1115
sed i [atque] euoca illam; si eae meae sunt filiae,
si illarum est nutrix, me continuo nouerit.
Mil. Heus, ecquis hic est? nuntiate ut prodeat
foras Giddeneni. est qui illam conuentam esse uolt.

Giddenes Quis pultat? **Mil**. Qui te proxumust. **Gidd**. Quid uis? **Mil**. Eho, 1120
nouistin tu illunc tunicatum hominem qui siet?
Gidd. Nam quem | ego aspicio? pro supreme Iuppiter!
eru' meus hic quidem est, mearum alumnarum pater,
Hanno Carthaginiensis. **Mil**. Ecce autem mala!
praestrigiator hic quidem Poenus probust, 1125
perduxit omnis ad suam sententiam.
Gidd. O mi | ere, salue, | Hanno, insperatissume
mihi tuisque filiis, salue atque . . . eho,
mirari noli neque me contemplarier.
cognoscin Giddenenem | ancillam tuam? 1130
Han. Noui. sed ubi sunt meae gnatae? id scire expeto.
Gidd. Apud aedem Veneris. **Han**. Quid ibi faciunt? dic mihi.
Gidd. Aphrodisia hodie Veneris est festus dies:
oratum ierunt deam, ut sibi esset propitia.
Mil. Pol sati' scio, impetrarunt, quando hic hic adest. 1135
Agor. Eho an huius sunt illae filiae? **Gidd**. Ita ut praedicas.
tua pietas nobis plane | auxilio fuit,
quom huc aduenisti | hodie in ipso tempore;
namque hodie earum mutarentur nomina
facerentque indignum genere quaestum corpore. 1140
Puer *Auamma illi.* **Gidd**. *Hauon bane silli mustine.*
mepstaetemes tas dum et alanna cestimim.
Agor. Quid illi locuti sunt inter se? dic mihi.
Han. Matrem hic salutat suam, | haec autem hunc filium.
tace atque parce muliebri supellectili. 1145
Agor. Quae ea est supellex? **Han**. Clarus clamor. **Agor**. Sine modo.
Han. Tu abduc hosce intro et una nutricem simul
iube hanc abire hinc ad te. **Agor**. Fac quod imperat.
Mil. Sed quis illas tibi monstrabit? **Agor**. Ego doctissume.
Mil. Abeo igitur. **Agor**. Facias modo quam memores mauelim. 1150

patruo aduenienti cena curetur uolo.
Mil. *Lachanna* uos, quos ego iam detrudam ad molas,
ind' porro ad puteum atque ad robustum codicem.
ego faxo hospitium hoc leniter laudabitis.—
Agor. Audin tu, patrue? dico, ne dictum neges: 1155
tuam mihi maiorem filiam despondeas.
Han. Pactam rem habeto. **Agor.** Spondesne igitur? **Han.** Spondeo.
Agor. Mi patrue, salue. nam nunc es plane meus.
nunc demum ego cum illa fabulabor libere.
nunc, patrue, si uis tuas uidere filias, 1160
me sequere. **Han.** Iamdudum equidem cupio et te sequor.
Agor. Quid si eamus illis obuiam? **Han.** At ne interuias
praeterbitamus metuo. magne Iuppiter,
restitue certas mi ex incertis nunc opes.
Agor. Ego quidem amores meos mecum confido fore. 1165
sed eccas uideo ipsas. **Han.** Haecine meae sunt filiae?
quantae e quantillis iam sunt factae. **Agor.** Scin quid est?
tragicae sunt: in calones sustolli solent.
[**Mil.** Opino hercle hodie, quod ego dixi per iocum,
id euenturum esse et seuerum et serium, 1170
ut haec inueniantur hodie esse huius filiae.
Agor. Pol istuc quidem iam certum est. tu istos, Milphio,
abduce intro. nos hasce hic praestolabimur.]

Adelphasium Fuit hodie operae pretium quoiuis qui | amabilitati animum
 adiceret,
oculis epulas dare, delubrum qui hodie ornatum eo uisere uenit. 1175
deamaui ecastor illi [ego] hodie
lepidissuma munera meretricum, 1176a
digna diua uenustissuma Venere,
neque contempsi eius opes hodie. 1177a
tanta ibi copia uenustatum aderat, in suo quique loco sita munde.
aras tus, murrinus, omnis odor
complebat. haud sordere uisust 1179a
festus dies, Venus, nec tuom fanum: 1180
tantus ibi clientarum erat numerus, 1180a
quae ad Calydoniam uenerant Venerem.
Anterastilis Certo | enim, quod quidem | ad nos duas 1181a
attinuit, praepotentes pulchre
pacisque potentes, soror, fuimus, 1182a
neque ab iuuentute inibi inriditculo
habitae, quod pol, 1183a

soror, ceteris omnibus factum est.   1183b

Ad. Malim istuc aliis uideatur, quam uti tu te, soror, conlaudes.

Ant. Spero equidem. **Ad.** Et pol ego, quom, ingeniis quibus sumus   1185
   atque aliae, gnosco;

eo sumus gnatae genere, ut deceat nos esse a culpa castas.

Han. Iuppiter, qui genus colis alisque hominum, per quem ueiuimus ueitalem
   aeuom,

quem penes spes uitae sunt hominum | omnium, da diem hunc sospitem
   quaeso,

[rebus meis agundis,] ut quibus annos multos carui quasque <e> patria
   perdidi parvas

redde is libertatem, inuictae praemium ut esse sciam pietati.   1190

Agor. Omnia faciet Iuppiter faxo,

nam mi est obnoxius et me   1191a

metuit. **Han.** Tace quaeso.   1191b

Agor. Ne lacruma, patrue.

Ant. Vt uolup est homini, mea soror, si quod agit cluet uictoria;   1192a
sicut nos hodie inter alias praestitimus pulchritudine.

Ad. Stulta, soror, magis es quam uolo. | an tu eo pulchra uidere, opsecro,

si tibi illi non os oblitum est fuligine?   1195

Agor. O patrue, o patrue mi. **Han.** Quid est,

fratris mei gnate, gnate, quid uis? expedi.

Agor. At enim hoc uolo agas. **Han.** At enim ago istuc.

Agor. <O> patrue mi patruissume.   1197a

Han. Quid est? **Agor.** Est lepida et lauta. ut sapit.

Han. Ingenium patris habet quod sapit.   1198a

Agor. Quae res? iam diu edepol sapientiam tuam haec quidem abusa est.

nunc hinc sapit, hinc sentit, quidquid sapit, ex meo amore.   1200

Ad. Non eo genere sumu' prognatae, tam etsi sumus seruae, soror,

ut deceat nos facere quicquam quod homo quisquam inrideat.

multa mulierum sunt uitia, sed hoc e multis maxumum est,

quom sibi nimi' placent minu'que addunt operam, uti placeant uiris.

Ant. Nimiae uoluptati est quod in extis nostris portentum est, soror,   1205

quod[que] haruspex de ambabus dixit . . . **Agor.** Velim de me aliquid dixerit.

Ant . . . . nos fore inuito domino nostro diebus paucis liberas.

id ego, nisi quid di aut parentes faxint, qui sperem hau scio.

Agor. Mea fiducia hercle haruspex, patrue, his promisit, scio,

libertatem, quia me amare hanc scit. **Ad.** Soror, sequere hac. **An.** Sequor. 1210

Han. Priu' quam abitis, uos uolo ambas. nisi piget, consistite.

Ad. Quis reuocat? **Agor.** Qui bene uolt uobis facere. **Ad.** Facere occasio est.

sed quis homost? **Agor.** Amicus uobis. **Ad.** Qui quidem inimicus non siet.

Agor. Bonus est hic homo, mea uoluptas. **Ad.** Pol istum malim quam malum.

Agor. Siquidem amicitia est habenda, cum hoc habenda est. **Ad.**   1215
   Hau precor.
Agor. Multa bona uolt uobis facere. **Ad.** Bonu' bonis bene feceris.
Han. Gaudio ero uobis . . . **Ad.** At edepol nos uoluptati tibi.
Han . . . . libertatique. **Ad.** Istoc pretio tuas nos facile feceris.
Agor. Patrue mi, | ita me di amabunt, ut ego, si sim Iuppiter,
iam hercle ego illam uxorem ducam et Iunonem extrudam foras.   1220
ut pudice uerba fecit, cogitate et commode!
ut modeste orationem praebuit! **Han.** Certo haec mea est.
sed ut astu sum adgressus ad eas! **Agor.** Lepide hercle atque commode.
Han. Pergo etiam temptare? **Agor.** In pauca confer: sitiunt qui sedent.
Han. Quid istic? quod faciundum est quor non agimus? in ius uos uoco.   1225
Agor. Nunc, patrue, tu frugi bonae es. tene. uin ego hanc adprendam?
Ad. An patruos est, Agorastocles, tuos hic? **Agor.** Iam faxo scibis.
nunc pol ego te ulciscar probe, nam faxo . . . mea eris sponsa.
Han. Ite in ius, ne moramini. antestare me atque duce.
Agor. Ego te antestabor, postea hanc amabo atque amplexabor.   1230
sed illud quidem uolui dicere . . . immo [hercle] dixi quod uolebam.
Han. Moramini. in ius uos uoco, nisi honestiust prehendi.
Ad. Quid in ius uocas nos? quid tibi debemus? **Agor.** Dicet illi.
Ad. Etiam me meae latrant canes? **Agor.** At tu hercle adludiato:
dato mihi pro offa sauium, pro | osse linguam obicito.   1235
ita hanc canem faciam tibi oleo tranquilliorem.
Han. It' si itis. **Ad.** Quid nos fecimus tibi? **Han.** Fures estis ambae.
Ad. Nosn' tibi? **Han.** Vos inquam. **Agor.** Atque ego scio. **Ad.** Quid id furtist?
   Agor. Hunc rogato.
Han. Quia annos multos filias meas celauistis clam me,
atque equidem ingenuas liberas summoque genere gnatas.   1240
Ad. Numquam mecastor reperies tu istuc probrum penes nos.
Agor. Da pignus, ni nunc perieres, in sauium, uter utri det.
Ad. Nil tecum ago, apscede opsecro. | **Agor.** Atque hercle mecum agendum
   est.
nam hic patruos meus est, pro hoc mihi patronus sim necesse est;
et praedicabo quo modo [uos] furta faciatis multa   1245
quoque modo \<uos\> huius filias apud uos habeatis seruas,
quas uos ex patria liberas surruptas esse scitis.
Ad. Vbi sunt eae? aut quas, opsecro? **Agor.** Sati' iam sunt maceratae.
Han. Quid si eloquamur? **Ag.** Censeo hercle, patrue. **Ad.** Misera timeo,
quid hoc sit negoti, mea soror; ita stupida sine animo asto.   1250
Han. Aduortite animum, mulieres. primum, si id fieri possit,
ne indigna indignis di darent, id ego euenisset uellem;
nunc quod boni mihi di danunt, uobis uostraeque matri,

eas dis est aequom gratias nos agere sempiternas,
quom nostram pietatem adprobant decorantque di immortales.   1255
uos meae estis ambae filiae et hic est cognatus uoster,
huiusce fratris filius, Agorastocles. **Ad**. Amabo,
num hi falso oblectant gaudio nos? **Agor**. At ita me di seruent,
ut hic pater est uoster. date manus. **Ad**. Salue, insperate nobis
pater, te complecti nos sine. **Ant**. Cupite atque exspectate   1260
pater, salue! **Ad**. Ambae filiae sumus. **Ant**. Amplectamur ambae.
Agor. Quis me amplectetur postea? **Han**. Nunc ego sum fortunatus,
multorum annorum miserias nunc hac uoluptate sedo.
Ad. Vix hoc uidemur credere. **Han**. Magi' qui credatis dicam.
nam uostra nutrix prima me cognouit. **Ad**. Vbi ea, amabo, est?   1265
Han. Apud hunc est. **Agor**. Quaeso, qui lubet tam diu tenere collum?
omitte saltem tu altera. nolo ego istunc enicari
prius quam te mi desponderit. **Agor**. Mitto. **Ad**. Sperate, salue.
Han. Condamus alter alteram ergo in neruom bracchialem.
quibu' nunc in terra melius est? **Agor**. Eueniunt digna dignis.   1270
Han. Tandem huic cupitum contigit. **Agor**. O Apella, o Zeuxis pictor,
quor estis numero mortui, hoc exemplo ut pingeretis?
nam alios pictores nil moror huius modi tractare exempla.
Han. Di deaeque | omnes, uobis habeo merito magnas gratias,
quom hac me laetitia adfecistis tanta et tantis gaudiis,   1275
ut meae gnatae ad me redirent in potestatem meam.
[**Ad**. Mi pater, tua pietas plane nobis auxilio fuit.
Agor. Patrue, facito in memoria habeas, tuam maiorem filiam
mihi te despondisse . . . **Han**. Memini. **Agor** . . . . et dotis quid promiseris.]

Antamynides Si ego minam non ultus fuero probe quam lenoni dedi,   1280
tum profecto me sibi habento scurrae ludificatui.
is etiam me ad prandium ad se abduxit ignauissumus,
ipse abiit foras, me reliquit pro atriensi in aedibus,
ubi nec leno neque illae redeunt, nec quod edim quicquam datur.
pro maiore parte prandi pignus cepi, abii foras;   1285
sic dedero: aere militari tetigero lenunculum.
nanctus est hominem, mina quem argenti circumduceret.
sed mea amica nunc mihi irato obuiam ueniat uelim:
iam pol ego illam pugnis totam faciam uti sit merulea,
ita <eam> replebo atritate | atrior multo ut siet   1290
quam Aegyptini, qui cortinam ludis per circum ferunt.
Anter. Tene sis me arte, mea uoluptas; male ego metuo miluos
(mala illa bestia est) ne forte me auferat pullum tuom.

Ad. Vt nequeo te sati' complecti, mi pater. **Antam.** Ego me moror.
propemodum | hoc opsonare prandium potero mihi. 1295
sed quid hoc est? quid est? quid hoc est? quid ego uideo? quo modo?
quid hoc est conduplicationis? quae haec est congeminatio?
quis hic homo est cum tunicis longis quasi puer cauponius?
satin ego oculis cerno? estne illaec mea amica Anterastilis?
et ea est certo. iam pridem ego me sensi nihili pendier. 1300
non pudet puellam amplexari baiolum in media uia?
iam hercle ego illunc excruciandum totum carnufici dabo.
sane genus hoc mulierosum est tunicis demissiciis.
sed adire certum est hanc amatricem Africam.
heus tu, tibi dico, mulier, ecquid te pudet? 1305
quid tibi negoti est autem cum istac? dic mihi.
Han. Adulescens, salue. **Antam.** Nolo, nihil ad te attinet.
quid tibi | hanc digito tactio est? **Han.** Quia mihi lubet.
Antam. Lubet? **Han.** Ita dico. **Antam.** Ligula, i in malam crucem!
tune hic amator audes esse, hallex uiri, 1310
aut contrectare quod mares homines amant?
deglupta mena, sarrapis sementium,
manstruca, halagora, sampsa, tum autem plenior
ali ulpicique quam Romani remiges.
Agor. Num tibi, adulescens, malae aut dentes pruriunt, 1315
qui huic es molestus, an malam rem quaeritas?
Antam. Quin adhibuisti, dum istaec loquere, tympanum?
nam te cinaedum esse arbitror magi' quam uirum.
Agor. Scin quam cinaedus sum? ite istinc, serui, foras,
ecferte fustis! **Antam.** Heus tu, si quid per iocum 1320
dixi, nolito in serium conuortere.
Anter. Qui tibi lubido est, opsecro, Antamynides,
loqui inclementer nostro cognato et patri?
nam hic noster pater est; hic nos cognouit modo
et hunc sui fratris filium. **Antam.** Ita me Iuppiter 1325
bene amet, bene factum. gaudeo et uolup est mihi,
siquidem quid lenoni optigit magni mali,
quomque e uirtute uobis fortuna optigit.
Anter. Credibile ecastor dicit. crede huic, mi pater.
Han. Credo. **Agor.** Et ego credo. sed eccum lenonem optume, 1330
[credo. **Antam.** et ego credo. **Agor.** edepol hic uenit commodus.]
bonum uirum eccum uideo, se recipit domum.
[**Han.** Quis hic est? **Agor.** Vtrumuis est, uel leno uel Lycus.
in seruitute hic filias habuit tuas
et mi auri fur est. **Han.** Bellum hominem, quem noueris.] 1335

Agor. Rapiamus in ius. **Han**. Minime. **Agor**. Quapropter? **Han**. Quia
iniuriarum multo induci satius est.

Lycus Decipitur nemo, mea quidem sententia,
qui suis amicis narrat recte res suas;
nam omnibus amicis meis idem unum conuenit,   1340
ut me suspendam, ne addicar Agorastocli.
Agor. Leno, eamus in ius. **Lyc**. Opsecro te, Agorastocles,
suspendere ut me liceat. **Han**. In ius te uoco.
Lyc. Quid tibi mecum autem? **Han**. Quia <enim> hasce aio liberas
ingenuasque esse filias ambas meas;   1345
eae sunt surruptae cum nutrice paruolae.
Lyc. Iam pridem equidem istuc sciui, et miratus fui,
neminem uenire qui istas adsereret manu.
meae quidem profecto non sunt. **Antam**. Leno, in ius eas.
Lyc. De prandio tu dicis. debetur, dabo.   1350
Agor. Duplum pro furto mi opus est. **Lyc**. Sume hinc quid lubet.
Han. Et mihi suppliciis multis. **Lyc**. Sume hinc quid lubet.
Antam. Et mihi quidem mina argenti. **Lyc**. Sume hinc quid lubet.
collo rem soluam iam omnibus, quasi baiolus.
[**Agor**. Numquid recusas contra me? **Lyc**. Haud uerbum quidem.   1355
Agor. Ite igitur intro, mulieres. sed patrue mi,
tuam, ut dixisti, mihi desponde filiam.
Han. Haud aliter ausim. **Antam**. Bene uale. **Agor**. Et tu bene uale.
Antam. Leno, arrabonem hoc pro mina mecum fero.—
Lyc. Perii hercle! **Agor**. Immo haud multo post, si in ius ueneris. 1360
Lyc. Quin egomet tibi me addico. quid praetore opust?
uerum opsecro te, ut liceat simplum soluere,
trecentos Philippos. credo conradi potest:
cras auctionem faciam. **Agor**. Tantisper quidem
ut sis apud me lignea in custodia.   1365
Lyc. Fiat. **Agor**. Sequere intro, patrue mi, ut [hunc] festum diem
habeamus hilare, huius malo et nostro bono.
multum ualete. multa uerba fecimus;
malum postremo omne ad lenonem reccidit.
nunc, quod postremum est condimentum fabulae,   1370
si placuit, plausum postulat comoedia!—]

[**Agorastocles** Quam rem | agis, miles? qui lubet patruo meo
loqui inclementer? ne mirere, mulieres
quod eum sequontur: modo cognouit filias

suas esse hasce ambas. **Lyc.** Hem, quod uerbum aures meas   1375
tetigit? nunc perii. | **Antam.** Vnde haec perierunt domo?
Agor. Carthaginienses sunt. **Lyc.** At ego sum perditus.
illuc ego metui semper, ne cognosceret
eas aliquis, quod nunc factum est. uae misero mihi!
periere, opinor, duodeuiginti minae,   1380
qui hasce emi. **Agor.** Et tute ipse periisti, Lyce.
Han. Quis hic est? **Agor.** Vtrumuis est, uel leno uel Lycus.
in seruitute hic filias habuit tuas,
et mi auri fur est. **Han.** Bellum hominem, quem noueris.
Antam. Leno, rapacem te esse semper credidi,   1385
uerum etiam furacem <aiunt> qui norunt magis.
Lyc. Accedam. per ego [te] tua te genua opsecro
et hunc, cognatum quem tuom esse intellego:
quando boni estis, ut bonos facere addecet
facite ut <uos> uostro subueniatis supplici.   1390
iam pridem equidem istas esse sciui liberas
et exspectabam, si qui eas assereret manu.
nam meae <eae> prosum non sunt. tum autem aurum tuom
reddam, quod apud me est, et ius iurandum dabo,
me malitiose nil fecisse, Agorastocles.   1395
Agor. Quid mihi par facere sit, ego mecum consulam.
omitte genua. **Lyc.** Mitto, si ita sententia est.]
Antam. Heus tu leno! **Lyc.** Quid lenonem uis inter negotium?
Antam. Vt minam mi argenti reddas, priu' quam in neruom abducere.
Lyc. Di meliora faxint. **Antam.** Sic est: hodie cenabis foris. 1400
aurum argentum collum, leno, tris res nunc debes simul.
Han. Quid me <in> hac re facere deceat, egomet mecum cogito.
si uolo hunc ulcisci, litis sequar in alieno oppido,
quantum audiui ingenium et mores eius quo pacto sient.
Ad. Mi pater, ne quid tibi cum istoc rei sit pessumo, opsecro.   1405
Anter. Ausculta sorori. abi, diiunge inimicitias cum improbo.
Han. Hoc age sis, leno. quamquam ego te meruisse ut pereas scio,
non experiar tecum. **Agor.** Neque ego; si aurum mihi reddes meum,
leno, quando ex neruo emissu's . . . compingare in carcerem.
Lyc. Iamne autem ut soles? **Antam.** Ego, Poene, tibi me purgatum uolo. 1410
si quid dixi iratus aduorsum animi tui sententiam,
id uti ignoscas quaeso. et quom istas inuenisti filias,
ita me di ament, mihi uoluptati est. **Han.** Ignosco et credo tibi.
Antam. Leno, tu autem amicam mihi des facito aut [auri] mihi reddas minam.
Lyc. Vin tibicinam meam habere? **Antam.** Nil moror tibicinam;   1415
nescias, utrum ei maiores buccaene an mammae sient.

Lyc. Dabo quae placeat. **Antam**. Cura. | **Lyc**. Aurum cras ad te referam tuom.
Agor. Facito in memoria habeas. **Lyc**. Miles, sequere me.— **Antam**. Ego uero
    sequor.—
Agor. Quid ais, patrue? quando hinc ire cogitas Carthaginem?
nam tecum mi una ire certum est. **Han**. Vbi primum potero, ilico.   1420
Agor. Dum auctionem facio, hic opus est aliquot ut maneas dies.
Han. Faciam ita ut uis. **Agor**. Age sis, eamus, nos curemus. plaudite.

Commentary

Abbreviations Used in This Commentary

Although a full list of abbreviations can be found before the Introduction to this book, I have for the most part employed the author/work abbreviations found in the *Oxford Classical Dictionary (OCD)* or the Greek lexicon of Liddell, Scott, and Jones, with the following exceptions: Menandrian, Plautine, and Terentian comedies are generally limited to the title's first three to four letters or a single syllable, and those comedies not listed by the *OCD* should be easily deducible. Comparanda from Plautine comedies are always listed first (and among them the *Poenulus* first), and thus the abbreviation "Plaut." is omitted.

1-tr./intr. = Shorthand for the principal parts of a completely regular first-conjugation verb. Thus *commentor* (1-tr.) indicates that the transitive verb has the principal parts *commentor, commentārī, commentātus sum*, while *litō* (1-intr.) indicates that the intransitive verb has the principal parts *litō, litāre, litāuī, litātum.*

A&G = Allen and Greenough's *New Latin Grammar*. The numbers cited refer to the section number therein, not to the page number.

K-A = Kassel and Austin's *Poetae Comici Graeci*.

Drāmatis Persōnae

Ăgŏrastŏclēs: *adulescens (amāns)*. The plight of the young man in love is frequently the focus of Greek New Comedy and hence Roman comedy as well. These young men are usually witless and rely on advice from others to get what they want, yet they nevertheless receive the audience's sympathy. The name Agorastocles, from the Greek ἀγορά ("marketplace") + κλέος ("glory"), means "Glory of the Agora." The accent in his name falls on the antepenultimate syllable since the penult scans short.

Milphĭŏ: *seruus (callidus)*. The stock character of the clever slave usually helps his younger master obtain access to the girl he loves, often against the wishes of his elder master, the young man's father. These slaves proudly use deception and trickery to attain their goals and—like most Plautine slaves—are generally "talktative, impudent, inquisitive, indiscrete, [*sic*] [and] gossipy," while nonetheless serving their young masters loyally (Starks et al. 1997b 39). Many clever slaves seem to be much older than their charges, Tyndarus in the *Captiui* being a notable exception. The name Milphio means "One Whose Eyelashes are Falling Out"; it derives from the Greek term μιλφῶσις "the falling off of eyelashes." (The condition may be caused by stress, so the name is unfortunately suitable for a slave character.) Perhaps his name was reflected in the appearance of his mask?

Ădelphăsĭŭm: *uirgo*. The elder of the two Carthaginian sisters and the beloved of Agorastocles. Although she and her sister start the comedy as prostitutes-in-training (for which the stock role *meretrix* would be appropriate), their freeborn status and eventual recognition necessitates their more innocent classification as maidens—though given their eagerness to adopt a trade, we might wonder how innocent they actually are. The name "Adelphasium, from the the Greek ἀδελφή "sister," means "Sisterling" or "Little Sister Girl."

Antĕrastĭlĭs: *uirgo*. The name Anterastilis means "Little Love Rival." It comes from the Greek ἀντεραστής "rival in love."

Lўcŭs: *lēno*. The pimp and slave dealer who owns Adelphasium and Anterastilis. His name comes from the Greek λύκος "wolf." It was a legal business enterprise to run a brothel in Greece and Rome, though slave-dealers who sold women into prostitution were considered disreputable. Pimps in Roman comedy tend to be easily tricked because of their greed, while their frequent impiety helps cast them as the villians the audience loves to hate. Lycus displays less personality than Plautus' other four pimps: Ballio of the *Pseudolus*, Cappadox of the *Curculio*, Dordalus of the *Persa*, and Labrax of the *Rudens* (Marshall 2006 140).

Antāmўnĭdēs: *mīles*. The often boastful and pompous mercenary soldier is another stock character in Greek New Comedy and Roman comedy. In this play Antamynides wishes to purchase Anterastilis. The name Antamynides means "Son of Defender" and comes from the Greek ἀνταμύνομαι, "defend oneself, resist; requite" with the patronymic suffix -ίδης. The name is appropriate both because "a soldier needs to defend himself and because Antamynides takes revenge on Lycus" (de Melo 2012 6n2). Perhaps this stock character does represent a real threat in the years after the Second Punic War when so many citizen soldiers, both young and old, had died (Marshall 2011). While the name is written as "Antamoenides" in the surviving manuscripts, that spelling likely derives from the hypercorrection of the original Antamunides since it was well known that early Latin *oe* later became *u*, and *u* was also Plautus' usual transcription for the Greek υ (de Melo 2012 6n2).

Advŏcātī: *lībertī.* Freedmen are rather rare in Roman comedy. Because manumission was so rare in Greece there are few no freedmen in the surviving lines of Greek Comedy, cf. Men. *Sam.* 238. (See more on freedmen below at note 504–614.) Freed characters in Roman comedy thus represent other types of characters who were modified or reclassified by Plautus or Terence during the adaptation process. The freedmen of the *Poenulus* are referred to as "Advocates" because they agree to act as court witnesses for Agorastocles against Lycus. These freedmen serve almost as a chorus in this comedy; the fishermen of the *Rudens* are the only other such group in Roman comedy.

Collўbiscus: *uīlicus.* The slave manager or overseer of Agorastocles' country properties. The *uīlicus* is another rare role in Roman comedy, likely because most plays take place in a city, where the overseer of a country estate is unlikely to venture. Olympio in the *Casina* is the only other surviving example. The name Collybiscus means "Little Cakes" or "Small Change" from the Greek κόλλαβος "cake, roll." Henderson (1994 44) punningly calls him "Johnny Cash."

Syncĕrastus: *seruus.* An unhappy slave belonging to Lycus. The name Syncerastus means "Mixed Up In" or "One Who Mixes Things Up" and derives from the Greek συνκεραστός "mixed drink," which in turn comes from συνκεράννῡμι "to mix together."

Hānnō: *senex Poenus.* A Carthaginian version of the "old man searching for lost children" subset of the "old man" stock character category. Hegio of the *Captiui* and Periphanes of the *Epidicus* are his closest parallels. Hanno shares the name of a famous Carthaginian general in the First Punic War (one whom his own side had crucified in 241 BCE after he lost a battle, according to Dio Cassius 12), as well as multiple Carthaginian officers and officials in the Second Punic War. Furthermore, Faller (2004 174) identifies "Hanno" as a shortened form of "Hannibal," the name borne by the brilliant and devastatingly effective Carthaginian commander in that recent war. Palmer (1997 31–34) and Starks (2000) read Hanno as a sympathetic character; Franko (1995 and 1996) sees him as unsympathetic. Both are probably correct—few characters are portrayed entirely positively on the comic stage. See Leigh (2004 28–37) on the similarity between Hanno and Hannibal.

Giddĕnĭs: *nūtrix.* The former wet-nurse of the two Carthaginian sisters, likely a slave, who was kidnapped along with them. Unlike the nurses in tragedy, who advise their charges (albeit often incorrectly), Giddenis appears only because her role in the recognition of the lost daughters is dramatically necessary. Thus, if a girl can be recognized as freeborn by means of tokens (cf. the *Cistellaria* and *Rudens*), no nurse need appear in the play. Giddenis is a Carthaginian name that may mean "Good Fortune" (Faller 2004 177–78). She is the only character explicitly labeled a nurse in Plautine comedy—there are old women in similar roles in the *Aulularia* and *Mercator* though, and nurses do appear in Terence's *Adelphoe* and *Eunuchus*.

Puer: *seruus*. An unnamed slave of Hanno's, he is the son of Giddenis. Between Milphio, Collybiscus, Syncerastus, Giddenis, the *puer*, and Hanno's silent attendants, we are given only a glimpse of the huge range of tasks and occupational roles that slaves performed in Rome. With the exception of Tyndarus in the *Captiui*, Roman comedy never displays the most oppressed types of slaves, such as agricultural laborers, miners, and the slaves who pushed the grindstones at mills. (See, e.g., Thompson 2003 chapters 3, 4, 6.)

Argūmentum

This "argument," or summary of the comedy's plot, which is also an acrostic of the work's title, is a post-Plautine addition to the manuscripts. At least one *argūmentum* survives for each Plautine comedy: the acrostic summaries survive in the P manuscripts for each play (except for the *Bacchides*, which is missing its beginning), while the nonacrostic summaries (usually fifteen lines long) only survive for the *Amphitruo*, *Aulularia*, *Mercator*, and *Miles Gloriosus* (in manuscript A and a few from P), and the *Pseudolus* (in manuscript A). These *argūmenta* were clearly added to the manuscripts a few centuries after Plautus' time, since the phrasing and terminology of the Latin isn't too different from Plautus' own—likely in the early or mid-second century CE.

1   **septuennis** From *septuennis, -e* "seven-year-old."

2   **osor** The rare noun *ōsor, ōsōris* (m) "hater" (from the perfect participle of *ōdī, ōdisse* "to hate") only appears in pre- and postclassical Latin.

4   **raptae** Supply *sunt*. Plautus often omits (or elides) forms of *esse*.

6   **obtrudit** From *obtrūdō, obtrūdere, obtrūsī, obtrūsus* "to thrust X upon Y," where X is accusative and Y is dative. **eum furto alligat** *alligō* (1-tr.) "to bind, lay under obligation" refers to the act of bringing someone to court.

furtō is ablative of cause (A&G 404). Cf. note at 737. Maurach (1988 42) notes that *alligāre* usually takes the genitive in early Latin, and the ablative is used starting in Cicero's time—another sign of the later composition of the play's *argūmentum*. Both *obtrūdit* and *alligat* employ different spellings here in the *argūmentum* than in the play proper.

7 **gnatum** Archaic spelling of *nātus* from *nāscor, nāscī, nātus sum* "to be born."

8 **adgnoscit** Archaic spelling of *agnoscō, agnoscere, agnōuī, agnitus.*

Prologue

The *Poenulus* features an impersonal prologue—the prologue's speaker (the *prōlogus*) does not possess any specific identity. (Impersonal prologues in comedies were a Roman innovation—Christenson 2008 147n1.) Because the prologue-speaker lacks an identity, scholars debate whether he wore a mask or costume. Beare (1964 194) proposes that the *prōlogus* wore all of the usual costume elements (tunic, cloak, slippers) except the mask, since that could indicate that he was speaking "in his own person and on behalf of the dramatist." Illustrated manuscripts of Terence's comedies do show masked prologue speakers, though the illustrations cannot be taken of proof of such a practice in Plautus' day. (Jones and Morey 1930–31 vol. 1 shows masked prologue-speakers in manuscripts C: Vaticanus Latinus 3868, P: Parisinus Latinus 7900, and O: Bodleianus Auct.F.2.13. See, e.g., fol. 3v of O, the mid-twelfth-century MS.Auct.F.2.13 from Oxford's Bodleian Library: http://image.ox.ac.uk/images/bodleian/ms.auct.f.2.13/3v.jpg.) As Slater (1992 135) argues, the lack of mask on the prologue-speaker here would be "striking" and would a) allow the actor to be identified and b) "subvert the joke of the opening lines" of tragic parody.

In the course of the prologue, observes Slater, the *prōlogus* tries on different roles ("tragedian, praetor, humble taxpayer") and thus helps place the actors and the audience into their appropriate roles. As in other Roman comedies, the prologue as a whole serves as "an induction" drawing the audience into the action of the play (Slater 1992 145). Furthermore, Moore (1998 16) asserts that his *prōlogus* is the most dictatorial of Plautine prologue-speakers: he calls himself *imperātor histricus*, announces a list of decrees, and assigns himself the role of a public official before finally subordinating both actors and audience to the power of the magistrates.

The *Poenulus* prologue is also unique amongst Plautine prologues, since it reflects the "challenging conditions" in which the actors performed: because performances were outdoors, in spaces temporarily adapted for a show, spectators could wander in and out of the "theater," sit up onstage, enter late, or just make a lot of noise in general (Moore 1998 10).

1   **Achillem Aristarchi** A reference to the play *Achilles* by the fifth-century BCE poet Aristarchus. Ennius, a contemporary of Plautus, had recently adapted this tragedy (Richlin 2005 251). **mihi . . . lubet** Archaic spelling of *libet*, an impersonal verb with dative of reference: "it is pleasing to me." **commentari** From *commentor* (1-tr.) "perform, recite."

2–4   Line 2 sets up a quotation from Aristarchus' tragedy *Achilles*, which quickly takes a turn toward comedy with the final word of line 4.

3   **aduortite** Archaic spelling of *aduertīte*.

4   **histricus** While *histricus, -a, -um* means "of the stage," the phrase *imperātor histricus* is a pun on the imaginary adjective **(H)Istricus* "Istrian" and *(h)istriō, (h)istriōnis* (m) "actor." The commander is a histrionic/Histrian one—cf. *imperiō histricō* at line 44. (Rome fought a series of three short wars against the Histrians, who were located across the Adriatic Sea from the Italian peninsula, between 221 and 178 BCE.) Plautus likes puns on adjectives in *-icus* in general: cf. *Capt.* 86–7; *Cas.* 98; *Men.* 12; Ter. *Eun.* 264 (Fontaine 2010 157, 206). Thus *histricus* "either equivocates on, or is a surprise for, **(H)Istricus* 'Istrian,'" in the context of a prologue "more given to puns and other verbal surprises" than other Plautine prologues (Fontaine 2010 206). While Moore (1998 161) declares the *prōlogus* "pompous and silly" here, Manuwald (2011 314) suggests that the word *histricus* finally reveals that the audience is about to watch a comedy—everything thus far has implied that the play is a tragedy. Similarly, in lines 54–55 of the prologue to the *Amphitruo*, Mercury jokes that he can change the play from a tragedy to a comedy without changing any of its lines. Passages like these remind us that we do not know how much Plautus' spectators knew about the play when they sat down for a performance—did they know the genre? the title? the author?— and thus we do not know how they would interpret such jokes. Without more information about how *lūdī scaenicī* were organized, such aspects of Plautine comedy must, alas, remain a mystery.

6   **uenerint** Subjunctive by attraction.

8   **fabulis** Pun on *fābula, -ae*, "the story" and *fabālis, -e*, an adjective meaning "belonging to beans, beany" and referring to snacks (little beans or lupines) often eaten at the games—the aediles sometimes even funded such snacks themselves (Gowers 1993 59n38). Note the difference in length between the initial vowels of *fābula* and *fabālis* and see the note on 1370. A modern equivalent might be "Storybursts," punning off the name of Starburst candy.

9   **quoi** Archaic form of *cui*, the dative relative pronoun. **paratum est** This phrase, when pronounced aloud, undergoes prodelision: elision in which the second word loses its first vowel. (See section 4c of the introduction.) Prodelision of *est* and participles or nouns is very common in Plautus (as is contraction in general). **edit** The archaic form of the present subjunctive of *edō, edere/esse, ēdī, ēsus* "to eat" (A&G 201). **nostra gratia** "For our sake."

10   **sessum** Accusative supine expressing purpose with a verb of motion: "to sit down" (A&G 509). Cf. line 20.

11   **praeco** The *praecō, praecōnis* (m) is a "herald," or even "bouncer" (Starks 2000 165). **fac populo audientiam** The phrase *facere audientiam* means "to make people pay attention, demand silence." *populō* is dative of reference (A&G 376).

12   **iam dudum exspecto** When accompanying the present tense, *iamdūdum* indicates that the action was begun in the past but has continued into the present (A&G 466). The present *exspectō* should therefore be translated as a perfect (in its present completed aspect). **tuom** is the archaic neuter accusative singular spelling of *tuus, -a, -um*. **officium** *officium, -iī* (n) "duty," also implies a "role," which thus introduces the metatheatrical theme to the play.

15   **reside** Potentially an obscene joke about a particular sexual position— cf. *Per.* 284–85 (Traina 1989 71–74, cited at Fontaine 2010 206). Cf. 268. Presumably the *praecō* has now called for silence. **duplicem** As Slater (1990 106n12) remarks, the prologue-speaker now offers the *praecō* double wages to be quiet!

16   **facesse** Singular imperative of *facessō, facessere, facessī, faccessītus* "to perform eagerly" (Welsh 2007 109). De Melo (2012) prints *bonum factum est*, which is also possible given the common use of the phrase *bonum factum* to precede edicts (see Suet. *Iul.* 80). Cf. line 44. **ut** introduces a substantive clause of result as the object of *facesse* (A&G 568).

17–35   This section gives insight into the diverse composition of the
Roman audience, mentioning in particular male prostitutes (17); lictors and
their magistrates (18); slaves and freedmen (23–24); wet nurses with infants
(28–31); and married women and their husbands (32–35). (Lictors were
freeborn attendants granted to magistrates as a sign of their office. A lictor
carried the *fascēs*, a bundle of rods tied together with an axe, and compelled
people to move out of the magistrate's path.) These groups are portrayed as
typical causes of disruption to a dramatic performance. Plautus' omission of
other potentially disruptive groups—female prostitutes, for example—should
be seen as unintentional (Marshall 2006 75–76).

17   **exoletum** From *exolescō, exolescere, exolēuī, exolētus* "to grow up;
become obsolete." **proscaenio** The *proscaenium, -iī* (n) is the "stage." See note
on line 20 below too.

19   **dissignator** "Usher." This is the only mention of the term in all of
Plautus' plays. The sentence suggests that there would be more than one
dissignātor and that they would assist the herald (Marshall 2006 31).

20   **sessum** See note for line 10 above. **histrio** One of the earliest uses of
the term. Cf. *Amph.* 69, 77, 82, 87, 91; *Capt.* 13—all for comic actors—and
Truc. 931 for a tragic actor. Terence never uses the term, but in Plautus it
is applied to any actor in a dramatic company. There seems to be no strong
distinction between *histriō* and *actor*, but usually *histriō* is used for any
member of a company, while *actor* is (in the singular) used for the troupe's
head actor. *histriō* may also possess a more disreputable connotation than
actor (Zucchelli 1964 34–35, 37, 41). **in scaena** Though there is a distinction
between *proscaenium* and *scaena*, the latter term is surprisingly ambiguous.
The phrase could therefore mean "before the stage building" or "in the
performance area" as at *Capt.* 60 (Marshall 2006 33n75). **siet** Disyllabic form
of *sit*, the third-person singular present active subjunctive. (Though see de
Melo 2011 323 on the potential for such a spelling for monosyllabic forms as
well.) Here *siet* is subjunctive by attraction, expressing action simultaneous to
the future sense of the jussive subjunctives (A&G 439) in the main clause.

22   **stent ... temperent** Subjunctives in substantive clauses of result
(A&G 569.2) after *decet* on 21.

24   **aes pro capite dent** To "give copper or money in return for one's head"
means to pay for one's own manumission. The slaves should either give up
their spots to the free men or purchase their freedom if they wish to stay.

25 **uitent** In Plautus the verb *uitō* (1-tr.) often takes an object in the dative case.

26 **hic varientur virgis et loris domi** Chiasmus with adverb/locative and ablative nouns. **domi** Locative, "at home."

27 **minus** Translate as if it were *nōn*. **curassint** Archaic sigmatic form of the perfect subjunctive of *cūrō* (1-tr.) "to take care of, attend to." De Melo (2007 206) notes that this sigmatic form of the subjunctive need not indicate action in the past and declares that here *cūrāssint* could be replaced either "by *cūrāuerint* ('they have done') or by *cūrent* ('they are doing')." **quom** Archaic spelling of *cum*, "when." **eri** Plautus is fond of the term *erus, -ī* (m) "master." Don't confuse its forms with forms of *esse* or *Eros*!

28-35 This prologue is a rare piece of evidence for the presence of women and slaves in theatrical audiences at Rome. Hurka (2013 47–49) discusses how the prologue-speaker a) is presented as the ideal spectator, b) validates the point of view of the adult male Romans, and c) attempts to assimilate all Others (non-Romans and women) into the point of view of the ideal adult-male-Roman spectator.

29 **ut** Introduces another in the series of jussive subjunctives from above (now positive in contrast to *nē opsideant* at 23). **quae** After *sī, nisi, num*, and *nē* (or *nēue/neu*), the indefinite pronoun *quis, quid* is used more often than *aliquis, aliquid*, though with much the same meaning: "some/any one/thing" (A&G 310). **spectatum** Accusative supine expressing purpose: "to watch." Cf. lines 10, 20.

33 **canora** *canōra, -ōrum* (n pl) means "melodiousness."

34 **fabulandi** Appositive genitive (A&G 343d) with *sermōnēs*: "their conversations of speaking."

36 **ludorum curatores** The aediles, "the ones in charge of the games."

37 **palma** Literally means "palm (branch)," the prize given to a winner of the Olympic games. The word, which appears at *Amph.* 69 and *Trin.* 706 as well, suggests that actors or plays may have been in competition at the Roman games (as at Athenian festivals), but no other evidence for such a competition exists. The allusions to a victory palm may instead refer to a kind of informal popularity contest among troupes as they competed for audience approval, which would help foster future contracts with Roman magistrates (Marshall 2006 84–85). **quoiquam** Archaic spelling of *cuiquam*. Cf. lines 9, 27. **artifici** *artifex, artificis* (m) is the most generic of the terms for actor and is often interpreted as a translation of the Greek term τεχνίτης, which designated members of the religious/professional organization of actors in the Hellenistic period: the Technitai of Dionysus (Zucchelli 1964 51).

38   **ambitionis causa** When used in the ablative, *causa, -ae* (f) means "for the sake of" and takes an object in the genitive, which usually precedes it.

39   **quo** Understand as *ut eō* "that thereby" or "in order that."

40   **fui** In Plautine Latin, the perfect tense of *sum* often replaces the present when constructing perfect passive forms. Translate *oblītus fuī* as the perfect tense.

41   **pedisequi** Male slaves who followed their masters around, charmingly translated by Richlin (2005 252) as "personal assistants."

43   **scriblitae** A *scriblīta, -ae* (f) is a type of cheese tart. See Cato *Agr.* 78.

45   **bonum . . . factum** See note on 16. **meminerit** Refers to line 44.

47   **gnarures** is a colloquial and archaizing form of *gnārus, -a, -um*, which means "knowing, knowledgeable."

49   **finitor** "Surveyor"—the public official who measured land.

50-2   The *prōlogus* reminds the audience that the presiding magistrates have the power, not the actors or the spectators (Moore 1998 16–17).

51   **comoediai** The disyllabic *-āī* is an archaic genitive singular ending of the first declension (A&G 43). **sin** "But if." **odio** dative of purpose (A&G 382): "a cause for hatred."

52   **siquidem** An adverb meaning "if in fact." **illos** The presiding magistrates mentioned in line 36.

53   **Καρχηδόνιος** *Karchedonios* is the Greek term for "Carthaginian." Plautus is referring to Alexis' comedy of that name. (See section 2a in the introduction.)

54   **latine Plautus patruus pultiphagonides** Understand a verb
such as *uortit*, "translated"—the absence of such a verb, and the bizarre
disjunction between lines 53 and 54 leads de Melo and Geppert to believe
that we're missing at least one line containing a form of *uortere* in between
them. (Trappes-Lomax suggests to de Melo (*per litterās*) the emendation
latine Patruom <uortit> Pultiphagonides for line 54—de Melo 2012 25.)
Furthermore, the meaning of these lines is debated. Some take *patruus* as
an alternate title for the play: *The Uncle*, but the term must refer to Plautus.
First, even though Hanno is occasionally called Agorastocles' uncle in the
play, he is actually Agorastocles' first cousin once removed. Second, de Melo
(2012 3) notes that *patruus* is in the wrong position and wrong case to be
considered the title of the play if we assume the omission of some form of
uortere. Whether *pultiphagonides*, "son of porridge-eater," is to be applied to
Plautus or to the uncle has also been debated, though the problem is solved
if Plautus and the uncle are one and the same. *puls, pultis* (f) "porridge" is
made of mashed grain and was a staple food for poor Italians—at *Most.* 828
Plautus actually mocks this staple of the Roman diet (de Melo 2012 3). The
term *pultiphagonides* also incorporates a Greek root (*phag-*) and a Greek
patronymic suffix (*-ides*), so Richlin (2005 201, 253) translates the name as
"Plautus de Cornpone-Jones." Surprisingly, instead of using *barbarē/barbarus*
(as is common in many of his plays—cf. *Asin.*10–11, *Trin.* 18–19) to refer to
the Latin language or to the Romans, Plautus uses *Latinē* here and at 1029
(Fantham 2004 238). Cf. *Rōmānī* at 1314.

55–58   The metaphor drawn from the Roman census shows the *prōlogus'*
dependence on the audience. The spectators are to be *iūrātōrēs* ("sworn judges,
assistants to the censors," 58) to evaluate the prologue-speaker's *argūmentem*
just as censors evaluate citizen wealth (Moore 1998 12–13).

57   **argumento** Dative of reference with the subject *locus* and the
predicate *suom* (archaic neuter nominative singular) *prōscaenium*. The
prōlogus is saying that the place for the plot is its own stage. **sibi** is somewhat
redundant because of *suom*.

58   **quaeso** Literally "I ask," it is more often used, as it is here, as a means
to say "please." **operam date** The idiom *operam dare* means "to pay attention,
do one's best."

59–67   The beginning of the *argūmentum* (plot summary), which in
the *Poenulus* "has a difficult job . . . [to] hold the two disparate halves of the
action together." It must attract spectators who like conventional Roman

plot elements (i.e., deception and disguise) as well as those "who prefer the sentimental recognition plot" of the second half. Thus the *argūmentum* focuses on "the pivotal figure from each plot: Lycus and Hanno respectively" (Slater 1992 141). Hanno and Agorastocles' familial relationship is mentioned at 59–67 but explained again at 1042–55 and 1060–71—there is plenty of repetition to ensure that the audience grasps important concepts. Similarly, the relationship between Hanno and his daughters appears at 83–97, 894–906, 961; Agorastocles' kidnapping and adoption are mentioned at 68–70, 894–906, 950–60, 1042–55, 1058–59; and the existence of a guest-host relationship between Hanno and Antidamas is repeated at 950–60, 1042–55, 1058–59 (Arnott 2004 66). The only prologues to incorporate plot summaries are those of the *Captiui*, *Menaechmi*, and *Truculentus* (Marshall 2006 195).

59   fratres patrueles *pātruēlis, -e* means "descended from a father's brother." Taken with *frāter*, the phrase means "father's brother's son." As a substantive *pātruēlis, -is* (m/f) means "cousin" on the father's side. Cf. 70, 1069.

60   fuere Alternative third-person plural perfect indicative of *sum, esse, fuī, futūrus*. **summo genere et summis ditiis** Ablative of respect.

61   emortuos Archaic nominative masculine singular of the perfect participle of *ēmorior, ēmorī, ēmortuus* "to die."

63   quia ... pollinxerat *pollingō, pollingere, pollinxī, pollinctus* means "to wash a corpse in preparation for a pyre." This is an odd joke when taken literally. Fontaine (2010 204, 206–7) may be right about *pollinctor, pollinctōris* (m) "undertaker" as a scribal error for *pol, linctor* (where *linctor* = "one who licks"), which suggests a sexual joke about Carthaginians via the Greek verb φοινικίζειν "to imitate the Carthaginians by performing *cunnilingus*."

64   mortuost Prodelision of *mortuos est*. See note on 61.

65   ab According to Lewis and Short, *ab* was still used before consonants (instead of *ā*) until the middle of the first century BCE.

66   puer septuennis surripitur Carthagine This entire line has been lifted to form the first line of the play's acrostic argument. **septuennis** The statement here that Agorastocles was seven years old when kidnapped is contradicted at 902 and 987, where he's almost or around six. Plautus has probably just loosely translated similar Greek phrases (Arnott 2004 71).

67 **prius ... quam** Tmesis. Translate as if *priusquam* were located where *quam* is. **quidem** The second syllable of the word shortens before the caesura (Maurach 1988 56).

69 **gnatum** Archaic spelling of *nātus* from *nāscor, nāscī, nātus sum* "to be born."

71 **Acheruntem** *Acherun, Acheruntis* (f) = Acheron, a river in the underworld, and by extension the underworld itself. Plautus treats it as a place rather than a river (which may explain why it's feminine for Plautus but masculine elsewhere—de Melo 2011 337). Thus, like the names of cities, towns, and small islands, it doesn't require prepositions to express motion to, motion from, or location in. Cf. 344, 431, 831. The first syllable of the word usually scans long for Plautus too (de Melo 2011 337).

72 **Calydonem** Calydon was a city in Aetolia, in west-central Greece, located near the mouth of the Gulf of Corinth. (See the map on p. 23.) See sections 2a and 2bii of introduction for Rome's war with the Aetolians in the 190s and 180s BCE, as well as the reasons for Plautus—or Alexis—to set the play there.

73 **hic** "Here" is Calydon in the world of the stage.

74 **liberorum ... mulierum** Objective genitives with the preceding participle and adjective.

77 **obiit diem** A periphrasis for "died."

78 **illisce** The emphatic demonstrative suffix *-ce* (sometimes shortened to *-c*) is added to demonstrative pronouns in many different cases. Cf. *ecce* (at 352).

79–82 A metatheatrical "commission" joke helps to spice up a long prologue (Slater 1992 139n22). The *prōlogus* teases the audience by claiming that he could cheat the spectators—cf. *Cas.* 67–78, *Men.* 51–55 (Moore 1998 20).

79 **reuortor rursus denuo** Pleonasm, though not necessarily colloquial (Gaertner 2010 250). Perhaps the translation "re-re-return" might be in order.

80   **quid** The indefinite pronoun *quis, quid*, used after *sī, nisi, num, nē* more often than *aliquis, aliquid*, still means "some/any one/thing" (A&G 310). Cf. *quī* on 81. **uoltis** Archaic spelling of *uultis*. **curarier** Archaic form of the present passive infinitive (which used *-ier*—A&G 183.4).

83   **illi patruo** Dative of possession (A&G 373). **huius** Refers to Agorastocles.

85   As Gratwick (1971 28) notes, the age of the two sisters is included in the prologue "to explain why the girls are accompanied by a nurse; being less than seven years of age, and having no recognition tokens, they need someone to remind them of their true identity."

86   **periere** Alternative third-person plural perfect form of *pereō, perīre, periī, peritus* "to be lost, perish, die." **Magaribus** The exact meaning of the term is unclear. There are three common hypotheses: a) Magaria was the traditional harbor for the city of Carthage (Maurach 1988 58); b) the term refers to the area to the west and north of Carthage—the sparsely populated outskirts of the city (Faller 2004 179; de Melo 2012 27n7; Zehnacker 2000 416); or c) "The Magara" is used to refer to a location inside Carthage and is perhaps "derived from Latin *magalia*, a Roman stereotype-word for African housing" (Richlin 2005 254).

87   **Anactorium** Anactorium, a colony of Corinth, was a port city of Acarnania. It was located on the Ambracian Gulf of the Greek peninsula, about sixty miles northwest of Calydon.

89   **praesenti argento** Ablative of price (A&G 416): "ready cash."

90   **sacerrumo** Archaic spelling of the superlative adjective *sacerrimus, -a, -um* (from *sacer, sacrī*). Aside from "sacred, holy," *sacer* can also mean "infamous," or "forfeited to a god due to an offense against divine law."

91   **uosmet** The emphatic suffix *-met* "___self" on pronouns is a marker of colloquial Latin. Cf. 251. **facite coniecturam** sets up an erudite riddle game to interpret the name *Lycus* in 92. "Wolf" is the obvious answer (it's the meaning of the Greek λύκος). But lines 93–95 mention Anactorium in Acarnania, the home of the wolf-fish known as λάβραξ ("labrax") and ἀκαρνάν ("akarnan") in Greek, *lupus* in Latin! So the pun suggests that Lycus will be easily caught, but also, because the *lupus* fish is a bottom feeder living near the exit of the *Cloaca Maxima*, that Lycus is a filthy "scatophage" (cf. 157–58, 825–26, where he is also associated with filth) (Fontaine 2010 150–52). Similarly, Labrax is the name of the pimp in Plautus' *Rudens*. **ceterum** An adverb meaning "for the rest."

92 **hominis** Partitive genitive (A&G 346) with *quid*: "what (of) a man." **Lyco** Lycus is the only character to be named: "as bestial sub-human, he is the motor of the farce's derision, our othered inferior and—favourite character" (Henderson 1994 36). Menander often names only one character in his prologues: cf. *Asp.* 110 (Kleostratos), *Dys.* 6 (Knemon), *Sam.* 56 (Chrysis). Such restraint might derive from a fear of encumbering the audience with too much information right at the start. Perhaps Alexis, whose play Plautus adapted, followed this rule of thumb too? (Arnott 2004 74). On the other hand Lycus is the perfect name for the owner of a *lupānar* "brothel" since *lupa* means both "she-wolf" and "prostitute" in Latin (Schmidt 1960 275).

95 **quaesti** Archaic genitive of *quaestus, quaestūs* (m): "profit; occupation." **aedibus** Ablative plural of *aedēs/aedis, -is* (f) "building." In the singular this noun often refers to a temple (which has only one room), while the plural refers to a "house, home" with its multiple rooms.

96 **perit** The verb *perīre* (see note on 86) also means "to be desperately in love." Cf. *dēperit* on 103.

99 **stupri** Partitive genitive (A&G 346) with *quicquam* "anything," the direct object of *fēcit*.

100 **duxit** With *uxōrem* the verb *dūcere* means "to lead a wife home, marry;" with *scortum* or *merētrīcem* the same verb means "to take home, hire" (cf. *Most.* 36, *Truc.* 678). Thus this phrase implies that Agorastocles has never achieved any union with Adelphasium at all. Likewise, Antamynides cannot succeed with Anterastilis before Hanno arrives because she needs to remain a virgin for a happy ending to be possible. A young woman who has had only one sexual partner but is discovered to be a citizen is able to marry her lover in *Cistellaria* (and perhaps in *Curculio* and *Rudens*), but Plautus avoids such a scenario here, perhaps to add to the humor through Agorastocles' over-the-top language and Adelphasium's tart commentary. Thus Lycus, who would otherwise want money, and who runs a very disreputable establishment (829–38) must oppose Agorastocles, who actually does possess both the independence and money that most young men in comedy lack. Similarly, Adelphasium must oppose doing anything improper for the same plot-oriented reason. (Even though the two sisters are referred to as *merētrīcēs*:

see 107, 155, 298, 304, 305, 498, 849, 1094.) This arrangement is funny and efficient, although not necessarily believable or psychologically consistent (Blume 2004 205n8). Such an explanation makes more sense than Segal's attempt to pin Agorastocles' failure to buy Adelphasium from the pimp on Milphio's pride in his own abilities—i.e., the slave considers simply purchasing Adelphasium a far too ordinary means of acquisition (Segal 1968 62–63).

101   **tangere ... bolo** *tangō, tangere, tetigī, tactus* can mean simply to "touch," but also to "trick, cheat out of." A *bolus, -ī* (m) is a "throw of the dice/net," and thus "haul, profit, gain." Take *bolō* here as either a dative of purpose (A&G 382) or an ablative of means, depending on your translation of *tangere*.

103   **miles** Manuwald (2004 222) notes that, although the soldier is not named in the prologue (he is anonymized as *mīles quīdam* as opposed to Agorastocles), he is not presented either as a boastful soldier elsewhere in the play or as a customary client of pimps (cf. 491b–98). He thus appears as a more positive example of the stock character than is usual in Plautus. **deperit** See note on 96. Note too the difference between the relationships of the two sisters and their lovers: Agorastocles wants to free Adelphasium (and perhaps marry her—see 360–61), while Antamynides wants to buy Anterastilis to serve as his concubine (Manuwald 2004 229). But because Anterastilis is discovered to belong to a rich and high-ranking family, she and Antamynides cannot have married at the end of the *Karchedonios*, as some scholars have suggested: "differences in both race and social status effectively rule out any marriage" between the two characters (Arnott 2004 84).

104   **Poenus** "Punic," not "Carthaginian" (a term with fewer negative connotations). *Poenus* is *not* the Latin equivalent of the Greek title Καρχηδόνιος (line 55): "The two adjectives were not coextensive, and Plautus could have opted for the national rather than the ethnic term had he wanted" (Fontaine 2010 205).

105   **usquequaque** "Everywhere, in every place."

107   **omnis** The alternative accusative plural ending for third-declension i-stem nouns and adjectives. Cf. 112 and throughout the play.

108   **ducit noctem** "Spends/passes the night." Most scholars interpret these lines as indicating that Hanno only asks prostitutes about their birth after having sex. (Attractive kidnapped children were often sold as prostitutes across the ancient Mediterranean). "Whether Hanno merely risks incest or actively seeks it, the audience's first piece of information about him reveals that he is crafty (*docte atque astu*) and so lecherous as to countenance sleeping with his daughters" (Franko 1995 251—where he also observes in n5 that at *Truc.* 49 "*noctes ducit* clearly means to spend the night with a *scortum*"). Plautus thus refers to the cliché of the sensualist Carthaginian (Faller 2004 169). Concern about potential incest (cf. *Epid.* 650–51) appears often enough in comedy that it "may indicate a real tension for the Romans" (Franko 1995 252n9). Finally, the hiring of prostitutes in order to question them may have been a trope in ancient Mediterranean popular culture, since the same plot appears in the novel *Apollonius, King of Tyre*, and the *Life* of St. Mary the Harlot (Richlin 2005 192–93). Whether or not Hanno the *senex* would be considered capable of sleeping with anyone may depend on how old he looked—but the fathers in the *Asinaria, Casina*, and *Mercator* are certainly all too lecherous for their own good, and the sight of Hanno does inspire a jealous reaction from Antamynides at 1297–1306. Hanno is the only character in extant Roman comedy to adopt this method of searching for his lost relatives.

109 **quoiatis** Archaic form of *cūiās, cūiātis* (pronoun): "of what country/ town?" As it often does, here the pronoun introduces an indirect question (one in a long series of them). Cf. 993.

111 **docte atque astu** The adjective *doctus, -a, um* in particular is often applied to the clever (or much-rehearsed) characters in Plautine comedy, such as slaves and prostitutes, and implies "mental agility" and adaptability (Brotherton 1926 33). *as(tū)tus, -a, um* also develops a "tricky force" in Roman comedy. Cf. the use of the related noun *astus, astūs* (m) "adroitness, craft," here and at 1223, where it refers to "the sort of shrewdness that 'puts something over' on the other person" (Brotherton 1926 31). To Segal, the prologue emphasizes Hanno's cleverness and deceit, though Hanno's behavior in the play does not necessarily match the prologue's description. Plautus seems to be giving the audience—at least in the prologue—what they want: a disreputable *Graeculus* character (Segal 1968 187n74).

112 **dissimulat** May carry a metatheatrical resonance, given the preceding line. Outside of lines 106–13, Hanno's portrayal is not entirely unsympathetic.

113 **opust** Prodelision. *Opus est* ("there is work with," hence "there is need of") usually employs the ablative case for the thing or person required (an ablative of instrument/means) and the dative case for the person who

needs that item/person. *quid uerbīs opust* "why is there a need for words"
points "toward verbality and its veiling" as a major weapon in the play
(Henderson 1994 36).

114   **portum** As Blume (2004 203) notes, Calydon was several miles
inland. The length of the journey might explain why Hanno reaches Calydon
a day after he reaches the harbor—one wonders whether he spent the night
pursuing his inquiries (cf. 108) with any prostitutes near the harbor.

115   **harunc** Archaic feminine genitive plural form of *hīc, haec, hoc*, the
original form of which was *hīce, haece, hōce* (it later lost its final "e" through
apocope). **patruos** Archaic form of the nominative *patruus*, "uncle." "Given
Roman objections to first-cousin marriages . . . it seems almost certain that
Plautus altered the story to make Hanno and Agorastocles' father cousins
(*fratres patrueles*, 59; cf. 70) rather than brothers, but here at the end he slips"
(Slater 1992 141n25). Agorastocles repeatedly refers to Hanno as his uncle
throughout the end of the play as well, perhaps as a sign of respect for the
elder man.

116   **si tenetis ducite** *teneō, tenēre, tenuī, tentus* should be understood as
"hold (mentally), grasp" here, which turns *dūcō, dūcere, dūxī, ductus* "draw,
pull" into an allusion to masturbation—cf. *Capt.* 10–14 (Moore 1998 17).
Given Plautus' suggestive language elsewhere (cf. 15), this interpretation is
more likely than de Melo's (2012 29n10) suggestion that it refers "to a dance in
which the participants hold a rope."

117   **caue dirumpatis** The imperatives of *caueō, cauēre, cauī, cautus* "to
beware, take care" are often used with a simple subjunctive to give a command
"be careful not to X; don't Y," even (as here) mixing singular and plural verbs
(A&G 450).

118   **relicuom** Archaic form of *reliquus, -a, -um* "remaining."

119–22   Henderson (1994 37) observes that these lines—like 75–76, 83,
104, 115—feature a plethora of pronouns.

120   **hospes** In both Greek (ξένος, ὁ) and Latin (*hospes, hospitis* [m]), the
term for "host" is also the word for "guest" or "stranger." In both cultures there
were strong ties of hospitality between hosts and guests (both of whom were
"strangers" before the host offered food, shelter, and perhaps even a bath).

121–22   In Greek New Comedy, a nondivine prologue speaker would not have the authority to declare the final outcome of the play; Arnott notes that predictions about what will happen in the play "are made only by divine prologues in Menander, obviously because mortals cannot so predict what will happen at a later stage of the play." He argues that Plautus probably changed the divinity who delivered Alexis' prologue (perhaps Aphrodite, Eros, or Tyche) into the unnamed *prōlogus* (Arnott 2004 74, 75). On the other hand, a nondivine prologue speaker predicts a happy ending in the *Casina's* prologue, although it may be post-Plautine.

122   **didici** From *discō, discere, didicī, discitūrus* "to learn."

123   **ornabor** The *prōlogus* probably did not wear any special costume at all, and thus the actor declares that he must go change into the costume of the character he will play next. *ornō* (1-tr.) "to dress"—and especially its compound *exornō*—carries resonances of "to disguise" since *ornamenta* was "the technical term for theatrical costumes" (Saunders 1909 19). The role-playing theme and self-aware actors appear throughout the *Poenulus* as a whole, so it is appropriate that its "prologue calls attention to its own status as dramatic performance" (Slater 1992 142). Manuwald (2011 322–23) proposes that a brief pause occurred between the prologue and the rest of the play, but much depends upon whether the actor delivering the prologue is also playing Agorastocles or Milphio.

124–6   I have bracketed these lines because they're unnecessarily repetitive and because the use of *ornābor* on 123 seems more Plautine. Leo brackets none of 121–26, Lindsay and de Melo bracket 121–23.

127   **palam** Adverb: "openly."

128   **Salus** The Roman goddess of health, welfare, and safety. Her temple stood on the Quirinal hill in Rome. Like the Greeks, the Romans were fond of creating gods for abstract concepts (Chance, e.g.). Plautus sometimes asks a deity to protect the city and/or audience in his prologues. Cf. *Asin.* 15; *Cas.* 2; and—a variation on the theme—*Rud.* 82.

129–209   The first scene of the play. (All scene breaks, i.e., places where new characters enter, are marked by spaces in the Latin text, though the concept of acts and scenes is anachronistic for Plautine comedy.) Milphio constantly and humorously undermines his master, Agorastocles, here. While some "contrast between helpless lover and ingenious slave" likely already appeared in the *Karchedonios*, Plautus would have exaggerated their differences (Lowe 2004 254). Such a relationship is common in Roman comedy, where a "male slave never identifies himself with his master's feelings, typically keeping a 'mocking distance.'" Cf. *Asin.* 591–745; *Curc.* 1–95; *Epid.* 337–81; *Men.* 226–50; *Pseud.* 1–131 (Dutsch 2008 120n75). The plot exposition's failure (at 129–58) to sufficiently clarify the relationship between Agorastocles, Adelphasium, and Lycus may be a sign of Plautine "omissions and rewriting" (Lowe 1988 102). The numerous references to whipping at 138–51 may represent Plautine additions as well.

130   **inopiosas** *inopiōsus, -a, -um* + genitive = "bereft of, in want of."

131   **cate** *catus, -a, um*, and *catē* usually connote "undersirable or tricky" cleverness (Brotherton 1926 32). Cf. 1107.

137   **gerrae germanae, αἱ δὲ κολλῦραι λύραι** Greek λύραι are "lyres, hymns," while κολλῦραι are "elongated loaves" (Brinkhoff 1935 151). While the line is somewhat obscure, there is wordplay on several levels, with sound repetitions in both halves of the line, and a potential pun with *gerrae* and κολλῦραι. De Melo (2012 31) reads the Greek literally: "loaves are the real lyres," and explains in note 11, "empty words mean nothing, while presents mean true praise." Richlin (2005 255) notes that *gerrae* "twigs; nonsense" may also mean "penis," and κολλῦραι may either nod to that meaning or simply suggest "nonsense" in this context. Given Plautus' penchant for exploiting polysemy elsewhere, the best translation of *gerrae germanae*, αἱ δὲ κολλῦραι λύραι might thus be "real nonsense, the songs and schlongs."

138–50   Milphio is versatile, and marked as the intellectual superior to Agorastocles. Their Saturnalian relationship (i.e., the inversion of the expected power structure) is made clear from their first lines to one another (Lefèvre 2004 42). Both Milphio and Agorastocles can be interpreted as fundamentally dishonest in this scene: Milphio plans to entrap the pimp to gain a legal hold on his property, while at 138–39 Milphio declares that Agorastocles "suits his words and behaviour to the occasion." Although this complaint is pretty standard about *adulescentēs amantēs* in Roman comedy, Maurice sees Agorastocles as a particularly flagrant offender—cf. lines 374, 376 (Maurice 2004 269–70). Milphio's own reminder of how much leather has been wasted on his back represents an extreme example of the comic slaves' "splitting of the self into the teller and the object of the joke" when they claim not to care about physical punishment—slaves often address their own body parts independently, as though they were separate from the slave. Cf. *Asin.*

276; *Capt.* 650; *Men.* 275; *Pseud.* 1325; but *Epid.* 348 offers the most extreme example (Dutsch 2008 125).

138   **es** The second-person singular form of *sum* often scans long in Plautus, according to Lewis and Short.

140   **si quid** See note on 29.

141   **Haud uidi magis** A very elliptical form of *haud quicquam uidī magis aequom.*

142-43   Similar to lines 189-90 of the *Persa*, an earlier play. Woytek (2004 131-32) notes the small connections between the two plays—cf. 174-75.

144   **post id locorum** "Afterwards," since *locōrum* is a partitive genitive (A&G 346) here.

145-46   Many Plautine *adulescentēs* allow their slaves to have *patria potestas* (complete control over their person, which normally belongs to Roman fathers). Here Agorastocles offers to let Milphio beat him—cf. *Most.* 407 (Segal 1968 113).

145   **lubido** Archaic form of *libīdo, libīdinis* (f) "longing, wish, fancy." **uoluptati** Dative of purpose (A&G 382) with the dative of reference *tibi* (A&G 376).

148   **sies** A disyllabic form of *sīs*, the present subjunctive of *esse*.

149   **istuc** Another form of the neuter *istud*. **ausim** An archaic, sigmatic subjunctive of *audeō, audēre, ausus sum* "to dare." Used potentially here.

151   **hercle** In Roman comedy, with the exception of *Cas.* 982, *Cist.* 52, and *Per.* 237, male characters alone swear by Hercules (using *hercle* or *mehercle*). In contrast, only women swear by Castor (either using *ēcastor* or *mēcastor*). Characters of both genders swear by Castor's brother Pollux. See Gell. *NA* 11.6, Donat. on Ter. *And.* 484, Adams 1984.

155   **maiusculam** is ambiguous. *māius* + *-culus* can mean both "a little larger" (in terms of height or perhaps chest size—see note on 1145-46) and "a little older." Richlin (2005 204) perfectly captures both senses with "slightly bigger."

158   **uin** Crasis (contraction) of *uīsne*, i.e., *uīs* + *ne*.

159   **nequam dare** "To make trouble." Milphio plays with the two senses of *nēquam* and *malum* (respectively, the adjectives "worthless" and "bad" vs. the substantives "injury, mischief" and "misfortune, calamity") from 159–62.

160   **dierectus** The word's meaning is uncertain, but it's used when one person tells another to leave. *abī diērectus* means something like "go and be hanged."

161   **malum** In Roman comedy, the substantive *malum* often implies "punishment."

162   **faxo** An archaic sigmatic form of the first-person singular future indicative of *facere*, *faxō* may have begun as a "parenthetic causative construction," since it can introduce a future indicative, a present subjunctive, a future perfect indicative, or even (rarely) a perfect subjunctive, an *ut* clause, or a double accusative (de Melo 2007 180–81).

163   **iocare** The alternative form of the second-person singular present passive indicative of *iocor, iocārī, iocātus sum*.

165–70   Concepts important to the plot against Lycus are presented here for the first time, but repeated frequently later so the audience won't miss them: Collybiscus is referred to as *uīlicus* at 415, 558, 779; the 300 gold coins are mentioned again at 415, 558, 594, 670, 771, 781 (Arnott 2004 66).

165–66   **faciam ut facias** Note the contrast with the use of *faxō* on 162, as well as the wordplay: "I'll take care that you take care to . . ." Cf. *Capt.* 409; *Cist.* 62 (Brinkhoff 1935 104). *ut faciās* is a substantive clause of result (A&G 568). **aurei . . . nummi Philippi** translates to "gold Philips." The phrase refers to the coinage of Philip II of Macedon, whose descendant (Philip V) Roman armies had fought between 216 and 197 BCE. Richlin (2005 195) wonders if the phrase "300 gold Philips" becomes a running joke in this play since it's repeated so often.

167   **facturu's** Prodelision of *factūrus es*.

169–73   Milphio, like many cunning comic plotters, starts out with only the briefest outline of his plan, but will be forced to elaborate further (173–80) given Agorastocles' confusion. Once Milphio's coconspirator Agorastocles understands the plan, he'll agree to it immediately (180, 188). This "seems to be one conventional device for the introduction of a scheme." Cf. Men. *Asp.* 329–47, *Epit.* 510–16 (Arnott 2004 77). Note therefore the prevalence of knowledge terms like *scīre* and *intellegere* (Lefèvre 2004 42).

169   **dono** Dative of purpose of *dōnum, -ī* (n) "gift." **qui** *quī* "how," is an adverb from the ablative of the interrogative *qui, quae, quod* "who? which? what? what kind of?"

170   **tuos** The adjective undergoes iambic shortening or synizesis.

171   **satin** Crasis of *satis + ne*.

172   **quo** Adverb, "where."

174–75   Similar to *Per.* 135–36 (Woytek 2004 132).

175–76   Role-playing, the central plot device of the *Poenulus*, appears for the first time. Cf. plays-within-plays in *Amph., Asin., Capt., Cas., Mil., Per., Pseud.,* and *Trin.* (and small deceptions in *Epid.* and *Men.* too).

177   **praeberier** Archaic form of the present passive infinitive *praebērī*, here used in the long indirect statement following *dīcat* in line 175.

178   **ne quis** See note on 29.

183   **quin** Translate as "that" to introduce the doubting clause (A&G 558) after *dubitās*.

186   **praetor** The *praetor, -ōris* (m) was the Roman magistrate in charge of administering justice, among other duties. After the First Punic War there were two praetors: one for Roman citizens (*praetor urbānus*), and one for foreigners (*praetor peregrīnus*). **addicet** comes from *addīcō, addīcere, addīxī, addīctus* "to deliver," meaning a judge's handing over of a debtor as slave to his creditor—the penalty for theft in Rome. Cf. 521, 564, 720, 1361.

187   **fouea** A *fouae, -ae* (f) is a "small pit," especially one used to capture wild animals (i.e., a pitfall). Milphio is either speaking metaphorically or making a bad pun about catching "Mr. Wolf" the pimp (Brinkhoff 1935 164).

189 tum demum "Only then."

191 Aphrodisia hodie sunt The Aphrodisia (*Āphrodīsia, -ōrum* [n] "festival of Aphrodite/Venus") and other large festivals appear in or serve as the setting for many Greek New Comedies: Men. *Aphr.*, e.g., or the monthly feast of Aphrodite Pandemos in Men. *Kol.* fr. 1 Sandbach. Cf. Timocl. *Dion.*, Theocr. *Adon.*, Ar. *Eccl.* and *Thesm.* (Fantham 2004 240–41). According to Athenaeus 13.572–80, *hetaerae* celebrated many different festivals other than that of Aphrodite in many different cities, e.g., in Magnesia, Samos, Corinth. And according to Alexis' *Philousa* (at Ath. 13.573c), prostitutes celebrate the Aphrodisia differently from married women, since they celebrate for the day and get drunk together. It is not clear whether Calydonian prostitutes did celebrate any Aphrodisia, but we can imagine the types of things prostitutes would pray for: "Whether the festival of Calydonian Aphrodite was an anthropologically observed fact, or a generic fiction, if it was a festival of *hetaerae*, they would pray to the goddess for profit in their trade, and conversely, if girls sacrificed at the festival, it would be to mark their maturity and readiness for business. For *hetaerae* the goddess would show her favour by bringing them rich lovers, or lovers willing to pay for their freedom and become their patrons" (Fantham 2004 241).

In Plautus' time, we know of two festivals to Venus held in Rome. The Veneralia (held April 1st) began early in the city's history, but in 212 BCE the April 23rd feast of Venus Erycina (held at the Colline Gate) was added to the calendar as well. According to Ovid, the Veneralia was for the wellborn *matrēsque nurūsque* (Ov. *Fast.* 4.133) who prayed to Venus Verticordia for *forma et mōrēs et bona fāma*; though there was also a "ritual to Fortuna Virilis for humbler women," who asked for their (physical) flaws to be concealed from men. The feast of Erycina, on the other hand, was for *uolgārēs . . . puellae* (*Fast.* 4.865—i.e., prostitutes), who "offered incense and wreaths of flowers in return for *formam populīque fauōrem . . . blanditiās dignaque uerba iocō* (*Fast.* 4.867–68) (Fantham 2004 241–42). A temple of Venus Erycina stood on the Capitoline hill from 215 BCE (it was built after Rome's disastrous defeat at Lake Trasimene), so a performance location near the temple would have emphasized the references to the Aphrodisia (Henderson 1994 28) and may also have reminded the audience of the Second Punic War (Richlin 2005 193). Jeppesen (2013 241–315) posits a revival performance of the *Poenulus* at the dedication of a new temple to Venus Erycina outside Rome's Colline Gate in 181 BCE.

192 munditiis *munditia, -ae* (f) is "elegance achieved through the toilette" (Richlin 2005 255).

195   **hanc . . . ut ferat fallaciam** "How to carry out this deception." *fallācia, -ae* (f) is a common term used to refer to the deceptions typical of Roman comedy. Cf. 577, 580, 605, 774; *Asin.* 250, 266; *Capt.* 226; *Pseud.* 672, 705a, 765 (Moore 1998 228n35). The term is "convenient, colorless," and "a general word for trick, [that] covers deceit of all varieties. It is used for an indefinite stratagem of any sort" (Brotherton 1926 8). Its importance for the genre can also be seen in Caecilius Statius' choice of *Fallācia* as a title for a comedy.

196   **uorsatur** Archaic spelling of *uersō* (1-tr.) "to turn, twist" in the active voice, and "to dwell, stay" in the passive.

199   **ne utiquam** "By no means, not at all."

200–2   **ballista est . . . ballistario** Military imagery—see note on 919. The latter noun appears only here—but *ballista* appears at *Bac.* 709, 710; *Capt.* 796; *Trin.* 668; Caecil. *Dem.* fr. 1 (Ribbeck); and *exballistāre* appears at *Pseud.* 585. A *ballistārium* is best understood as the place from which a *ballista, -ae* (f) "projectile, large crossbow bolt" is fired or shot: a) the siege engine itself; b) the emplacement of the engine; or c) the protected spot the engine operators shot from—also known as the *prōpugnāculum* (Jocelyn 1990 5–8). It's not a humorous word in and of itself, but these lines can be interpreted as a "phallic threat": the *ballista* is *intenta* ("cocked") and ready to shoot with some force (Richlin 2005 256). Furthermore, we may also read these lines as a joke on the name of Ballio, the villain of Plautus' *Pseudolus*, staged in 191 BCE (Welsh 2009 97). While the audience may not have recognized the reference to that specific character, it may have been an in-joke for the playwright and actors— cf. *Bac.* 214–15.

202   **haud multo post** "Not long afterward."

203–444   Lowe believes that Plautus added Milphio to this scene in an attempt to significantly increase his role in the play. Cf. 961–1173 and Milphio's expanded role at 504–816 (Lowe 2004 262).

203   **eccam** "Here she is!" From *ecce* + *eam*.

205–9   The conversation between Milphio and Agorastocles before the sisters walk onstage "identifies [the women] as objects of both love and the gaze" (Dutsch 2008 156).

206–9   ludos … spectare … spectaculum Terms used to describe the festival games in Rome—like the one where the *Poenulus* was first performed. The whole passage is therefore metatheatrical, reflecting on the play as a performance (cf. Henderson 1994 45, 49–50).

206   iucundissumos Archaic spelling of *iūcundissimōs*—such archaic spellings of superlative adjectives and adverbs are common in Plautus.

210–407 *Virginēs* ("[r]espectable unmarried girls") are usually kept off stage in Greek and Roman comedy. (See, e.g., *Aul.*, *Cas.*, *Trin.*, *Truc.*, Ter. *And.*, *Eun.*, *Hec.*, *Phor.*, *Ad.*). Less respectable young women (i.e., the love objects) can also be kept off stage. "But girls exposed to the life of a *meretrix*, whether they were merely emancipated, like Philocomasium in *Miles Gloriosus*, or Philematium in *Mostellaria*, or were subsequently revealed as citizen-born and married off, like Selenium in *Cistellaria* and Ampelisca in *Rudens*, were more articulate: the chief divergence between them is the extent to which their outlook has been coloured by their upbringing." Philematium in the *Mostellaria* provides a good contrast to Adelphasium and Anterastilis: she (a freedwoman) is "grateful and loyal to her lover," while "the citizen daughters of *Poenulus* are far more meretricious." Just as in the *Truculentus*, during the three scenes featuring the two sisters Plautus "exploits the audience's persistent fascination with the *ars meretricia*" (Fantham 2004 242–43). On Roman prostitution in general, see McGinn 2004.

The focus on extravagance and clothing may be a reference to Rome's recent repeal (195 BCE) of the Oppian Law, which forbade women from having more than half an ounce of gold or wearing multicolored clothing (Livy 34.1). According to Johnston (1980 150–53), the Carthaginian sisters represent a parody of the debates regarding the repeal of the Oppian Law, with Adelphasium arguing on the Catonian side and Anterastilis on the Valerian side. Johnston (1980 157) also sees Adelphasium's strictness as potentially intimidating, depending on the timing of the *Poenulus*' performance: "the ascetic strength of Adelphasium would further arouse that old familiar dread of the inherited, innate toughness which brought Hannibal so close to victory over Rome." Women's clothing is an important theme here regardless: Maurice (2004 274) notes that the verb *ornāre* and related forms appear thirteen times in this first scene with the sisters, and five times in Adelphasium's thirty-three-line opening speech (210–32). Finally, the high concentration of forms of *Venus*—not *Āphrodīsia*—in the scene suggests the influence of the cult of Venus Erycina on the composition process (Jeppesen 2013 275–76, and see note 191).

210-15   It is a common—and misogynistic—theme in Plautus (and Roman literature in general) that women spend a long time bathing and getting dressed. Cf. *Mil.* 1292-95; *Sti.* 744-47; Livy 34.7.7-10. Indeed, most generalizations about women in Roman comedy (even those by women about other women) are not complimentary: cf. 240-47, 1201-4; *Aul.* 123-26, 138-40; *Epid.* 546; *Mil.* 887-90; *Rud.* 685-86 (Moore 1998 223n28-29).

The duo of Adelphasium and Anterastilis represents "one among a series of pairs of women, one stronger, the other weaker, one a leader, the other a follower" in Roman comedy. (Cf. *Bac.*, *Cist.*, *Rud.*, *Sti.*) Usually the leader exhibits womanly virtues, and upbraids the other for her weaknesses (Dutsch 2008 131n105). That both sisters are brought up to be prostitutes is not surprising—it is likely that any slave or exposed girl who looked like she would grow up to be pretty would be raised in a house of prostitution. This speech begins a whole section (210-47) that Lowe (1988 108-9) argues was expanded significantly from the Greek version with "verbal jokes . . . comic business of a more physical nature . . . [and] comic stereotypes" to increase the humor of the play. Any resulting incongruities, he argues, were not as important to Plautus as the laughter the scene invoked. "To rig" is a good translation for all forms of *ornāre* at 214, 215, 220, 229, 283, 284, 285, 297, 299, 301 (Brinkhoff 1935 39).

211   The comparison between women and ships may also allude to the construction and expansion of the Roman navy in the First and Second Punic Wars (Richlin 2005 256).

213   occeperis From *occipiō, occipere, occēpī, occeptus* "to begin." **exornare** Even more metatheatrical than *ornāre*, the verb means "to 'deck out,' 'adorn elaborately' . . . Often the idea of 'disguise' is not far to seek." Cf. *Cas.* 769; *Mil.* 1184; *Per.* 335 (Saunders 1909 25).

215   satis satietas est may suggest a philosophical question. (At least what is *satis* seems to be a philosophical question in fr. 4 [Ribbeck] of the *Lindia*, a second-century BCE play by Turpilius.) This is the first sign that Adelphasium "will (just like Alcumena [in the *Amphitruo*]) usurp for herself the voice of a serious moralist." Adelphasium's "doctrine teaches respect for limits," but the rest of the speech, where a woman's and ship's needs are equal, "introduces erotic overtones that playfully undermine the moralist strain" in her sermon. Many Greek comedies compare women (especially prostitutes, because of their stereotypical enormous demands) to the sea. Similarly, some constant forces can wear down a woman's will. "The nautical motif inevitably evokes numerous Greek jokes comparing sexual intercourse to seafaring, and the allusions to vigorous scrubbing (*fricari*) in the description of the morning toilet also carry sexual connotations." The whole speech thus suggests that "it is constant sexual activity (driven by greed) that wears a woman out" (Dutsch 2008 157).

216   **domo** Best understood as a rare use of the ablative of place where, though we would expect a locative with this noun (A&G 427). **docta** See the note on 111 above.

217   **ad hoc quod diei** "To whatever point of the day."

221   Brinkhoff (1935 146) notes the asyndeton and general sound play here.

223   **lauando, eluendo** Dative gerunds after *dedērunt* (A&G 505).

225   **apage sis** *apage* comes from the Greek imperative ἄπαγε, "away (with you/it)!" or "begone," while *sīs* is a contraction of the phrase *sī uīs*, meaning "please."

227   **poplo** This archaic spelling of *populus, -ī* occurs frequently in Plautus.

231a   **neniam** A *nēnia (naenia), -ae* (f) is a "funeral song." Cf. *Truc.* 213.

232   **perculta** From *percolō, percolere, percoluī, percultus* "to cultivate; perfect, adorn." Dutsch (2008 158–59) observes that Adelphasium and Anterastilis' "physical filth (difficulty in ordering matter) is only the residue of the metaphysical dirt (difficulty in ordering the mind). *Cultus* is thus the ultimate and most elusive remedy for feminine dirt."

Line 232 is unusual due to its series of anapests. Leo brackets this line, though it has now been accepted by Lindsay, Questa, and de Melo. Schmidt (1960 74) points out the playful sound effects in *lauta est/perculta est/inluta est*.

234   **callida** "Clever," often associated with the deceptive slave in Roman comedy. **sis** Potential subjunctive (A&G 446).

236   **amatorculos** A diminutive of *amātor*, which carries either a disparaging sense ("silly little lovers") or an endearing one ("cute little lovers") depending on one's interpretation of Anterastilis' personality. Her claim is also demonstrably false, given that Agorastocles and Antamynides the soldier are already interested in the sisters (Fantham 2004 244).

238   **habitu** Supine of *habēre* with *optumus*. It is an ablative of respect/specification (A&G 418): "to have."

239   **nimia . . . nimium** From the noun *nimium, -iī* (n) "excess." Dutsch (2008 159) doubts whether Adelphasium actually understands the concept of limits—cf. lines 284–88.

241   **salsa muriatica** Comes from *saliō, salīre, —, salsus* "to salt, sprinkle with salt" and *muriāticum, -ī* (m) "pickled fish." In comedy "dirt and stench" are frequently connected to female characters: cf. *Asin.* 928; *Men.* 167–68; *Truc.* 378 (Dutsch 2008 158). See Richlin (2005 256) for the vulgar comparison of women and fish here and in Roman satire.

245a   **eius seminis** Genitive of description or quality (A&G 345): "of that stock."

248–49   Plautus is quite fond of two-part riddles in which the second part explains the wordplay of the first. Here Plautus plays with the double meaning of *insulsus* ("unsalted/without charm") when Milphio calls Anterastilis a cook. Cf. 384, 1168; *Asin.* 594; *Bac.* 1148; *Cas.* 360; *Curc.* 9, 397; *Per.* 288–89; *Pseud.* 614, 747; *Trin.* 1015 (Fraenkel 2007 29, 298n43).

249   **quid** Adverbial accusative (A&G 390n2): "why." **molestu's** Contracted form of *molestus es*. For the theme of quiet/silence, prevalent throughout the play, cf. 3, 261, 250–51, 295, 524–25, 741, 875, 890, 906, 913, 916, 1145–46, 1191b, 1234. The play seems aware that it has been "designed to be an unusually quiet one" without a lot of music (Moore 2004 142).

251   **in** "Against."

254   **deum** Genitive plural.

255–56   **diem . . . dignum** Accusative of exclamation (A&G 397d).

259   **cado** From *cadus, -ī* (m) "wine jar, jug," a Latinization of the Greek κάδος.

261   **ne opturba** *nē* with the present imperative means "stop doing X" (de Melo 2011 330). The sisters' *canticum* ends at 261 and is followed by a switch to trochaic septenarii, a "more forward-moving" meter that is still accompanied by the *tībia* (Moore 2004 153).

262   **gnatum** Archaic form of *nāscor, nāscī, nātus sum*, "to be born, be produced." **foret** A frequent substitute for *esset*.

263   **illo** Adverb, "(to) there."

264   **aedem Veneris** Temples in general were "evidently regarded as hotbeds of adultery and prostitution" (McGinn 2004 23). **maneat . . . mane** Polyptoton with *maneō, manēre, manuī, mansus* "to remain, stay."

265   **uorsarier** Such "medio-passive infinitives in *-ier*" are almost always used in iambic lines where infinitives in *-ārī* wouldn't fit the meter (de Melo 2011 327).

266   **proseda . . . pistorum . . . alicarias** From *prōseda, -ae* (f) "common prostitute" and *pistor, pistōris* (m) "miller." *alicārius, -a, -um* is best taken as "ground like spelt (a form of wheat)," where grinding is a metaphor for sex (Adams 1983 336). **reliquias** is the reading of MSS B and C, whereas T reads *rēgīnās*, which leads many to assume *alicāriās* means "spelt-grinding." Such an interpretation is then explained as referring to a supplemental source of income for prostitutes or their propensity to pursue their trade near the spelt mills, which may not be warranted (cf. Festus [Müller 1839] 7).

267   **schoeno delibutas** "Smeared with rush perfume."

268   **olant** Irregular present (potential) subjunctive from *oleō, olēre, oluī* "to emit a smell, smell of" something. **sessibulum** is a nonsense word (introduced by *stabulum*, "brothel"), likely with a sexual meaning: *sedēre* "indicates a sexual position." Cf. 15 (Fontaine 2010 41n8). One student suggests "barstools" as a translation. The scorn with which Adelphasium and Anterastilis discuss (other) prostitutes here and elsewhere suggests that the two women actually want to work as prostitutes (see line 1292), or at the very least desire to surpass their competition. Fantham argues that simple "snobbery, not morality" motivates Adelphasium's speech and points out that her next conversation with Anterastilis (at 283–88) is "equally materialist" (Fantham 2004 245).

270   **diobolaria** "Costing two obols," where an obol was one of the smallest units of money in Greece, perhaps with the buying power of $9 or thereabouts. Cf. note on 1287.

272 **eampse** Feminine accusative singular of *ipse*, an archaic form that shows how the pronoun started out as a compound of *is* and the emphatic suffix *-pse* (Hammond et al. 1963 52).

274 **quoius** Archaic spelling of *cuius*. **nebulai** An archaic disyllabic genitive ending (A&G 43). **cyatho** Ablative of price (A&G 416). A *cyathus, -ī* (m) is a ladle used to pour wine from the mixing bowl into a cup for drinking.

276 **qui** Introduces a relative purpose clause (A&G 531.2) with *crēdam* as its main verb (which itself introduces an indirect statement using *esse*). **siem** Archaic disyllabic spelling of the present subjunctive of *sum*.

277–82 The idea that Adelphasium is the real Venus contradicts Agorastocles' speech at 275–76, where he claims that he feels no less immortal on earth than the gods in heaven. Such incongruity of thought probably results from Plautus' additions, which tend to emphasize the ridiculous (including interruptions) over consistency of character (Fraenkel 2007 149–50).

278 Puns on Venus and *ueneror, uenerārī, uenerātus*. Venus is a frequent target of Plautine wordplay (cf. 1176–78, 1180–81), probably because love was such a common theme in Roman comedy (Mendelsohn 1907 37). Cf. notes on similar wordplay at 623–24, 845–46.

279 **adsum** Agorastocles intentionally mishears *assum*, "roasted," instead of *adsum* "I'm here." **elixus** "Boiled." Cf. the contrast between *assus* and *ēlixus* at *Most.* 1115. Furthermore, notes Fontaine (2010 59), this pun was probably in Alexis' play too since "boiled" and "roasted" also sound similar in Greek. For *eccum* see the note on 203.

280 **delicias** The word *dēliciae, -ārum* (f) means "delight, pleasure; sweetheart," and as the object of *facere* it means "to play tricks, joke." But the phrase also has sexual connotations in later Latin (cf. Catull. 45.24) so it may do so here as well. **tequidem** *Tē* + *quidem*, "indeed."

283 **ecastor** See note on 151.

286 The pimp recognizes that he must spend money to make money.

288   The line is corrupt, but I adopt Leo's proposed supplements here.
(Lindsay 1905 and Starks et al. 1997a print *eō illud satiust 'satis' quod satis
est habitū; <hoc> plūs quam satis est.*) **eo** Adverb: "for that reason." **satiust**
Prodelision of *est* and *satius* "better, preferable" (the comparative form of
satis). **habitu** Supine (see note on 238). Take it with the unstated *est*.

289   **ita me di ament** Religious language such as this is used, even abused,
frequently in Plautine comedy (Segal 1968 29). Either Agorastocles takes the
phrase too literally or the audience must, in order for the rest of the line to
make sense (Brinkhoff 1935 97).

292   **sis** See note at line 225. **limaui** From *līmō* (1-tr.) "to file, polish." The
phrase *caput līmāre* has been interpreted as a joking expression for "kiss"—cf.
Plautus *Schematicus* fr. 112, but it may also convey a more explicit sexual
meaning (Wright 1974 170).

293–94   Milphio creates a pun, deriving *līmāre* from *līmus* ("mud, filth")
rather than from *līma* ("file") (Schmidt 1960 145). Hence *līmāre* means
something like "to slime" here, much like *linō, linere, lēuī, litus*, which is
actually etymologically related to *līmus*.

295   **i in malam rem** "Go to hell." Milphio deliberately (and humorously)
misinterprets the command by taking it literally (Schmidt 1960 226). **perdis**
Either "you destroy [me]," or "you waste [time]!"

297   **soror** The word undergoes iambic shortening here.

299   **cordolium** "Grief," literally "pain in the heart." Richlin (2005 257)
nicely modernizes the term to "heart attack."

300   **malitia** "Wickedness," though the term is often the functional
equivalent of *dolus, fraus,* or *fallācia*. It is usually associated with slaves and
women in Roman comedy, though any character devising a trick will prize it
(Brotherton 1926 17–18).

301   **med** Archaic ablative singular of *egō*.

304–7   The moralizing speech from Adelphasium is problematic: how
seriously should we interpret it? The sisters are certainly portrayed in a more
negative fashion than the other young-women-about-to-be-recognized-

as-citizens of Roman comedy: "[s]urely if Adelphasium thinks of herself as a *merētrix*, [Plautus] has not just muddied the maiden simplicity of the *Poenulae*, but has consciously professionalized the girls" (Fantham 2004 245). Perhaps this aspect of Adelphasium and Anterastilis' character is where the majority of Roman prejudices against the Carthaginians emerge, rather than in the (surprisingly pious) figure of Hanno himself? They seem to be the exception to Syed's (2005 367) claim that the "portrayals of all four Carthaginian main characters is in no way any more or less sympathetic than what the conventions of the genre require." Perhaps it is safer to joke about them because the Roman men in the audience are less likely to identify with them than with their father Hanno.

Overall, the conflict between Adelphasium's status and her ideals is quite funny: "[a]s her sermon continues, the moralizing voice brings up other philosophical questions, for example, the difference between natural goodness (*bonum ingenium*) and prosperity based on luck (symbolized by *aurum*). Ultimately, [at lines 301–2] the two strains, the moralizing and the sexual, converge into an oxymoronic aphorism on whorish chastity" (Dutsch 2008 159). That prostitutes exhibit *pudor* is a "hilarious paradox"; also incongruous is the moral speech appropriate to a Roman matron emerging from the mouth of a "Phoenician" in a "Greek" city (Dutsch 2008 160).

304   purpuram Purple clothing was quite expensive (the dye comes from the mucus secretions of the *mūrex* shellfish) so was a sign of wealth and high status.

310   audibis The use of *-ībō, -ībis,* etc. (cf. the first/second-conjugation endings) for the future tense of the fourth conjugation is a mark of archaic Latin, as is the use of *-ībam, -ībās,* etc., for the imperfect. Cf. the future of *eō, īre, iuī/iī, itus*. Cf. 462, 509.

312   passa From *pandō, pandere, pandī, passus* "to spread out (to dry)." **pensilis** From *pēnsilis, -e* "hanging."

313   esse Alternative infinitive of *edō, edere/esse, ēdī, ēsus* "to eat." Note Milphio's play with *amāre*: it gains a different nuance when an infinitive follows it (Schmidt 1960 230). Plautine and later romantic comedies often contrast a master's desire for love with the slave's desire for food. This contrast allows the slave's appetite to seem sensible in relation to the master's, especially since farces exaggerate the master's love (McCarthy 2000 117).

314   **Viden** *uidēsne* has undergone crasis. **sorderum** Here *sordēs, -is* (f)
"dirt, filth; rabble" is using the genitive plural of the fifth declension.

315   **sordist** Prodelision of *sordis est*. **cedo** *cedo* is an irregular imperative
meaning "give me, grant that, let me!" that is formed from the demonstrative
cē (which is usually a suffix) and the old imperative *dō*. Given its two short
syllables, *cedo* cannot be confused with *cēdō, cēdere* "to move (along)." **sis**
Crasis of *sī uīs*, "please." **deteram** Subjunctive from *dēterō, dēterere, detrīuī,
detrītus* "to rub" in a substantive clause of result after *cedo* (A&G 568).

316   **tu huius** *tū* elides with *huius*, which itself undergoes synizesis into a
single long syllable.

320   **sacruficatum** Accusative supine of purpose with a verb of motion.
Archaic spelling of *sacrificō* (1-tr./intr.).

321   **expergiscatur** With *priusquam*, a subjunctive of anticipated action
(A&G 551c) from *expergīscor, expergīscī, experrectus* "to wake up, bestir
oneself."

325-26   **opsecro** "I beg you," a sign of politeness, tends to be used more
by female characters than male characters (de Melo 2011 340). **ut** "How."
mulsa means "honeyed" and modifies the unstated *uerba*. **laterculos** A
laterculus, -ī (m) is a "little brick/tile," but here the term is used to refer to
baked goods. Milphio thus seems to be declaring his true opinion about
Adelphasium. He partially amends his tone by covering the "little bricks" with
roasted (from *frīgō, frīgere, frīxī, frīctus*) nuts and sesame and poppy seeds
(Richlin 2005 257–58).

327   **ecquid** Milphio intentionally misinterprets this word (the adverbial
accusative "at all") as the substantive "anything" (Mendelsohn 1907 131).

328   Cf. lines 613 and 861 for other reminders to the spectators that a
character is "fulfilling the expectations of their stock character." Cf. *Amph.*
986–87; *Bac.* 772; *Capt.* 778–79; *Cist.* 120–23, 150; *Curc.* 65–66, 280–81;
Epid. 194; *Mil.* 213; *Per.* 118–26, 280a, 291; *Rud.* 47–48, 341; cf. Ter. *Phor.* 848
(Moore 1998 14, 205–6n26).

329   **lubet** Archaic spelling of *libet* "it pleases." *ut libet* can often be
translated "as you please." **sequere** Second-person singular imperative. **hac**
The word *uiā* should be understood here.

330–409 At first this scene was thought to have been inserted from another Greek play (see, e.g., Fraenkel 2007 188–90), but it is dramatically necessary for the two sisters to appear early in the plays so the audience can see and connect with them (Lowe 1988 103). More likely is that Alexis' version of the scene included only Adelphasium and Anterastilis, but Plautus added in Agorastocles and Milphio's roles—both the eavesdropping at 210–329 and then the four-person dialogue from 330–409 (Lowe 1988 104–5).

332 **et oleum et operam perdidi** The slave is using a phrase ("to waste oil and effort") that usually applies to work done at night by lamplight (Brinkhoff 1935 58). The *ancilla* thus implies (probably sarcastically) in her only line of the play that she stayed up all night beautifying herself. Although the text of the play doesn't make it clear, she must have been onstage as long as Adelphasium and Anterastilis. What has she been doing the whole time? Marshall (2006 96) notes that it is likely that the actor playing this character doubled in another part—cf. line 1141.

333 **quo** "Whither, to where." **eo** "Thither, to there."

336 **illi** Archaic form of *illīc* "there."

338 **qui** "How"—see note on 169. **lubet** Cf. 329. Note the anaphora, assonance (and general sound and sense play) in this line (Schmidt 1960 51).

341–42 **merci** From *merx* (archaic *mers*—see line 342), *mercis* "goods, merchandise," it is dative with *oportet*. **sita** "Situated," perfect passive participle from *sinō, sinere, sīuī/siī, situs* "to allow, permit; lay down."

343 **λαλεῖς** "You chat, prattle." A manuscript variant has *mēcum caput et corpus cōpulās*, meaning "join your head and body with me," but Leo deems that variant too long for the meter (trochaic septenarii).

344 **Acherunte** See note on 71, cf. 431, 831.

345 **lymphatici** From *lymphāticus, -a, -um* "insane, watersick" (i.e., having hydrophobia). Referring to Agorastocles' passion, and to give the sense at 346 that the gold coins, like a current, can't stop moving (Brinkhoff 1935 108).

346 **deferto** Future imperative singular of *dēferō, dēferre, dētulī, dēlātus* "bring (down)." **faxo** Archaic sigmatic future of *facere* (see note on 162) setting up the remainder of the sentence as an object clause (i.e., a substantive clause of result—A&G 568). Such clauses are normally introduced by *ut*, but that word has undergone ellipsis here.

347   bellula Rare diminutive of *bellus, -a, -um*, also used at *Cas.* 848 and *Mil.* 989 to describe a young woman (Marshall 2006 65).

348   quam magis . . . tam magis "The more . . . the more." **nimbata** Related to *nimbus, -ī* (m) "cloud," this rare adjective probably means something like "frivolous." **nugae merae** *nūgae, -ārum* (f) "jokes, trifles, nonsense" only appears in the plural.

349   amiculum From *amīculus, -ī* (m), the diminutive of *amīcus*. Agorastocles may be referring to himself or—via the pun on *amiculum, -ī* (n) "cloak"—his genitalia.

350   comperce Imperative from *comparcō/compercō, comparcere, compersī, —* "to save," or with an infinitive "to refrain from."

351   facere compendi "To save, abridge, shorten" something in the accusative case. *compendī* is a predicate genitive (A&G 343b). Adelphasium (here and at 359–63) blames Agorastocles for promising, but failing, to buy her freedom.

352   ecce odium meum *ecce* may derive from the neuter *ed* (i.e., *id*) and the demonstrative suffix–*ce* (see 78). Here it appears with an accusative of exclamation. This is Milphio's final aside to the audience for almost five hundred lines (Moore 1998 40).

354   nam qui istaec magis mea est curatio Leo, Lindsay, and de Melo print *namque*, though some make the sentence a question and some a statement. **qui** is Ritschl's (1881 43) emendation. Another appearance of the interrogative adverb meaning "how"—cf. 169. **istaec** is a feminine nominative singular pronoun referring to Adelphasium.

356   alcedo *alcēdo, alcēdinis* (f) "kingfisher, halcyon." **pullos** *pullus, -ī* (m) can mean both "young animal, chicken," and "young fowl, chick." Halcyons were thought to build floating nests on the ocean, and their eggs were thought to hatch in the period of calm weather ("halcyon days") around the winter solstice.

358 **oratorem** Milphio's jokes here and on 384 depend on the double meaning of *ōrātor* (from *ōrō* [1-tr.] "to speak" but also "to pray, beg"—see line 386): it means "speaker, orator," but also "ambassador" or "spokesman" for an embassy, and "suppliant, entreater" in general. Suppliants in the ancient world were supposed to be protected from physical harm because they were sacred to Zeus/Jupiter. **pectas** From *pectō, pectere, pexī, pectus* "to comb." It is used with *pugnīs* "with one's fists" to mean "to thrash, beat." Cf. *Men.* 1017; *Rud.* 661; and a pun on this phrase at *Amph.* 320 (Fontaine 2010 120, 120n55).

359 **morare** Second-person singular indicative from *moror* (1-tr.) "to delay" with the unstated object *nōs*.

360–63 Here lies one major flaw in the plot construction of the *Poenulus*. (The "implausible coincidences" later in the play are simply part of the genre of New Comedy—Arnott 2004 70.) According to Adelphasium (here and at 399–400), the wealthy (72–77, 165–66, 345, 516–17, 904) Agorastocles hasn't done anything to obtain Adelphasium as his mistress. While 98–101 does say Lycus is tormenting Agorastocles by not permitting him to touch Adelphasium at all (cf. 548, 818, 879, 1097), such claims don't make sense given that pimps elsewhere in comedy are marked by a strong desire to make money. (See note on 100.) Arnott declares that this inconsistency likely arose in Alexis' comedy as well: "If Agorastocles had been presented as a poverty-stricken young man unable to satisfy Lycus' demands for money, it would have been difficult for him to satisfy a wealthy parent such as Hanno that he was a suitable match for Hanno's daughter. Alternatively, if Agorastocles had been presented as a miser reluctant to spend his money or a ditherer who habitually postponed decisions, he would have been an unattractive *jeune premier* for any audience" (Arnott 2004 73). And as one of my students has noted, at 974 Agorastocles does declare that it is easier to start things than to complete them! On the other hand, Agorastocles' financial status does change for the better once he gains access to his inheritance from his biological father at 1080–85. (It's his second inheritance, since he'd already been named heir to his adoptive father—see 77.) Finally, it is also quite unrealistic that Agorastocles never mentions Milphio's new plan for acquiring Adelphasium—her anger is therefore justified, but its main purpose is to prompt the amusing dialogue in this scene (Lowe 1988 105).

For Fantham on the other hand, Plautus' failure or refusal to exploit the sisters' impending initiation into the ranks of Lycus' merchandise (Adelphasium exhibits no sense of urgency regarding the "deadline" of the Aphrodisia here) helps him portray Adelphasium as "a real gold-digger after the style of Phronesium in *Truculentus*, without a thought of constructing an acceptable set of attitudes and beliefs for this future bride." Neither sister "think[s] of herself as freeborn or fear[s] the loss of status which sex will bring her." Instead, the mercenary *meretricēs* "provide the *frisson* of spying on the demi-monde which seems to have been a major factor in Plautus' appeal to his public" (Fantham 2004 246). One wonders whether the sisters' status as Carthaginians is related to their somewhat unsympathetic—albeit potentionally humorous—portrayal. (See note 304–7 above.)

360   **in cassum** *cassus* means "empty, void," and thus the phrase *in cassum* (sometimes spelled *incassum*) is used adverbially to mean "in vain, uselessly."

363   **seruio** From *seruiō, seruīre, seruiuī/seruiī, seruītus* "to serve, be a slave." **nihilo minus** "Nevertheless"—sometimes written as one word.

365–67   Milphio's list of pet names in Latin are, alas, not pet names when translated literally into English. **sauium** Plautus uses two words for "kiss" and according to the *OLD*, *s(u)āuium, -iī* (n) is the more erotic of the two—the other is *osculum, -ī* (n). **colustra** The archaic spelling of *colostra, -ae* (f) "the first milk [usually of a cow] after birth, beestings." **molliculus** is both literal and figurative here: the cheese is both "soft" and "voluptuous" cf. *Cas.* 492 (Brinkhoff 1935 94).

369   **carnuficem** Archaic spelling of *carnifex, carnificis* (m) "executioner."

371   **ninnium** is "a word of uncertain meaning," according to the *OLD*. Richlin translates it as a "bejillion dollars" (2005 258), while Maurach and de Melo think it more likely as a vocative of some term of endearment for Adelphasium, thus Maurach suggests "little horsey" (1988 100) and de Melo "my little doll" (2012 55). It seems best to take it as a direct object of *dabit*, which otherwise would lack one. You may invent your own meaning for *ninnium* here, as long as it makes sense with *prō tē dabit*, which refers to Agorastocles purchasing Adelphasium's freedom.

372   **ut sis ciuis Attica atque libera** This makes no sense, given that all these characters are current residents of Calydon. Arnott (2004 71–72) thinks it possible that Plautus has simply translated loosely, using *attica* as the Latin equivalent of Ἑλληνική (cf. *Men. Kith.* 39) due to the prevalence of the phrase *cīuis attica* elsewhere in Roman comedy: Ter. *And.* 221; *Eun.* 805; *Phor.* 114. Compare de Melo (2012 4): for Plautus "Athenian citizenship means no more than 'best citizenship.'" Alternatively, one could interpret Milphio as so self-aware and knowledgeable about the traditions and customs of New Comedy (and hence Roman comedy) that he refers here to the common practice of recognition at the end of those plays.

373   **quin** As an interrogative particle it means "why not?" and is used in an exhortatory or remonstrative sense. **bene uis item** The main clause of the sentence, with an unstated dative of reference such as *eīs*, which is the antecedent of *quī*. *tibī* (which undergoes iambic shortening) is the parallel dative of reference with *uolunt*.

374   **mentitust** Prodelision of *mentītus est*.

375   **sine** From *sinō, sinere, sīuī/siī, situs* "to allow, permit." It can take an infinitive object, or an object clause employing the subjunctive. **auriculis** *auricula, -ae* (f) is the diminutive of *auris, auris* (f), and refers either to the "earlobe," or as a term of endearment to the "ear" in its entirety.

376   **sycophanta** Originally a Greek term (συκοφάντης) denoting someone who informed the authorities about illegal fig exports, it came to be used to refer to informers and slanderers generally, and thence to mean "deceiver, trickster, con-artist." It is a word with strong metatheatrical associations in Plautine comedy due to its use for characters who don costumes and perform roles in the "play-within-a-play" deceptions common to the genre. See especially the *Trinummus*, where a character who refers to himself as a *sycophanta* (680) appears onstage for more than 150 lines. In the *Poenulus* see lines 425 and 654, as well as *Amph.* 506; *Asin.* 546; *Bac.* 764; *Per.* 325; *Pseud.* 527, 572, 672 (Moore 1998 214n47).

377   **ploratillum** Found nowhere else in Latin literature (a Plautine neologism), this word seems to be a diminutive adjective formed from the participle *plōrātus* and meaning something like "bawling, pathetically weepy" (Schmidt 1960 408), or as Starks et al. suggest, "sob-lime" (1997a 16). It modifies an unstated *eum* here (Schmidt 1960 408).

378   **ne** Translate as "that" in the fear clause (A&G 564) introduced by *formīdō* on 379. **uerberetillum** is another invented diminutive adjective, this time based on the Latin for "hit, strike, flog" (Schmidt 1960 408). Richlin (2005 258) translates it as "punchy," Starks et al. (1997a 18) as "wound-erful."

381   **trioboli** Genitive of indefinite value (A&G 417) of *triōbolus, -ī* (m) "piece of three obols, half a drachma; trifle." See note at 270. **mastigiae** From the Greek μαστιγίας, meaning "someone who deserves to be whipped (with a μάστιξ)," i.e., "scoundrel, rogue." Plautus employs several epithets that are associated with the torture of slaves. Cf. *Curc.* 567 (Richlin 2005 258).

382   em Like *hem*, an alternative form of the interjection *ēn* "behold! see there!" (and related to *eccum, eccam, ecce*). Agorastocles strikes Milphio for talking to Adelphasium inappropriately, but it's not clear how sincerely the young man beats (or attempts to beat) his slave. Milphio could also avoid Agorastocles' swipes; a lighter reading of the play suggests that Agorastocles may not be truly angry, given his pleas to Milphio for help soon after (Segal 1968 153–54). **uoluptatem** Accusative of exclamation.

384   oratorem uerberas See the notes on 358 (for the pun) and 248–49 (for the joke format, in which the second clause explains the joke set up in the first).

387   diceres Potential subjunctive in the imperfect tense. Translate "might have . . ."

393   mammeata "Large-breasted." A rare adjective (*mammōsus, -a, um* is more common), perhaps invented by Plautus.

394   oculus . . . lippitudo Also contrasted at *Curc.* 318; *Per.* 11 (Richlin 2005 259). **mel . . . fel** Assonance. Cf. *Cas.* 223, *Cist.* 69, *Truc.* 178–79 for play with the same words (Brinkhoff 1935 145).

395   tu huic Prosodic hiatus occurs between these two words.

397   uictitandum From *uictitō* (1-intr.) "to live, feed, subsist," the frequentative verb (A&G 263.2) formed from *uīuō, uīuere, uīxī, uīctus*. Here it's an impersonal gerundive of obligation (A&G 158d) with a missing *esse*, all in an indirect statement following *uideō*. **sorbilo** Adverb: "sippingly, bit by bit."

398   ostreatum Literally "covered with oyster shells [*ostreae*]," hence "scabby." **gestito** From *gestitō, gestitāre*, gestitāuī,— "to carry often, carry a lot," another frequentative verb (formed from *gestō* [1-tr./intr/]). Scars from whippings are shaped like oyster shells, so it was very obvious what they were. Here they are even understood as a marker of identity (Dutsch 2008 126n93).

**399–400   **Adelphasium calls Agorastocles a liar here, and Maurice (2004 269) argues that the first half of the play shows Milphio and his master "consistently depicted as dishonest." However, it is better to attribute Agorastocles' failure to purchase or rescue his beloved to the exigencies of the plot (see notes on 100 and 360–63 above) rather than to a defect in his character, or he will appear too unsympathetic to the audience. Incompetent but well-meaning is one thing, connivingly greedy is another. Nor is Adelphasium a completely unsullied "voice of virtue in the play" as Maurice (2004 270) claims.

400   **aduorsum** Archaic spelling of *aduersum*, adverb and preposition (taking the accusative) meaning "toward, against."

401   **incommodus** This adjective can mean both "troublesome" (as here) and "inconvenient, unseasonable" (cf. 1331).

405   **ab re diuina** "From the sacrifice, from the ritual."

406–7   **audin** Crasis of *audīs* and *ne*. **dicito** Future imperative singular of *dīcere*. **salutem** The phrase *salūtem dīcere* means "to say hello."

408–9   **respice. respexit.** Agorastocles uses *rēspiciō, rēspicere, rēspexī, rēspectus* in two senses: "to look back" (the literal meaning) and "to regard, be mindful of" (i.e., to answer your prayer). Cf. *Capt.* 834 (Mendelsohn 1907 93, 126).

410–48   Since this scene features four speaking characters, it cannot have been translated without modification from Alexis' *Karchedonios* since Greek New Comedy was limited to three speaking actors. It is likely, therefore, that the Greek version of Milphio either remained silent (and Plautus gave him the lines at 410–13 and between 427–45) or that he was absent for the entire scene and the Greek version of Agorastocles simply watched the two sisters on his own (Lowe 2004 254–55).

410–11   **quid nunc mi es auctor** The question roughly means "What should I do?" or "What do you advise me?" But it also plays metatheatrically with the idea of playwriting and producing because *auctor* can mean "creator, author, inventor" (Maurice 2004 275). Cf. 146, 721. **Vt me uerberes atque auctionem facias** Understand a verb such as *suādeō* or *fac* to introduce this indirect command/substantive clause of result (A&G 563/568).

413   **maiorem partem** Accusative of duration of time (A&G 423)—supply *temporis* or something similar. Milphio refers to the frequent beatings (and insults?) he receives from his master (de Melo 2012 61, 61n26).

414   **Supersede** From *supersedeō, supersedēre, supersēdī, supersessum* "to desist from," which takes an ablative of separation (A&G 402). **ueis** Archaic spelling of *uīs*.

421   **mi** The masculine vocative singular of *meus* "my," it is employed far more often by women than men—especially with names. It carries an intimate sense more like "my dear" (de Melo 2011 340). Its use both by Agorastocles here and by him and Hanno elsewhere in the play marks them as slightly unusual in the world of Roman comedy, and perhaps carries a negative valence. Cf. 1039, 1051, 1076, 1158, 1197. **Milphidisce** Vocative form of the diminutive *Milphidiscus*, "sweet little Milphio," or as Fontaine (2010 84) would have it, "Milphikins." Plautus frequently uses this -*sc*- infix "to create readily intelligible, ad hoc usages." Cf. *Cas.* 739. See note 382 on the likelihood of Agorastocles' anger being merely pretended.

422   **promisti** Syncopated form of *prōmīsistī* from *prōmittō, prōmittere, prōmīsī, prōmissus*.

425   **sycophantiis** See note on 376. An ablative of means of *sȳcophantīa, -ae* (f) "craft, cunning, deceit," a term with many metatheatrical implications in Plautine comedy. It is often associated with the tricks and deception of the clever slave, and along with *ornāmentīs* (425) and *exornābō* (426) is a key term for the upcoming play-within-a-play (Maurice 2004 274).

427–41   Agorastocles delivers a long, convoluted speech marked by anacoluthon (the change of syntax in the middle of a sentence). In contrast, Milphio humorously repeats himself while trying to calm his master and send him away (Schmidt 1960 54). Compared to other Plautine *seruī callidī*, Milphio seems quite unconcerned about the prospect of freedom. Segal (1968 165–66, 217n56) notes that such lack of excitement about the possibility of manumission is very un-Roman, according to Livy 8.21. Perhaps Milphio does not believe him, or perhaps Milphio—as appropriate for a broadly-drawn, unnuanced farcical character—is more concerned with defeating Lycus than serving his own interest. Maurice (2004 270) observes that Agorastocles' promises of freedom from 428–36 rest upon such ridiculous grounds that they're worthless, though it does not necessarily follow that Agorastocles intends "to tease and infuriate Milphio" as she claims—he may merely be ridiculously incompetent because of his extreme emotions.

427   **Fugio** *fugere* means both "run hard" and "run away" here, as is emphasized by Milphio's deliberate misunderstanding (Schmidt 1960 216).

Other Plautine lines playing with the double sense, as well as the idea that it's related to one's duty or theatrical role, include *Asin.* 380 and *Bac.* 760 (Brinkhoff 1935 40, 62). A similar runaway slave joke can be found at *Per.* 421 (Richlin 2005 259).

428   ecfexis Alternative form of *effēceris* (here likely the future perfect indicative rather than the perfect subjunctive).

429   emittam manu The combination *mittere* + *manū* means "to manumit, set free." Cf. *lībertātem* on 420.

431   Acherunte See note on 71. The first syllable scans long here.

432   aquai The archaic genitive ending—cf. 51. **Abiturun** Crasis of *abitūrus* + *ne*.

436   quid opust uerbis Prodelision of *opus est*. Maurice (2004 276–77) discusses the importance of the phrase (cf. 579) and the similar *quid uerbis opust* at 113, and *quid multa uerba* at 483, 702. These phrases occur more often in the *Poenulus* than in any other Plautine comedy, and are often used ironically or to refer to dishonesty. *quid uerbis opus* also appears at *Amph.* 445, 615, 777; *Aul.* 468; *Bac.* 483, 486, 1164; *Capt.* 937; *Cist.* 94; *Curc.* 79; *Men.* 484; *Mil.* 1213; *Most.* 993; *Rud.* 85, 135, 590; *Trin.* 553.

437   quiduis From *quīuīs, quaeuīs, quoduīs/quiduīs* "who/what you wish, anyone/thing," which is generally used in an affirmative sense (A&G 312). Compounds with *uīs* are common in Plautine Latin. Cf. 831, 1174, 1333, 1382.

443   isti orationi Dative of reference. **Oedipo** Cf. *Bac.* 275 and Ter. *And.* 194 for the mention of Oedipus as a kind of metaphor (Fraenkel 2007 9). That Milphio explains his allusion to Oedipus suggests that some Greek mythology was new to his Roman audience (Moore 1998 109, 217n8). *Oedipo* is an ablative of means/instrument with *opus est* "there is need of" in the following line.

446   meamet Intensive form of *meā*. The reinforcing suffix *-met* appears only here in Plautus (de Melo 2010 71n3). **obiexim** Alternative spelling of *obiēcerim*, from *obiciō, obicere, obiēcī, obiectus* "to set before, put up."

447   **testis** Accusative plural. *testis, -is* can mean "witness" (as a masculine or feminine noun) or "testicle" (as a masculine noun). The word is thus the source of many puns, both here (at Agorastocles' expense) and at *Curc.* 31 (Richlin 2005 259, 97).

447–48   The Agorastocles-Milphio relationship echoes other master-slave reversals in Plautine comedy, such as that of Lysidamus and Olympio at *Cas.* 734–41. Agorastocles is portrayed as especially useless here since it was impossible to enslave a Roman in Roman territory. Slavery was considered the very worst of fates (death was preferable), so even being a slave to love was antithetical to Roman mores (Segal 1968 111).

455   **litare** *litō* (1-intr.) means "to offer acceptable sacrifice, obtain favorable omens." **illim** Early form of *illinc* "from that place." **ilico** "In that very place, on the spot," hence "immediately."

456   **uotui** An alternate spelling of the first-person perfect indicative of *uetō, uetāre, uetuī, uetitus* "to forbid, prohibit." **prosecarier** Present passive infinitive (cf. 265) of *prōsecō, prōsecāre, prōsecuī, prōsectus* "to cut away, cut off [parts to be sacrificed]."

457   **adii manum** *adīre manum* takes a dative object, and means "to deceive or trick [someone]." Richlin (2005 260) suggests that the phrase might be a metaphor from wrestling—cf. 462; *Per.* 796.

460   **faxo** Future tense. See note on 162.

462   **scibunt** See note on 310.

465   **malum** See note on 161.

466   **ei** Dative, referring to Venus. **diuini aut humani** Partitive genitives (of substantive neuters) with *quid*. **credere** has the sense "entrust" here.

471   **lenulle** Vocative form of the diminutive *lenullus, -ī,* "little pimp." The diminutive is pejorative here, much as in the title *Poenulus.* **Pentetronica** Many editors have hypothesized that this term, a made-up word from *pente,* "five," is actually the corrupt form of something funnier in Greek. Some guesses include *Ptenanthropica* ("Land of eagle-men"—Ritschl 1879 564) and *Ptenolatronica* ("Land of eagle-bandits"—Leo 1906 in the apparatus criticus).

472 **sexaginta milia hominum** "60,000 men" (*hominum* is a partitive genitive).

473 **uolaticorum** From *uolāticus, -a, -um* "flying, winged."

477 **dicam** Richlin (2005 260) notes that the word often introduces a lie—cf. *Curc.* 407–53. **uiscum** *uiscum, -ī* (n, but also in the masculine *uiscus, -ī*—see line 479) is "bird-lime." Made from holly or mistletoe berries, bird-lime is used to capture small birds; because it is very sticky it is spread onto twigs so that any small birds that land on them will not be able to fly away. **legioni** In Plautus' time there were 4,200 soldiers (including light infantry, heavy infantry, and cavalry) in a typical Roman legion.

478 **fundas** From *funda, -ae* (f) "a sling (for throwing stones)." **farferi** An alternate spelling of *farfarus, -ī* (m) "colt's foot," a plant in the aster family.

480 **periuras** *periūrō, periūrāre,* —, — is an older form of *peierō* (1-intr./ tr.) "to perjure oneself, lie."

481 **grandiculos globos** *grandiculus, -a, -um* "moderately large" is the diminutive of *grandis, -e*. A *globus, -i* (m) is a "ball" or "spherical mass."

482 **funditarier** Present passive infinitive from the frequentative verb *funditō* (1-tr.) "to hurl at, sling at." (Based on *fundō, fundere, fūdī, fūsus*.)

483 **quid multa uerba** Cf. 702 and parallels at 113, 436, 579. *quid multa uerba* is only found elsewhere in Plautus at *Truc.* 405 and *Vid.* 94 (Maurice 2004 276–77n29).

484–85 **tam . . . quam** Tmesis.

487 **turturem** The *turtur, -is* (m) is the "turtle-dove."

492 **Nil moror** *nīl/nihil morārī* means "to let a thing go, to care nothing about it."

494 **dilidam** From the rare verb *dīlīdō, dīlīdere,* —, — "to crush into pieces, break."

497 **die bono** "Well-omened," because the Aphrodisia was exactly the right time to buy a concubine (Henderson 1994 39).

500   **extollo** The verb usually means "to lift up," but in Plautus and other early writers can mean "to put off, defer."

501   **Profestos festos** Understand *diēs* with both. *profestus, -a, -um* means "non-festival," or (with *diēs*) "working day." *festus, -a, -um* means the opposite: "festive, belonging to the holiday."

503   **in hunc diem** "For this day." A *mercēnārius, -ī* (m) is a "hired man, servant." Cf. 720, though there Collybiscus speaks ironically (Richlin 2005 260).

504-614   The *aduocātī* enter; at least one of these freedmen delivers the lines assigned to them. They are called advocates because it was expected for friends and relatives at Rome to help one another in court—cf. *Cas.* 576; *Curc.* 685; *Epid.* 422; *Trin.* 621, 651; Ter. *Ad.* 645; *Eun.* 327; and a similar situation with witnesses at Plaut. *Bac.* 261-62 (Rosivach 1983 83). However, as Lowe (1990 281–82) notes, Plautus never clarifies why the *aduocātī* agree to help Agorastocles. They like to assert their independence, so may not be his *clientēs*, and therefore may act out of a desire for free food (529–35, 810) or out of hatred of Lycus/pimps in general (622, 815–16). Alternatively, they might simply be overly litigious (586–87) or skilled at deception (574, 603, 648, 653–54, 666).

   The advocates, like the fishermen at *Rud.* 290–324, represent a rare example of a chorus in Roman comedy—they may even have been modeled somewhat on the "choruses of contemporary Roman tragedy" (Lowe 1990 296). They differ from the choruses of Greek New Comedy, however, because they actually play an important role in the plot and do not merely provide a musical interlude between acts (Lowe 1990 275). The advocates are unlikely to have had a speaking role in Alexis' play, as that would have resulted in more than four speaking parts in one scene. Furthermore, their lines show many features uncharacteristic of Greek New Comedy, such as "breaches of realism and consistency" (Lowe 1990 284, 277). A nonspeaking role in the Greek version would be understandable since Athenian advocates—συνήγοροι—in the fourth century BCE were men who made a living by being hired for law court appearances (Arnott 2004 66). That they are freedmen is a definite sign of Plautine modification since freed slaves in Athens couldn't be witnesses at a trial, and Milphio talks about their time in the *comitium* at 583–85. Thus their status as freedmen, perhaps even *clientēs* of Agorastocles, and their concern with class and power are both Plautine innovations (Rosivach 1983 89).

   Interestingly, although we are never told their motivation, as Arnott (2004 66–67) notes, Plautus gives us more detail about the advocates than about any other character in the *Poenulus*: they are poor (515, 536), not old (508), freedmen (519–20), slow-moving (506, 507, 508, 510, 513–14, 575), independent/proud (515–18, 537–39, 573, 610), and "unscrupulous jurymen" (584–87). Furthermore, as comic characters the *aduocātī* mix the stock roles of *edax parasītus* and *sȳcophanta impudēns* too, but their entrance mocks the typical fast entrance of the *seruus currēns* (Lowe 1990 282–83). The similarity between the *aduocātī* and the parasite character—both are poor, hungry, and want an invitation to lunch—helps to account for the metatheatrical nature of these freedmen, since parasites, like slaves, often represent comic poets or other theatrical personages (Petrone 1983 18). By enlarging the role of the *aduocātī* and giving them lines to deliver, Plautus created additional "potential for visual effects," created an opportunity for "mild social comment" from the perspective of the poor (see the note on 517)—which would have appealed to some of the audience, and also created an opportunity for more metatheatrical commentary from Collybiscus, an internal audience for the freedmen (Lowe 1990 295–96). In turn, they serve as meta-spectators of the play-within-a-play deception, and compete with Milphio for comic supremacy (Henderson 1994 44).

Note that (assuming the six actors required to perform lines 1120–54 and 1338–1422) there are at least three actors available to play the *aduocātī* if the actor playing Milphio also played Lycus. Three would be sufficient to represent a stage crowd (Marshall 2006 112), but additional advocates would be possible if more than six actors were available.

Finally, *tībia* music starts up again for the entrance of Agorastocles and the *aduocātī* since the meter switches to trochaic septenarii. (The music will end when the pimp Lycus enters at 615.) While the freedmen are necessary components of the overall plot, this particular scene doesn't move it forward at all, and the slow movements of the advocates reflect this stasis (Moore 2004 145). There is also irony in the fact that while this normally "forward-moving" meter is often used for clever and running slaves, the freedmen don't hurry at all: it's an unusually heavy section of trochaic septenarii (Moore 2004 153–54, 2012 174n4). In fact, their refusal to run (522) amounts to a refusal to play the role of the *seruus currens* (Petrone 1983 18). The advocates' scene illustrates the connection between music and metatheater in this play as well (Moore 2004 145).

506   spissigradissumos "Slow."

507   corbitae A *corbīta, -ae* (f) is a "slow freight boat, barge." Cf. 543.

508   **dedita opera** An ablative absolute formed from the expression
operam dāre, "to pay attention, do one's best."

509   **scibam** See note on 310. **tardiores** Take it with an unstated *eōs esse*.
amori moram A bit of anagram wordplay with *amor* and *mora* next to each
other (Brinkhoff 1935 151).

510   **procos** *procus, -ī* (m) means "suitor," but is also an early form of
procer, proceris (m) "nobleman," used to describe the upper class of citizens in
early Roman history. The latter form is operative—ironically—here, but with
a pun on the former operating in the background as well (Richlin 2005 260).
loripedes From *lōripēs, lōripedis* "bandy-legged," a compound adjective made
from *lōrum, -ī* (n) "leather, thong, whip" and *pēs, pedis* (m) "foot."

512   **datum** Supine.

513   **gradus** *gradus, -ūs* (m) can mean both "step" and "pace." **succretust**
Prodelision. The verb is *succernō, succernere, succrēvī, succrētus* "to sift
through, to sift." **cribro** Ablative of means from *crībrum, -ī* (n) "seive."
pollinario "of or belonging to fine flour," i.e., their steps are small (de Melo
2012 71) and perhaps infrequent. Agorastocles' metaphorical language helps
explain *lōripedēs* three lines earlier, but the terms also evoke images of poor
treatment of slaves in shackles (cf. 514), or dreaded work at a flour mill, where
shackled slaves powered the millstones (Petrone 1983 21).

514   **pedicis** From *pedica, -ae* (f) "shackle, fetter (for the feet)."

515–99   The freedmen remind the audience of their low social position
as well as their need to entertain. There is no attempt to make the explanation
seem natural: they tell the audience that the money is only *aurum cōmicum*
"stage money" at 597–99 and openly acknowledge that they must not bore
the audience (550–52; cf. 920–22, 1224). The advocates—like many other
comic characters—thus display a paradoxical mix of subservience and "mock
haughtiness" in their approach to the audience (Moore 1998 15).

516   **diues** Vocative of *dīues, dīuitis* "rich."

517   **mactare** De Melo (2011 340) notes that *mactō* (1-tr./intr.) originally
appeared only in religious contexts and meant "to endow/honor someone
with something," but that Plautus uses it "mock-solemnly" in phrases such
as *mactāre aliquem infortūniō*. **infortunio** Ablative of means. Here the

aduocātī declare their propensity for punishing rich men with trouble. It's an interesting line because of the rare verb and the contrast (unusual for Plautus) between rich and poor. (Plautus tends to contrast young/old, free/slave, slave/master, father/son.) Thus the remark may be an indirect attack on the wealthy, since it showcases the author's ability to skewer the wealthy politicians and destroy their fortunes—as the poet Gn. Naevius allegedly had (Petrone 1983 22–23).

518   **istuc** Seems to be an accusative of respect from *iste, ista, istud* + the demonstrative suffix *-ce*: "in respect to that thing," which sets up the indirect question in the following clause.

519   **quom argentum pro capite dedimus** Archaic spelling of *cum*. The *aduocātī* have bought their freedom from slavery (*caput* can mean "person" or "life" in addition to "head").

520   **nihili** Genitive of indefinite value (A&G 417).

521   **addictos** An *addīctus, -ī* (m) is a "debt slave." Cf. 186, 564, and 720; contrast 184, 1351.

522–23   These lines and 525 are thought to be an adaptation of two lines from Alexis fr. 265 K-A (which should probably be attributed to the *Karchedonios*). Cf. Alexis fr. 263 K-A, which also links slowness and free status, and the further parallel of unscrupulous jurymen, who appear in the comic tradition at least since Aristophanes' *Wasps* (Arnott 2004 62, 66–67).

523   **seruoli** Genitive of characteristic/predicate genitive (A&G 343c) with *esse* in the indirect statement introduced by **duco** "I consider."

524   This line is used to date the performance of the *Poenulus* to a time after 197 BCE (when the Romans defeated Philip at Cynoscephalae) or after 189 BCE (when the Romans defeated Antiochus).

528   **cerritis** *cerrītus, -a, -um* clearly means something like "frenzied, mad," but its nuance depends upon which derivation one trusts. Nonius 44 (at Lindsay 1903 64) asserts that it derives from possession by Ceres, so the *OLD* translates the adjective as "[p]ossessed by Ceres." But Lewis and Short consider it a contraction of *cerebrītus*, from *cerebrum*, "brain," which gives the sense "having a crazed brain." **insectabit** From the rare frequentative *insectō, insectāre, —, —* (usually *insector* [1-tr.]) "to pursue, attack."

529–30   **aedem** In the singular, *aedēs* refers to a temple, not a house. "In temples animals were sacrificed, and most of the meat was consumed by those making the sacrifices and by their guests" (de Melo 2012 73n32). **gralatorem** A *gralātor, -ōris* (m) is a "stilt-walker." There is alliterative play with *cervom/cursū* and *gralātōrem/gradū* (Schmidt 1960 70).

532   **podagrosi** "Gouty." Gout is brought on by the incomplete metabolism of uric acid, and the disease causes painful inflammation as urate crystals accumulate in the small joints of the feet and hands.

533–35   The sense is, "Why wouldn't we hurry on our way to a place we could eat and drink for free and not have to return anything to a master?"

533   **curratur** Impersonal passive (A&G 208d) potential subjunctive from *currō, currere, cucurrī, cursum* "to run."

534   **ueis** Archaic spelling of *uīs*. **ad fatim** Usually written as one word, it's an adverb meaning "to one's satisfaction, enough."

535   **quoio** Archaic spelling of *cūiō* from *cūius, -a, -um* "pertaining to whom? of whom? whose?"

536   **cum eo cum quiqui** "At any cost"; literally "with that thing, with whatever thing" (Lindsay 2010 [1894] 448). *quīquī* is a rare i-stem ablative form of *quisquis* "whosoever, whatsoever." The phrase is a "technical term of legal language" which de Melo (2012 73n33) translates as "taking this and any other consideration into account."

537   **conteras** From *conterō, conterere, contrīuī, contrītus*, which here means "to grind down, wear out [by asking]." Cf. *Cist.* 609–10 (Schmidt 1960 404). The entire phrase *nē nōs tam contemptim conterās* may allude to Naevius fr. 27 (Mariotti): *superbiter contemptim conterit legiōnēs*, which would support the Naevian themes that Petrone (1983 24) sees throughout the entire *aduocātī* scene, with the freedmen representing Naevian theater.

539   **flagitamus** *flāgitō* (1-tr.) "to importune, demand, summon," is often used to describe the process of publicly shouting at a thief to force him to return stolen goods. Cf. *Curc.* 145; *Per.* 406–26, 569 (Richlin 2005 261).

540   **ramites** The alternate spelling of the plural accusative of *rāmex, rāmicis* (m) "(blood vessels of) the lungs."

542   **habeto** Future imperative singular. **quae** The plural pronoun refers to the singular *dictum* with the sense "many" (Maurach 1988 116).

543   **celocem** *celox, celōcis* (f) "clipper, yacht" is used because it sounds similar to *celer, celeris, celere* (although they're not related etymologically). Cf. *Mil.* 986 for another use of *celox* (Schmidt 1960 387). **corbitam** See note on 507. Here the noun gains the additional sense of *tardus* and thus modifies an unstated *operam* (Schmidt 1960 205). **ne . . . date** "Stop giving." See note on 261.

546   **meliust** Prodelision.

550–54   Self-aware language from the *aduocātī* here: they're role-playing for the spectators! Cf. 577, 580–81, 596–99 (Maurice 2004 274). While these lines reveal that there were rehearsals to prepare for live performances, they do not reveal anything about the nature of the rehearsals—or even whether the actors used physical texts (Marshall 2006 30n63, 29). The lines can also help reconstruct Plautine poetics: the spectators are forewarned and given the necessary information to follow the action, but are not bored with needless repetition just to make the plays seem longer (Petrone 1983 26–27).

551–52   **agitur . . . agas . . . agas** Forms of *agere* are repeated three times, with three different meanings: "to act out, to perform as an actor, and to do" (Schmidt 1960 124).

553   **curassis** Archaic sigmatic perfect subjunctive from *cūrō* (1-tr.) "to care for, attend to."

557   **ratu's** Prodelision. The verb is *reor, rērī, ratus sum* "to reckon, think." Dramaturgically speaking, Agorastocles' mistrust might merely result from Plautus' desire to repeat the details of the deception one last time to ensure that the audience understands it (Petrone 1983 25, 27).

559   **quos** Introduces a relative clause of purpose (A&G 531.2).

561   **quaesitum** Supine.

564   **leno addicetur tibi** This line presents bond-slavery (cf. note on 521), with the judgment delivered by the praetor, as a punishment for Lycus, who will be caught in *furtum manifestum* at 785. (Cf. 186, 727, 790, 1361; contrast 1351.)

565   **rem** means both "the matter in hand" and "money." Cf. *Epid.* 116–17; *Most.* 653. **tenetis** means both "understand" and "hold." Cf. 116; *Curc.* 44–45, 600 (Mendelsohn 1907 91, 123, 129, 136, Schmidt 1960 221).

566   The *aduocātī* seem to be implying that Agorastocles has a small penis. Cf. 116–17 and *Curc.* 44–45 (Richlin 2005 261).

570–71   **deciderint** Perfect subjunctive in a substantive clause of purpose without *ut* (A&G 565) after the potential *uelim*. Supply a parallel *uelīmus dēcīdere* for line 571. **femina** From *femur, femoris/feminis* (n) "thigh." **solum** From *solum, -ī* (n) "ground, sole (of the foot)."

572–73   **uostrum** is the equivalent of a genitive of characteristic/predicate genitive (A&G 343c) with *esse*. Cf. **tuom . . . loqui** in the following line.

574   **Callemus probe** *calleō, callēre*, —, — literally means "to be callous/thick-skinned," but comes to mean "to be skillful" and "to know by experience, understand, be *callidus* (clever)." Cf. *Per.* 305 (Richlin 2005 261).

576   **euge** A Greek interjection (εὖγε) meaning "well done! bravo!"

577   **basilice** Plautus uses the adjective and adverb *basilicus, -a, -um* and *basilicē* ("magnificent/ly," rather than the expected "kingly, kinglike") frequently. The terms are used to describe an unusually splendid appearance. To take a Greek adjective and attach Latin adjective and adverb endings onto it is quite unusual and is perhaps a sign of colloquial Latin (de Melo 2011 337). These terms are likely Plautus' addition to the text since the Greek equivalent βασιλικός/βασιλικῶς does not appear in Greek comedy (Fraenkel 2007 131) and Plautus employs this term for slaves and parasites who speak or act "beyond their station": *Capt.* 811; *Per.* 29, 31, 462, 806; *Pseud.* 458; *Rud.* 431; *Trin.* 1030 (Moore 1998 89). Here the adverb helps emphasize Collybiscus' excellent costume and his professionalism in his play-within-a-play performance (Petrone 1983 30).

578–816   Milphio's role in these scenes is likely larger than that of his Greek equivalent in Alexis' *Karchedonios* (Lowe 2004 262.)

578–79   **Vide sis calleas** In later Latin *calleās* would be preceded by *ut*, marking it more clearly as part of a substantive *ut* clause, the object of *uidē sīs* "please see to it" (A&G 560, 565). Here the second meaning of *callēre* (see above, note 574) is appropriate, but line 579 puns on the first meaning. **callum**

callum, -ī (n) is the "thick skin" or "hide" of an animal. **aprugnum** is an adjective meaning "of or belonging to the wild boar." Mary-Kay Gamel thinks the reference might be to a back scarred by multiple whippings. Cf. *Per.* 305, 380, 455 (Richlin 2005 36, 169).

580–81 **condocta** From the extremely rare word *condoceō, condocēre, condocuī, condoctus* "to train, instruct," which is only used by Plautus and perhaps by the author of the *Bellum Africum* at 19.3.14. **tibi . . . dicta** *tibi* should be understood as dative of possession here, modifying *dicta*. Note the self-aware language from Collybiscus too: now he is role-playing for the spectators! (Maurice 2004 274). Henderson (1994 44) calls him "a meta-*actor*." Cf. *Per.* 465 for the same joke, plus *Bac.* 649–50; *Cas.* 685–88, 855–61; *Most.* 1149–51; *Pseud.* 401–8 (McCarthy 2000 147n70).

582 **Adsunt testes** Lindsay reads the phrase as a statement, not a question, and gives the line to Agorastocles (and *tōt quidem* to Milphio), but there is no reason for Milphio to have yet seen the *aduocātī* behind his master. With a small, shallow stage it's easy for some characters to stay "out of sight" behind another character if required to be so by the script.

584 **nefastust . . . comitiales** Here both *nefastus* (which has undergone prodelision with *est*) and *comitiālis* can be understood literally as, respectively, "unlucky, sacrilegious, nefarious" and "relating to the *comitia*," maybe even "afflicted with epilepsy." But the words can also be understood as a pun referring to *diēs nefastī* "days closed to assembly business" and *diēs comitiālēs* "assembly days" (Brinkhoff 1935 57, Schmidt 1960 191–92). When Milphio continues on 585 *comitiālis* then evolves to mean something like "spending too much time at the assembly," which suggests that here "[t]he words *nefastus* and *comitialis* are used solely to make a word-play" (Mendelsohn 1907 113). In addition, there may be a pun on *comitiālis* and *incomitiō* (to abuse)—see the note on *in comitiō* on 807.

586 **iuris coctiores** The manuscripts offer two alternatives: *doctiōrēs* or *coctiōrēs*. The latter reading (where *coctus, -a, -um* means "skilled in" and takes the genitive) is preferable because it produces delicious wordplay with *iuris*: there are two neuter words spelled *iūs, iūris*, which mean either "law" or "meat juice!" Mendelsohn explains, "one who is *coctus* in the law would be quite similar, though in a bad sense, to one who is *doctus* in the law. The phrase *qui lites creant*, which follows, refers to the habit, common among *aduocati*, of helping to stir up lawsuits, and it may be that in *coctiores* we have a pun" on *coctor* as *coquus*. See line 1349; *Epid.* 522–23 for *iūs* too (Mendelsohn 1907 106). *coctiōrēs* also allows Plautus to again connect the themes of cooking and deception. On *iūs* (law) as corruption, see Gowers (1993 77). **litis** Accusative plural of *līs, lītis* (f) "quarrel, lawsuit."

587   quicum "With whom." **litis emunt** means either that they hire themselves out as advocates when they lack cases of their own (Maurach 1988 119) or they act like modern collection agencies, buying the opportunity to sue someone in order to make a profit (Richlin 2005 262).

588   cum eo cum quiqui See note at 536.

593   demonstretis Subjunctive after *uolō*, which doesn't require the use of *ut*—the subjunctive in such cases began as an independent hortatory or optative subjunctive (A&G 565).

594-99   These lines contain an unstated pun about using *lupīnī* (lupines— see notes on 8 and 598) to catch a *lupus*, i.e., Lycus (Fontaine 2010 153). As discussed above, the trickery is technically superfluous considering Agorastocles should be able to buy whatever he desires. Here Milphio uses the money as a stage prop in their play-within-a-play. In fact, Plautus has one of the *aduocātī* further emphasize the theatrical nature of the entire performance by breaking the dramatic pretense of the *Poenulus* to emphasize that the "money" is actually a bag of seeds (Segal 1968 63–64). This passage also reflects on the theater's simultaneous "resplendence and poverty": something banal and everyday is dressed up/trans-substantiated into something it isn't. This metatheatrical "openness" is a marker of Plautine comedy, as opposed to Terence's, which is instead "absolute drama" (Petrone 1983 31–32).

598   macerato ... auro Soaking is necessary for lupine seeds, which contain toxic alkaloid compounds (de Melo 2012 80n35). Lupines were also snacks for the theater—see the note on line 8. **barbaria** *barbarus, -a, -um* is the word Plautus uses to mean "Italian," and he intends it to be as insulting as "elsewhere" (Richlin 2005 262).

599   agundam Archaic spelling of the gerundive *agendam*. **Philippum** Scans as *Phĭlĭppum* here (despite the double consonant), with the third syllable elided as expected. **adsimulabimus** *adsimulō* (1-intr.—later assimilated to *assimilō*), meaning "to pretend, act," can adopt a metatheatrical resonance.

600   adsimulatote Future imperative plural.

603 **potes** From *pōtō, pōtāre, potāuī, pot(āt)us* "to drink." **pergraecere**
From *pergraecor, pergraecārī, —,* which means "to Greek it up, act really
Greek," i.e., to eat and drink to excess and to hire prostitutes. The word
supposedly came into Latin after increased contact with Greeks. See Gowers
(1993 61–62) for more regarding the connections between Greekness, food,
and revelry. The link between Greeks and excessive behavior also allows
Plautus to safely portray such activities on the Roman stage, since no Roman
citizens are associated with such behavior. That nominally Greek characters
use the term without any apparent irony may disrupt the dramatic pretense
of the *Poenulus* as well. Cf. complaints about such behavior at *Most.* 64 and
Titinius incert. fr. 13 (Ribbeck).

604–7 **Agite . . . abite . . . uos . . . facite** Collybiscus and the advocates
refer to both Agorastocles and Milphio together with their plural verbs
and pronoun. Milphio apparently exits on 607 without saying anything.
Although Maurice (2004 270–71) wishes to see Milphio's quick departure—
and absence from the stage until the conclusion of the trick on Lycus—as a
sign of Agorastocles' "supremacy in craftiness," it seems instead as though
Agorastocles is again having trouble leaving the stage (cf. 427–44), while
Milphio better understands the necessity of hiding himself for the duration
of the pimp's deception. In fact, Milphio's absence allows the actor playing the
slave to play the role of Lycus as well (Barsby 2004 96).

604 **Quis te porro** A question in response to Agorastocles' previous
statement. Understand *docuit. porro* is an adverb with many meanings, best
understood as "then, in turn" here.

605 **fallaciae** See note on 195.

609a–10 **flagitium . . . Crepuerunt** *crepō, crepāre, crepuī, crepitum*
means "to rattle, creak," but because of *flāgitium, -ī* (n) "disgraceful act"
gains the obscene sense "to fart, make a noise like farting." This is always
the sound the stage doors open with in Plautus (Brinkhoff 1935 37). The
jokes in these lines are based on double meanings that only exist in Latin, so
they must be a Plautine addition to the script (Schmidt 1960 319). Plautus
has also personified the doors—cf. *Curc.* 147–55; *Most.* 829; *Sti.* 312; *Truc.*
350 (Fraenkel 2007 316n16). Personification of dead or abstract things is
a frequent source of humor in Plautus, but is seen only in dialogue, not in
monologues—cf. 704; *Cas.* 527; *Mil.* 1000; *Pseud.* 23, 952 (Fraenkel 2007
37). **perduint** is the archaic form of the present subjunctive of *perdō, perdere,
perdidī, perditus.*

611 **pone** is a preposition meaning "behind," but can sometimes be an adverb meaning "behind, after" as well.

612 **scurrae** are "dandies" or "jesters, parasites"—young men, potentially low-class, who say witty things, perhaps in order to eat and drink at someone else's expense (Richlin 2005 101). Cf. *Curc.* 296–97. Richlin (2005 105) takes *Curc.* 484 as a reference to *scurrae*, though the term isn't used there. **pone sese homines locant** Maurach (1988 120) takes *hominēs* as the object of *pōne* here to render the *scurrae* the followers of famous men, but both Richlin (2005 62) and de Melo (2012 83n37) take *sēsē* as the object of *pōne* to render the phrase an allusion to anal sex, although *scurrae* are not explicitly associated with sex elsewhere. *Most.* 15 does, however, link *scurrae* to *dēliciae*, which has its own sexual connotations (see note on 280), and the same sexual pun on *pōne* appears at *Aul.* 637 (Schmidt 1960 328). Similarly, Richlin (2014 188) argues that the terms *datō*, *patior*, *consuescō* all allow for sexual innuendo, but such interpretation depends on the behavior of the actors in such contexts. That the phrase can be interpreted both ways is no doubt Plautus' intention, given his play with ambiguous language elsewhere in the work (cf. 295, 313, 327, 427, 871–72, 990–1028).

613 **Bonus** here has a double reference: the first meaning has sense of "upright, honorable." But the words *similis malī est* "giv[e] to *bono* the force of 'good at his trade,' *i.e.,* a 'good' procurer, although not a good man" (Mendelsohn 1907 107). The line thus jokes metatheatrically about the stereotypical "evil pimp" in comedy (Richlin 2005 262).

615 **istuc** Adverb, "to there, to that."

616 **sient** Archaic disyllabic spelling of *sint*, here necessary for metrical reasons. Cf. 817, 1404, 1416.

617 **eadem** Shortened form of *eādem operā* "by the same work," therefore "at the same time."

619 **tantum hominum incedunt** The collective adjective *tantum* (here with a partitive genitive) can take a plural verb.

620 **chlamydatus** "Wearing a chlamys." The *chlamys, -ydis* (f) is a Greek-style woolen cloak, typically worn by soldiers in Roman comedy. Cf. *Curc.* 611, 632; *Per.* 155 (Richlin 2005 262).

621 **Aetoli** Masculine substantive of the adjective meaning "Aetolian, belonging to Aetolia," an area in central Greece, south of Thessaly. (See map on p. 23.) In the current events of Plautus' time, it had been allied with Rome against Philip V of Macedon before switching sides and then being conquered by Rome in 189 BCE. **ciues** That the advocates, as freedmen, became citizens shows that their freed status is due to Plautus' modifications of the Greek model—freed slaves became citizens only in Rome, not in Greece. **salutamus** A "delocutive" verb since it derives from the phrase *dīcere 'salūtem'* and not from not *salūs* itself, *salūtō* (1-tr.) both extends greetings and describes the act of greeting (Poccetti 2010 119).

622a **leniter** While the adverb can mean "gently, moderately" it is best understood as "half-heartedly" here. **lenonibus** Assonance with *lēniter*. See note at line 639.

623–24 **Fortunati ... Fortunam** Polyptoton. For similar play (with verb and adjective pairs, name and adjective pairs, etc.), see 278, 845–46, 1176–78; *Asin.* 506–7; *Aul.* 586, 616–18; *Bac.* 115–16, 240; *Cas.* 759–62; *Cist.* 515, 644; *Merc.* 9–11, 601; *Most.* 161; *Pseud.* 229, 712; *Rud.* 305, 624–25, 1348–49; *Trin.* 975–77 (Schmidt 1960 250–52). **situram** From *sinō, sinere, sīuī/siī, situs*. It governs *fierī* and should be translated with an unstated *esse* as the second verb of the indirect statement introduced by *sciō*.

626 **ut ... habeant** In this result clause, translate *habeant* as "consider" with *loquī* as its object and supply the missing *esse*. **quaestui** Dative of purpose from *quaestus, quaestūs* (m) "profit, gain, advantage."

633–36 Plautus likes to show his deceptive characters preaching about morality. Cf. *Amph.* 938–43; *Curc.* 494–515; *Epid.* 225–35; *Mil.* 477, 563–65, 1292–95; *Per.* 563; *Pseud.* 460–61, 492–93; *Trin.* 924, 946–47 (Moore 1998 212n6).

633–34 **tantundem est ... quantum** The correlative pair (A&G 152) *tantundem* and *quantum* mean "just as much . . . as." **qui** "How"—see note on 169.

636 **aetatem expetit** "Outlasts his lifetime."

639 **leniter lenonibus** Cf. 622a. While the repetition could indicate that 622a resulted from a scribal error, this line could also be a catch-phrase of sorts for the freedmen, who would have real reasons to dislike slave-dealers.

641   **Boni** Partitive genitive with an unstated *aliquid*. Cf. 640.

642   **adeo** "Moreover," a meaning unique to the comic poets, according to Lewis and Short.

644   **Hunc chlamydatum** Translate as though it were dative along with *eī* in the following line.

645   **ei Mars iratust** The phrase *Mars īrātus est alicui* usually refers to a soldier who's been unlucky in battle and has been captured or has had either to flee or leave behind his armor or weapons (Schmidt 1960 195). **Capiti uostro istuc quidem** Supply *fīat* or a similar verb.

646   **hunc . . . ad te diripiundum adducimus** *dīripiundum* is an accusative supine of purpose with a verb of motion (A&G 509) meaning "for ripping apart/plundering/destroying." *tē*, as Lycus understands it, is the only object of *ad* (with *hunc dīripiundum*—i.e., Collybiscus—as the direct object of *addūcimus*). However, Collybiscus and the *aduocātī* understand *tē dīripiundum* as the entire object of *ad*. Dramatic irony results, as the audience can also understand the intentionally deceptive language. There is also play with the original (Greek) meaning of Lycus here (and at 187 and 660), where the man is trapped in a pit, captured/snared, or described as prey (Schmidt 1960 275).

648   **lupum** Palimpsest A and Codex P read *lycum* instead. The use of *lupum* is preferable here as it allows for bilingual wordplay on the pimp's name.

653-54   Collybiscus presents himself as internal audience, thus allying himself with the real audience of the play against Lycus, who's constantly overheard—see Moore (1998 34–35) on eavesdropping as a means of gaining rapport with the audience. But the *aduocātī* serve as another internal audience for Collybiscus as actor too (Maurice 2004 275).

657   **liberum** The adjective *līber, lībera, līberum* means "free of any restraint, free-and-easy" here (Mendelsohn 1907 89n15). **praeberier** See note on 265.

658   **ubi** Here equivalent to *ut ibi*, it sets up a relative clause of result (A&G 537.2).

659   tu . . . agere tuam rem occasio est Anacoluthon (change of syntax) can be a sign of colloquial or everyday Latin (Chahoud 2010 51, 59–60). The advocates begin by making *tū* the subject of their sentence, but after the protasis interrupts their train of thought *occāsio* becomes the subject.

660   Ille est cupiens Lindsay 1905 and Starks et al. 1997a assign this phrase to Lycus, but it works better as a statement by the *aduocātī* since *aurum habet* doesn't directly answer *ille est cupiens?* **praeda haec mea est** Lycus puns on his own name when talking about Collybiscus (Mendelsohn 1907 28). Cf. Lycus again at 668, Collybiscus at 647.

662   At enim "But surely, but indeed." **clam** "Secret," when used (with *furtim*) as the predicate with *esse*.

**663–66   **Plautus expands Collybiscus' role from what it must have been in Alexis' play: he gets to play the role of a braggart soldier. The advocates claim he has been at Sparta but fled from King Attalus to Calydon (663–66, 769–71, 780), then he mentions King Antiochus (694) and Sparta (719) himself. Many boastful soldiers talk (or threaten to) about their famous previous employers and generals: see Antiphanes fr. 200 K-A; Plaut. *Mil.* 14–15; Ter. *Eun.* 397–98, 401, 407–8 (Arnott 2004 67). Plautus uses such seemingly precise details to render the scene more realistic—cf. *Men.* 409–12 (Fraenkel 2007 381n106). Attalus was the king of Pergamum. Pergamene troops fought in the war against Sparta in 195 BCE, though he had died in 197. That the *aduocātī* get the details wrong isn't necessarily important—it could indicate confusion on their part, or ignorance on Lycus' part, since he doesn't object at all.

669   quo "In order that." Like *ut*, it can introduce a purpose clause, but only when accompanied by a comparative adjective or adverb.

671   adlexero Unassimilated form of the verb *alliciō, allicere, allexī, allectus* "to draw to one's self, attract."

678   quid quod "What about that which . . ."

679   adulescens Unlike most *seruī callidī*, who are much older than their young masters, Agorastocles' *uīlicus* seems to be a young man as well. (*Puer* is used to address male slaves of any age in a derogatory manner.) While the only other *uīlicus* in surviving Roman comedy (*Casina*'s Olympio) opposes the slaves in his master's urban household, Collybiscus allies with his fellow slaves in the city.

681–82   These lines must be spoken as asides, so that Lycus cannot overhear.

684   **Illud** refers to *lūcrum, -ī* (n) "profit" in line 683—Collybiscus overhears Lycus' comment to himself, which is a sign of the *uīlicus'* supremacy over the *lēno* in this deception (cf. 653–54). Supply another *it* as the verb with *lucrum*. **quorsum** means "whither, to which place." Collybiscus is being ironic.

688   **quaeritare** *quaeritō* (1-tr.) is a frequentative meaning "to seek earnestly." It is based on *quaerō, quaerere, quaesiī/quaesīuī, quaesītus*.

689–92   **muscis** The interpretation of these lines has been much debated. Most of the confusion stems from the interpretation of the phrase *hospitium quaeritāre ā muscīs*: does it mean "seek lodging from flies" (or, by extension, "from pests") or "away from flies/pests?" De Melo (2012 91n41) translates the phrase in the latter sense, stating simply that flies "symbolize overcurious people," as *Merc.* 361 makes clear. Alternatively, editors have suggested modifying only the first appearance of the word (on 690): Lindsay prints *muschis* (a rare Greek word for "genitals"), whereas Maurach (1988 124) suggests *amustis* (from ἄμυστις "deep drinking"). These replacement words would set up a joke that depends on Collybiscus misinterpreting Lycus' words and hearing *musca, -ae* (f) "fly" instead. What seems simplest, however, is that Lycus means "away from pests" and Collybiscus reinterprets both elements of the phrase *ā muscīs* to produce the meaning "from flies."

690   **Minime gentium** The partitive genitive of *gens, gentis* (f) "clan; people" can be used like *terrārum* to mean "in the world." Thus *minimē gentium* means something like "not at all, by no means."

692   **carcerem** refers to "the prison" in the Roman Forum where citizens were executed on occasion. Cf. 1409; *Curc.* 692 (Richlin 2005 263).

694   **regi Antiocho** King Antiochus, the Seleucid king of Syria, was involved in fighting in Greece during this period. He was known for extravagant, luxurious living and died in 187 BCE (Richlin 2005 263, de Melo 2012 91n42). **oculi** is occasionally used to mean "testicles" (e.g., Mart. 3.92.2). Alternatively, Greeks referred to high-ranking members of the court of the Great King of Persia as the "King's Eye"—cf. Ar. *Ach.* 91–97 (Richlin 2005 263).

695 **ne** *nē* as an interjection just means "indeed." **festiuom** See line 686.

696 **te** Direct object of *esse* and *contrectāre* (698). **pati** A complementary infinitive after *potes*, it takes the remainder of the sentence as its direct object. **lepido** Its use twice in two lines reveals the pimp's excitement (Schmidt 1960 52).

698 **complexum** Participle from *complector, complectī, complexus sum* "to embrace." It modifies *tē* in line 696. **contrectare** *contrectō* (1-tr.) "to touch, handle" gains the sexual sense "to fondle" here and at 1311 (Franko 1995 252). **uiam** Accusative of extent of space (A&G 425) with the verb of motion *īs*.

699 **Leucadio, Lesbio, Thasio, Chio** Cf. *Curc.* 78 (Richlin 2005 263). Leucadian, Lesbian, Thasian, and Chian are all different varieties of wine named for the Greek islands on which the wine was produced: Leucadia, Lesbos, Thasos, and Chios (whose wine was noted as especially good).

701 **unguentum** An archaic genitive plural (*unguentūm*) of the noun *unguentum, -ī* (n) "ointment, perfume." **geumatis** Ablative plural from the Greek noun γεῦμα, -ατος, τό "taste."

703 **balneator** A "bath-keeper, bath-attendant." **unguentariam** Along with an unstated *artem*, it means "the art of creating perfumes."

704–5 **latrocinantur** From *lātrōcinor* (1-intr.) "to serve as a mercenary, be a hired soldier." Another of Plautus' puzzle-jokes in which the second line explains the first (Schmidt 1960 323). Cf. line 609.

707–10 When Lycus demands immediate payment of the money from Collybsicus, the *aduocātī* call Agorastocles out of his house to watch the transaction. Lowe describes why this part of the play must derive from Plautus: a) it's unrealistic for Collybiscus to take six lines to hand it over, thus allowing Agorastocles time to enter; b) it's not part of Milphio's original plan; c) at 604–6 Collybiscus had been concerned that Agorastocles not be seen; and d) it's inconsistent with Agorastocles' speech at 763–64, where he never mentions to Lycus that he actually saw Lycus take money from Collybiscus. Instead the call for Agorastocles to come quickly (709) intentionally echoes Milphio at 205–9, when he calls Agorastocles so he can come see Adelphasium. Instead, Alexis' play probably called for the money to be given to Lycus inside the house (and gave time for a choral song between actions).

It's also unrealistic for Agorastocles to let Collybsicus walk into Lycus' establishment after he's witnessed the crime himself (Lowe 1990 285–87).

708   **ipsus** Archaic form of the nominative masculine adjective *ipse*.

709   **qui** Introduces a relative clause of purpose. **furem** Because Lycus will be in possession of another man's property: both Collybiscus and the gold coins. **captas** From the frequentative verb *captō* (1-tr), which is based on *capiō, capere, cēpī, captus* and means "to strive to seize, chase."

712   **tuos seruos** Archaic nominative masculine singular.

715   **hosce apsumi** The use of the emphatic demonstrative *hīce, haece, hōce* suggests a gesture or other movement pointing out the coins to which the pronoun refers. Note other places in which the demonstrative enclitic *-ce* is used, since it can provide a clue to movement onstage.

716   **promum** From *prōmus, -ī* (m) "distributor; steward, butler."

719   **eadem** See note on 617.

720   **addictum tenes** Ironically, Collybiscus is speaking about Lycus. An *addīctus, -ī* (m) is a "bondsman," someone in debt slavery. See the notes at 521, 1351.

721–29   The speech of the *aduocātī* is filled with "anaphora, alliteration, homoeoteleuton," and other literary devices, which ridicule both legal language and the advocates themselves (Sharrock 2009 177–78).

721   **Quid nunc, mi auctores estis** See note at 410. **Vt frugi sies** The dative of *frux, frūgis* (f) "fruits (of the earth)" is used as an indeclinable adjective meaning "useful, proper, honest." The advocates' answer to Agorastocles' question is a substantive *ut* clause understood as the object of that question (cf. line 410): "that you be useful/good."

722   **Esto ut sinit** *esto* "let it be" is the third-person singular imperative of *esse*.

725   **Rem aduersus populi saepe leges** Supply *scītis* and *esse* (724) again.

727   **praetorem** The word may have the sense "generic magistrate" in Plautus since characters mention the *praetor* so "casually and frequently." Cf. *Aul.* 317; *Capt.* 505; *Merc.* 664 (Moore 1998 62). **usus ueniet** *ūsus est* and *ūsus uenit* mean "there is need, it is necessary."

728–29   **pultem** The present subjunctive of *pultō, pultāre, —, —* "to beat, knock at" is here understood as the accusative of *puls, pultis* (f) "grain mush." Early Romans ate *puls* before they learned about bread. It retained a religious purpose as Rome developed, however: it was used at sacrifices and as food for the sacred chickens (which were used to determine the will of the gods). Cf. line 54. **frangito** Future imperative singular of *frangō, frangere, frēgī, fractus.*

730–45   **Quippini** "Why not?" The advocates' repeated use of this word is better explained as a humorous means of teasing Agorastocles (Schmidt 1960 54) rather than simply as a "filler" word as Sharrock (2009 177) claims. Sharrock does, however, point out the following similar passages: *Bac.* 6–12; *Cas.* 602–9; *Rud.* 1216–27; *Trin.* 583–91.

730–34   Agorastocles now shows his own cleverness by suggesting new facets to the deception of Lycus, but even though the *aduocātī* agree to them, they're never carried out. Agorastocles is actually more cunning than many other Plautine *adulescentēs amantēs*—he runs the trick in Milphio's absence and knowingly lies to Lycus at 763. Lycus himself seems to appreciate Agorastocles' abilities and calls him *malus* (like the *aduocātī*) at 765 (Maurice 2004 271). The "clever slaves" (*seruī callidī*) in Roman comedy often present their own badness as a virtue as well (cf. 856). On the other hand, his skill at deception could be taken as proof of stereotypical Carthaginian treachery—see the note on 1076–85.

734   **nummis** Ablative of degree of difference (A&G 414).

737   **Homo furti sese adstringet** Here *furtī* is likely a genitive of the charge (A&G 352) with the verb of accusation *a(d)stringō, a(d)stringere, a(d) strinxī, a(d)strictus* "to bind, place under obligation; charge." See the note on line 6 of the *argūmentum.*

738   **Quantumquantum ad eum erit delatum** Understand *dēnegābit* (736) again here. The word *quantumquantum* is the neuter nominative of *quantusquantus* "however much." *eum* likely refers to the praetor. Translate *dēferō, dēferre, dētulī, dēlātus* here as "indict, denounce."

739   **Diespiter** *Dĭespĭter, -tris* (m), from *dīuus* or *dĭes* + *pater*, is another
name for Jupiter. **perduit** Archaic present subjunctive of *perdere*—cf. 610.

743   **sine** See note on 375.

744   **operire capita** At *Curc.* 288, 293, 389 a covered head suggests
craftiness or deception (Richlin 2005 264).

745   **inlices** The unassimilated form of *illex/illix, illicis* "alluring, enticing,"
it is used substantively as "lure" here.

747   **quam** "Than." *potius* "rather" must be understood with *suspendant*.
creduam Archaic present subjunctive of *crēdō, crēdere, crēdidī, crēditus*.

750   **is** Plural ablative (of means) of the pronoun *is, ea, id*. **lucro** Ablative
of respect/specification (A&G 418).

752   **antidhac** Archaic form of *antehāc* "before this time." It is necessary
for the meter here.

754   **utquomque** Archaic spelling of *utcumque* "in whatever way." **exim**
Alternative apocopated spelling of *exindē* "from that place."

757   **si audes** The uncontracted form of *sōdēs* "please." Cf. 1075.

759-60   Lycus' joke depends both upon the literal meaning of *frīgefactō,
frīgefactāre, —, —* "to cool," as well as upon the metaphorical meaning
"to be silly/mad/not sane." As usual, the second line clarifies the initially
unintelligible first statement. Cf. *Rud.* 1326; both jokes must be inventions of
Plautus since they're based on a connotation of the Latin words that could not
have existed in the *Karchedonios'* Greek (Schmidt 1960 323).

762   **numquam factum reperies** Supply *id* and *esse* with *factum*.

764   **renuntiatum est** We are missing something like *ab illīs*, which
provides the antecedent for *quibus*.

765   **captatum** Supine. **testibus** Another joke about testicles? See notes on
447, 664; cf. *Curc.* 30–38, 565, 622, 695 (Richlin 2005 264).

768-76 Lycus totally misinterprets the situation—a sign that he's a true blocking character on the comic stage.

768 **Hahahae!** "Ha ha!"

771 **facturum lucri** With *facere* the genitive (of indefinite value) of *lūcrum* means "to gain, get the credit of."

773 **qui ... diceret** Relative purpose clause.

775 **eo** Ablative of separation: neuter singular to refer to the *aurum* of line 774.

776 **lupo** Lycus refers to himself as a wolf here, in a repeat of the frequent wordplay on the theme.

778 **aruio** According to the *OLD,* the onomatopoetic colloquial form of *rāuiō, rāuīre,* —, — "to be hoarse, talk oneself hoarse."

782 **adeo** "For in fact." The *aduocātī* may also be making another metatheatrical joke about the "bag of gold" prop, since they told the audience it was simply lupine seeds at line 598. **marsuppio** *marsūpium, -iī* (n) "pouch, purse" is often written with only one *p*.

783 **Vae** "Alas, woe, oh no!" It often takes the dative case. **in mundo est** Only used in early Latin, the phrase *in mundō esse* means "to be in readiness." *mundus, -a, -um* on its own means "neat, clean." **tuae** Supply *aetātī* again here.

784 **furcifer** "Fork-bearer," addressed to Lycus. A *furca* is a two-pronged frame to which slaves were bound as punishment. Cf. *Curc.* 193; *Per.* 11, 21–28, 278–79, 419–26, 795 (Richlin 2005 264). See Parker 1989 on additional insults threatening slaves with punishment. **marsuppium** Agorastocles seems to force Lycus to return his purse of gold, but Leo (in the apparatus criticus) and Lowe (1990 287) believe such an act would contradict the end(s) of the play. In the first (spurious) ending, 1351 and 1360–63 imply that Lycus must pay an additional penalty after returning the original sum: the double fine at 1351 is reduced to a single one at 1362. In the second (spurious) ending, Lycus admits to possessing Agorastocles' gold at 1393–94. The third (legitimate) ending likewise suggests that Lycus has the gold at 1408, but we might understand all of these passages as referring to the large penalty Lycus owes to Agorastocles.

785   **manufesto** Legal language: *furtum manifestum* was "theft proven by direct evidence." See the note on 1351–53.

786   **dum . . . uideatis** Subjunctive in a clause of anticipated action (A&G 553): "until you should see . . ."

787–95   This speech and Lycus' exit to the forum were likely added to the play by Plautus (Lowe 1990 291). Plautus seems to have rewritten the exits of Lycus, Agorastocles, Collybiscus, and the *aduocātī* between 787 and 816 (Lowe 1990 288–91).

788   **insidiae** Given the importance of other deception language, *īnsidiae, -ārum* (f) "ambush" may have a metatheatrical resonance in Plautus too.

789   **dubito** *dubitō* (1-intr.) "to hesitate, delay" is used most frequently with the infinitive, although also with *quīn* and the subjunctive (A&G 558).

790   **optorto** Assimilated form of *obtorqueō, obtorquēre, obtorsī, obtortus* "to turn around, twist."

792   **hariolos haruspices** Synonyms—repetition for comic effect. A *hariolus, -ī* (m) is a "soothsayer, prophet," and *haruspex, -icis* (m) refers to a "soothsayer, Etruscan diviner." You can read one as an adjective: "(real) prophetic soothsayers."

793   **perspisso** Adverb: "very slowly." Cf. *spissigradissumōs* at 506.

795   **suspendere** "To hang" is a surprise joke. The audience might expect something like *exsoluere* "to release, pay off" (Schmidt 1960 310). The black humor here (cf. 309–12) is typically Plautine—the pimp's exit has been reworked for the Roman stage (Lowe 2004 259).

798   **quicum** "With whom." Lines 798–800 contain the types of remark that Plautus liked to add during the adaptation process (Lowe 1990 288).

800   **subscribam** In legal contexts *subscrībō, subscriber, subscrīpsī, subscrīptus* means "to sign one's name to a charge," hence "to prosecute." **dicam** From *dica, -ae* (f) "lawsuit," the Latinized version of the Greek δίκη.

801   **Numquid** An untranslatable word used to introduce questions (similar to how the ¿ marks the beginning of a question in Spanish). It

expects a negative answer. **me** Supply *uīs* as the verb. **ornatum** Here ends
the *Poenulus*' play-within-a-play—cf. the note on 123. Since Agorastocles-
as-producer is done with his lead actor, he orders him to leave and don
another costume—perhaps a self-aware reference to the actor's next role in the
Poenulus. Maurice (2004 275–76) takes this as a command to the advocates to
leave and take their costumes off, but *sumere* refers to the opposite action.

802–4 These lines are probably Plautine additions. **praedae** A partitive
genitive with *paululum*. While appropriate to Collybiscus' role as a mercenary,
the use of military terminology for deceptions is particularly Plautine—
cf. *Epid.* 381; *Merc.* 498; *Most.* 312; *Per.* 608 (Fraenkel 2007 354n24). **extis**
Collybiscus' claim that he is full of *exta* both contradicts statements that
they've not been carried home yet (at 491, 617, 847, 863) and repeats what
Antamynides says at 1285 (Lowe 2004 259).

807 **cras** Agorastocles asks that the *aduocātī* meet him in court tomorrow
(for the prosecution of the pimp) since the courts would of course be closed
on a festival day. But as Syncerastus obliquely warns Milphio on 914, taking
the pimp to court on the following day (as planned) would not necessarily
prevent them from becoming prostitutes: "The whores *do* work on the
holiday, even if the law doesn't . . . What is to stop the dealer selling his
women, if not at the temple market, then to the next caller?" (Henderson
1994 46). The awareness of this possibility allows Plautus to incorporate an
additional trick—probably his own invention (see de Melo 2012 10–11)—into
his adaptation, and the introduction and execution of that second trick will
constitute the second half of the *Poenulus*. Agorastocles' deferral of court
proceedings here parallels *Pseud.* 1231, where a reference to the inevitable
judicial defeat of the pimp "tomorrow" allows the poet to streamline his play
by omitting part of the Greek model (Lowe 2004 259). Similarly, Plautus
exploits the *Poenulus*' dramatic setting, the Aphrodisia, in order to expand
and elaborate the comic plot. **in comitio** Cf. *Curc.* 400–3 for the pun on
in comitiō "in the meeting place in the forum" and *incomitiō* "to abuse" (F.
Coarelli at Steinby 1993 310–11, cited at Moore 1998 220n13). **estote** Plural
imperative of *esse*. **obuiam** "At hand, within reach." It can also mean "in the
way," which would work with the pun on *in comitiō*.

808 **sequere** To whom is Agorastocles talking? Although Collybiscus
has declared his intention to depart (at 805), he must still be onstage, as it
is unnecessary for Agorastocles to address any of the *aduocātī* individually
inside. The *uīlicus* may have delayed his exit in order to remove and pick up
all the elements of his soldier costume—cf. *ornātum tuum* on 801 (Maurach
1988 131).

808b–16   In their exit monologue, the *aduocātī* highlight their low status by complaining about the behavior of the wealthy towards the poor—cf. *Trin.* 847–50 (Moore 1998 12). As with 504–614, the speech's concern with status suggests Plautine authorship (Rosivach 1983 89). The advocates likely complain because Agorastocles has failed to compensate them adequately, not, as Lowe (1990 288) argues, because he has deferred all legal action until tomorrow (800, 807) and demanded their attendance in court then.

809   **illic** Here *illic* can either be the masculine nominative singular of the pronoun *ille* with the strengthening demonstrative particle *-ce* ("this guy"), or it can be the adverb from the same root "there, in this matter." **postulat** *postulō* (1-tr.) means "to demand," but also "to prosecute."

812–13   **pluma ... plumbeas** Parechesis—the letter *b* is probably not very easy to hear, thus making it difficult to distinguish between the two words (Fontaine 2010 114). The "leaden anger" of the rich may be an allusion to the chains the *aduocātī* mention at 514 (*pedicīs*) but may also refer to the punishment of the comic poet Naevius, who was jailed for his plays' *ad hominem* satirical attacks on a powerful Roman clan (Petrone 1983 23–24).

814   **sultis** Crasis of *sī uultis* "if you wish, please."

816   **perderemus** Subjunctive in a substantive clause of result (A&G 570) that explains *id* in the preceding line.

817–919   Milphio "addresses a series of self-conscious asides to the audience" both before he interacts with Syncerastus and again after Syncerastus leaves at 920–22. Syncerastus, however, like all members of Lycus' household, lacks any metatheatrical awareness—in contrast to those in Agorastocles' household (Maurice 2004 276). These asides help Milphio build rapport with the spectators during his scene with Syncerastus (Moore 1998 40).

   This scene doesn't advance the plot much (since the audience already knows that the sisters are freeborn); instead it emphasizes performance and silliness. As such, its meters—iambic octonarii (ia8), iambic septenarii (ia7), trochaic septenarii (tr7)—are all accompanied by music. Hanno will stop the music when he enters at 930 (Moore 2004 146, 154). Moore (2004 154–55) further discusses how the meter suits the action here: Milphio's initial iambic octonarii suggest "that Milphio is simply interested in finding out what happened in the previous movement," not in moving forward. Then two lines of iambic septenarii close off his monologue and help transition to Syncerastus' entrance. Syncerastus starts in trochaic septenarii, which are appropriate for clever and running slaves. This section of trochaic septenarii also moves particularly quickly, which suits the slaves' growing excitement.

817-20 Milphio's speech here is "typical of the tricky slave returning to the action"—cf. Ter. *Eun.* 923 (Barsby 2004 105). On the other hand, it's incompatible with recent events: Agorastocles has gone inside at 807 and could have explained everything then, though Barsby (2004 105n37, 98n17) notes that "implausible non-meetings of characters in the wings or the houses" do not seem to have bothered ancient playwrights. It seems best to take 817-20 as an example of careless writing on Plautus' part, even though the (interpolated) line 929 supports Milphio's claim here that Agorastocles is not at home (Barsby 2004 105). Because Plautus has added the *līberālis causa* ("a lawsuit regarding a person's freedom or freeborn status") trick and all passages associated with it, the error here is understandable—in Alexis' comedy Agorastocles would have left to find the praetor with his witnesses so he could prosecute Lycus (Lowe 2004 258, 1990 289-90).

817 **techinae** Alternate spelling of *techna, -ae* (f) "trick, cunning device."

821 **Syncerastum** The name's connection to mixing (it's derived from συγκεράννυμι "to mix up") is appropriate "because he gives information to Milphio concerning Adelphasium and Anterastylis, and thus puts Lycus' affairs into confusion" (Mendelsohn 1907 61).

823-44 Syncerastus' speech on the depravity of his master's household is one of many rhetorical monologues in Plautus. Cf. *Bac.* 385-403; *Men.* 127-34, 446-61, 571-89; *Merc.* 544-54; *Mil.* 21-24; *Most.* 93-100, 118-19; *Truc.* 209-45 (Moore 1998 26-28, 207n8). Here Syncerastus is worried about being punished by the gods for his master's bad behavior. It is improbable that Lycus has refused to sell Adelphasium to Agorastocles thus far, given the popularity of the pimp's business, but the plot of the comedy requires this refusal, however unlikely or out-of-character. (See note 100.) I am not convinced by Slater (2004 294n10) that Syncerastus is "a deluded prig" who doesn't understand the real situation.

823-38 The monologues of comic slaves, even as far back as the plays of Aristophanes, often open with complaints about the work their masters require from them. Cf. Milphio at 819-20; *Amph.* 166; *Pseud.* 767; Ar. *Plut.* 1. Thus the core of this speech is likely to come from Alexis' comedy (Fraenkel 2007 123). However, the list of the various classes of citizens at 832-33 is

quite Roman and has a parallel in *Capt.* 159–64. Syncerastus' indignant tone
probably doesn't derive from the *Karchedonios* either (Fraenkel 2007 101–2).
For parallels to the description of Lycus' establishment see *Pseud.* 173–229;
Truc. 98–111, 658, 760, 944 (Moore 1998 142, 222n8).

826   **luteus** means "dirty, besmeared; vile." **caeno conlitus** *caenum, -ī* (n)
is "dirt, filth." And *collinō, collinere, collēuī, collitus* (the assimilated form of the
verb) means "to besmear." See the note on 91–92 for the connection between
Lycus and filth.

827   **lautumiis** The *lautumiae, -ārum* (f) "quarry" was a place of difficult
labor and severe punishment for its slave workers; Plautus alludes to the
unpleasant conditions in his *Captiui*. **pistrino** The *pistrīnum, -ī* (n) "mill"
wasn't much better: slaves turned the millstones by pushing the beams
projecting from the axle and thus walking in circles all day. Syncerastus' claim
that he'd rather work in a mill or a quarry than in Lycus' house is almost
unbelievable, since the conditions there were so much worse than the usual
conditions for a house slave (Slater 2004 293). For quarry and mill conditions
see Thompson 2003 chs. 4 and 6 and Apul. *Met.* 9.11–13; the latter offers a
man-turned-donkey's perspective on his mill experience—sometimes donkeys
powered mills too.

828   **latere** A *later, lateris* (m) is a "brick; bar, ingot."

830   **di uostram fidem** "For heaven's sake! By the protection of the gods!"
It is the abbreviated, colloquial version of something like *dī obsecrō uostram
fidem*, or *dī uostram fidem date*, where *fidem* means "protection."

831   **quoduis** See note on 437. **Acheruntem** Cf. 71, 344, 431. Here the
first syllable scans short, as is usual for the word.

832   **Equitem, peditem** is a Latin expression that means "all male
citizens" because the reference to "knights and footsoldiers" covers the
majority of the citizen body (Richlin 2005 265). This mixing of the social
classes is what makes a *popīna* (a type of fast-food shop or "eating-house"—
see 835) or *taberna* ("bar, tavern") as potentially disgraceful for an upper-class
man as a brothel (McGinn 2004 19).

833   **det** Potential subjunctive. **utut** "Howsoever, in whatever manner."

835   **estur** Impersonal passive (A&G 208d) from *edō, edere/esse, ēdī, ēsum*
"to eat."

836–37   **litteratas** has two meanings ("with letters on it, branded; educated, learned"). Both are in play until *litterīs* in 837 clarifies which Plautus means (Brinkhoff 1935 121). **fictiles epistulas** Literally "messages/epistles made of clay," i.e., "amphorae with words on them." **pice signatas** From *pix, picis* (f) "pitch" and *signō* (1-tr.) "to mark; seal up." While the second meaning fits the context, it isn't particularly funny, and the second part of the line allows for alternative interpretations. **cubitum** The *cubitum, -ī* (n) is one's "elbow," and hence a "cubit," the length from the elbow to the tip of the middle finger. It's an accusative of extent of space here (A&G 425). Thus 837 could allude to gifts of wine with the names of givers written (with pitch) in letters a cubit high—cf. *Rud.* 1294–96 for letters a cubit high (Marshall 2006 202). Or customers are signing their names on the labels of the amphoras they buy so they can drink the rest of the wine during future visits (Slater 2004 294n11). Finally, that Syncerastus complains about the amphorae suggests that he is at least familiar with writing, but the humor and deception of the *Poenulus* don't depend on a slave's ability to read and write as we see elsewhere in Roman comedy—cf. *Pseud.* 20–75.

838   **uinariorum** A *uīnārium, -ī* (n) is a "wine-flask, wine-pot." **dilectum** Alternative spelling for *dēlectus, -ūs* (m) "selection, choice; levy."

840   **id** refers to Syncerastus' preceding speech, and is the direct object of *meditātur*. **illi** Dative of reference with *mortuō*, referring to Lycus. **meditatur** *meditor* (1-tr.) means "to muse over, consider; intend." **uerba faciet mortuo** Milphio presents Syncerastus' words as a parody of a *laudātiō fūnēbris* "eulogy, funeral speech." As Slater (2004 294n13) observes, this was a Roman practice without an obvious parallel in the Greek world. He notes that Milphio's remark is funny because, while Roman slaves could be freed in their masters' wills, the thanks for such manumission should be better than this series of insults! Milphio's aside is also similar to *Aul.* 496, *Trin.* 1041 (Fraenkel 2007 101).

842–44   **crucior** Syncerastus is so tormented by the thoughtless behavior of his fellow slaves that he uses a term that usually describes physical torture. **expeculiatos** "Stripped of private property." *pecūlium, -ī* (n) was the "private property" that a Roman *paterfamilias* gave to his son, daughter, or slave to be his/her own—see Stewart 2012 51–52. (Note that the concept of *pecūlium* means that this part of the speech was added by Plautus.) Syncerastus' main complaint is that his (expensive—*pretiīs emptōs maxumīs*) fellow slaves waste their peculium, and thus their means of buying their freedom, in Lycus' brothel—cf. similar behavior at *Sti.* 751 (Slater 2004 296). In contrast, Slater notes that Syncerastus' own desire for freedom can be seen at 909–11. **suis eris** is dative of advantage (A&G 376), not disadvantage (*pace* Maurach 1988 134). **male partum male disperit** The phrase's connotation is a bit unclear, even if the sense is simple. *partum* is a substantive from *pariō, parere, peperī, paritus/partus* "to bring forth, bear, produce." The rare compound verb *dispereō, disperīre, disperiī,* — "to go to ruin, perish" forms its future tense in the same way as its base verb *īre* (cf. 908). Have the slaves earned their peculium through theft or other illicit means? (See Stewart 2012 118.) Or is it just a proverb: "easy come, easy go"? Either way, the audience's sympathies could still lie with the foolish slaves (Slater 2004 296n20).

845–46   **frugi bonae** The indeclinable *frūgī* (cf. 721, 963) strengthened by an attributive adjective, hence "good and proper." Being *frūgī* and hence doing the right thing was a Roman virtue—cf. *Per.* 449 (Richlin 2005 265). **ignauiorem . . . Ignauiam** Plautus also plays with an adjective and the personification of the related abstract concept at *Asin.* 267–68 and *Pseud.* 669–70. Cf. note on 623–24 for similar play with pairs of related words (Schmidt 1960 250–51). This whole remark is an aside delivered out of Syncerastus' hearing.

848   **suo** An example of (nonreflexive) *suus* showing up where we might expect *eius,* it is probably used for emphasis here (de Melo 2010 94).

849   **meretrices nostrae** Were Adelphasium and Anterastilis the only women from Lycus' household to go to Venus' temple for the Aphrodisia? He seems to own other women at 1415. Or did all of the women from his household succeed in propitiating Venus immediately? The text is not clear.

851–58   The verbal sparring and "slow recognition" scene with Milphio and Syncerastus bears all the hallmarks of Plautine composition (Lowe 2004 259). The banter at lines 854–56 in particular delays their meeting despite Syncerastus' warning that he bears a heavy load. Cf. *Pseud.* 246 (Fraenkel 2007 155).

854   **pactam** The adjective *pactus, -a, -um* "agreed upon, settled," has a passive sense, even though derived from the deponent verb *paciscor, paciscī, pactus sum* "to agree, contract [to something]."

855   **uapulandum sit** comes from the verb *uāpulō, uāpulāre,* —, — "to be beaten, flogged," which retains its passive sense in all its forms. **corium** By metonomy, *corium, -iī* (n) "leather, hide" can mean "(leather) strap."

856 **quid uiri** The use of *quid* with a partitive genitive referring to a person is a colloquialism (Halla-aho and Kruschwitz 2010 146). **malus sum** A badge of honor for a clever slave, cf. 730–34 and *Per.* 221–22, where the adjective is *scelestus*. **tibi sis** Understand *malus* from the previous sentence too. *sīs* is simply a present subjunctive.

857 See also Ar. *Av.* 1494–1504 for a similar use of the motif of a slow recognition (Fraenkel 2007 414n155).

859 **deaeque** *deae* undergoes synizesis. **nec te nec me** See *Per.* 205 for a similar joke (Richlin 2005 265).

860 **meum adeo** A metrically tricky section: *meum* undergoes synizesis, then that single syllable elides with *adeō* (Maurach 1988 136). Cf. 1070. **id** *dignus, -a, -um* "worthy (of)" can take the accusative of a neuter pronoun.

862–63 **quid agis** Play with both meanings: "how is it going for you?" and "what are you doing?" (Schmidt 1960 225). **manufesti** Archaic spelling of *manifestus, -a, -um* "clear, evident, exposed." **moechi** *moechus, -ī* (m) is the Latinized version of the Greek μοιχός "adulterer." **vasa** (n pl) can mean both "jugs, dishes" and, by extension, "testicles, genitals." Syncerastus is referring to castration, the punishment for adultery; cf. *Curc.* 30–38 (Richlin 2005 265). Similar dialogic riddles with asyndetic answers can be found at 1145; *Asin.* 619; *Bac.* 50; *Cas.* 720; *Men.* 160; *Mil.* 321; *Rud.* 535. Because this double meaning only exists in Latin, Plautus must have been responsible for the joke (Fraenkel 2007 36).

864–65 Anacoluthon (change of syntax in the middle of a sentence) with two protases and a repeated purpose clause in the apodosis.

865 **cedo** Irregular singular imperative meaning "give me, grant that, let me!" Cf. 315, 896.

866 **male mihi est** "It's going badly for me." Play with the standard meaning of the phrase: "I feel unwell," and paronomasia with *malus* and *male* (Schmidt 1960 139; Brinkhoff 1935 115). **memoradum** *dum* is an intensifying particle that means "now" when used as an enclitic added to the ends of imperatives. (Lewis and Short think it originated as an accusative of duration of time.) Cf. 1049, 1063.

867 **edis** Archaic present subjunctive of *edō, edere/esse, ēdī, ēsus* "to eat."

868   **ductas** From the frequentative verb *ductō* (1-tr.) "to lead, conduct," hence "to take a concubine." **gratiis** This ablative plural form of *grātia, -ae* (f) "favor, thanks, charm" means "for nothing, free of cost."

869   **Diespiter** See note on 739, though the *ie* undergoes synizesis into a single long syllable here. **Vt quidem . . . dignus es** Milphio could undercut Syncerastus' apparent sincerity here, depending on the actor's intonation.

871   **meae alae** An *āla, -ae* (f) is a "wing; armpit." The word's double meaning permits Milphio's pun in 872 (Brinkhoff 1935 35). Here *meae* undergoes synizesis, then elides with *ālae*.

872   **Nolito** Future imperative singular of *nōlō, nōlle, nōluī, —*.

873   **tuae** undergoes synizesis. **hirquinae** An archaic form of *hircīnus, -a, -um* "of a goat, goaty, goatish." Armpit odor was considered repulsive by the Romans, and jokes tended to use "goaty" to refer to such odor—cf. Catull. 69.5–6, 71.1; Hor. *Epod.* 12.5; Ov. *Ars Am.* 1.522, 3.193. On the other hand, it was considered effeminate for men to pluck their armpit hair and thus attempt to improve their hygiene (by inhibiting the growth of odor-causing bacteria) (Richlin 2005 265, and see Richlin 1995).

874   **cito** "Quickly, soon."

878   **periclo** The contracted form of *perīculum, -ī* (n) "danger" is common in early Latin. The phrase *meō perīculō* means "at my risk," hence "I'll guarantee." Cf. Petron. *Sat.* 72.3 and Cic. *Att.* 4.7.2 (Smith 1975 200). **Male credam, et credam tamen** Plautus plays with two meanings of *crēdere*: "believe" and "entrust" (Schmidt 1960 116). Cf. line 889.

880   **Omnem operam** Understand *tuam*.

881   **Quid ergo** Scans *quĭd ĕrgō* here (Maurach 1988 138). **quin** "That." (As is usual after a verb of ignorance or doubt such as *dubitās*.) **lubenter** Archaic spelling of *libenter*.

882   **eius merito** Dative of purpose of *meritum, -ī* (n) "what one deserves; reward, punishment." *eius* refers to Lycus. The phrase *libens meritō* ("gladly and deservedly") is used when paying a vow to the gods (cf. *Per.* 254), so Plautus may be alluding to the justness of Milphio and Syncerastus' hatred for Lycus at 881–82.

884 **paritem** From the frequentative verb *paritō, paritāre,* —, — "to prepare, get ready," here a subjunctive of anticipated action (A&G 553)—cf. 786. **ne** "That," introduces a fear clause (A&G 564). **perduim** See notes on 609a, 739.

886 **Crurifragium** "Shinwreck." Syncerastus' pun on *naufragium* "shipwreck" is built on *crūs, crūris* (n) "shin" and indicates that the name-bearer would have his legs broken. In the process he provides a "false etymology for *Syncerastus*" as related to *sincērus* because that adjective can mean "whole" or "uninjured" (Mendelsohn 1907 21, 70). Another slave jokes about a name-change necessarily accompanying physical punishment at *Bac.* 362 (Fraenkel 2007 24).

888 **indicasso** An archaic first-person singular future perfect indicative form of *indicō* (1-tr.) "to point out, indicate." **ut ne** The equivalent of *nē*, it introduces an indirect command.

889 **ted** Archaic ablative singular form of *tē*.

890 **Fide non melius creditur** Perhaps a well-known maxim in Plautus' time. *crēditur* is an impersonal passive, while *fidē* is either a contracted form of the dative or an ablative of comparison: "one doesn't trust [anything] better to Faith" OR "than faith (or Faith itself)." The joke about a personified *Ignāuia* at 846 suggests that Plautus is again referring to the personification *Fidēs* (Richlin 2005 265).

891 **hic soli sumus** A funny self-aware joke, given that Milphio betrays his own awareness of the audience's presence when he addresses the spectators at 921. Because Syncerastus does not notice the audience, the joke's on him.

892 **meum erum perdet** This is a momentous line in the play, and perhaps one quite worrying for its audience, since it shows that "[a] slave has made the independent moral decision to reveal one of his master's most closely guarded secrets, and he does so based both on his own moral judgement and his belief that he can trust a fellow slave to protect him as a source" (Slater 2004 297). Syncerastus is in fact quite concerned that he receive protection for his betrayal from Agorastocles. **Qui** "How" again, both here and at line 896. Though Syncerastus thinks Milphio and Agorastocles can destroy Lycus with the information about the sisters' freeborn status, he has no proof of their free birth other than his word (or that of Giddenis). Furthermore, "[a]s a slave, he cannot legally give evidence except under

torture [nor can Giddenis]—and torture would require the permission of
his master Lycus." It's as if the slave believes that the mere knowledge of the
truth will free the young women (Slater 2004 291–92). That the knowledge of
their free birth would be enough to rescue them from the pimp's ownership
depends on something similar to the first-century BCE *lex Fabia de plagiāriīs*.
As Scafuro (1997 406–9) explains, this similar law, probably passed after the
battle of Cannae in 209 BCE, penalized kidnappers or people who bought
the victims of kidnapping, either free or slave. The law allowed an *adsertor ad
lībertātem*, a citizen with knowledge of the kidnapped person's true status, to
initiate the *uindicātiō in lībertātem*, by which he "made a symbolic seizure [of
the kidnapped person] and summoned the self-proclaimed owner to court."

894–900   Syncerastus' function in the *Poenulus* is to reveal to Milphio
that the sisters are freeborn and to reveal the story of their kidnapping
(Fantham 2004 240, 247). Fantham also notes that while Giddenis knows of
their free birth, and we would think it likely for her to have told them, the
young women never show any knowledge of their birth. Syncerastus' betrayal
of his master Lycus is the first time this knowledge appears onstage outside
of the prologue (Fantham 2004 246–47). If Syncerastus' Greek equivalent
also revealed the truth of their free birth in Alexis' *Karchedonios*, much of
the scene between him and Milphio could have derived from Alexis' play as
Lowe (2004 259) argues. But it is not clear that Alexis' version of Syncerastus,
and not the titular Carthaginian, must have revealed that information in the
Karchedonios. Much of this scene bears the marks of Plautine composition—
cf. notes on 823–38, 840, 842–44, 851–58, 862–63, 905–6, perhaps 886.

896   **cedo** See note on 315, 865. **qui** See note on 892. **Anactorio** See note
on 87.

897   **Siculo** *Siculus, -a, um* means "Sicilian." Several battles were fought
on the island of Sicily during the First and Second Punic Wars, which may be
why Plautus characterizes Sicily as a source of wickedness here and at *Capt.*
888, *Rud.* 49–56 (Richlin 2005 39). **Quanti** Genitive of indefinite value.

898   **Giddenenem** Giddenis (genitive: Giddenenis) is named for the first
time here, though she is mentioned at 86. Her name, meaning something
like "Good Fortune," is appropriate because she will be reunited with her son
(Faller 2004 178).

901   **lepidum ... facinus** *lepidus, -a, -um* "pleasant, charming, elegant,"
is often used with words referring to deception in Plautus. Cf. *Men.* 132; *Mil.*
767; *Per.* 463, 466; *Pseud.* 946; *Truc.* 964 (McCarthy 2000 147n69).

902 **surptus** Syncopated form of the perfect passive participle of *surripiō, surripere, surripuī/surrupuī, surreptus* "to snatch away secretly, steal." **sexennis** The adjective *sexennis, -e* means "of six years, six years old." Note that this conflicts with what the prologue says about Agorastocles' age at the time of his kidnapping (see note on line 66).

904 **diem obiit suom** "Met his (appointed) day," a periphrasis for "died."

905-6 **quo** Introduces a purpose clause—see note on 669. **manu eas adserat / suas popularis liberali causa** *manū aliquem asserere līberālī causā* means "to declare someone freed by laying hands on," thus "to free someone." (In Rome, a slave could be freed from his master if someone knew him to have been free—Scafuro 1997 406.) Since it relies on Roman law (see note on 892), Plautus himself must be responsible for inventing and introducing the *līberālis causa* motif—and thus all passages dealing with it (Lowe 2004 257, 259). *populāris, -e* means "of the people; of the same people, (fellow-)countryman."

907 **ad incitas ... rediget** With *ad incita/incitās* the verb *redigō, redigere, redēgī, redāctus* ("to drive back") means "to bring to a standstill," perhaps even "to put into checkmate." The meaning depends on the extension of the adjective *incitus, -a, -um* "immovable" to the word—unstated here—*calx, calcis* (f) "game-piece, chess-piece" (from the Greek χάλιξ, ἡ). That noun is not related to *calx, calcis* (f) "heel" (Brinkhoff 1935 76) although the meaning "heel" may also be in play here (Schmidt 1960 181).

908 **Quin** here means "indeed." **prius ... quam** "before" is often separated: translate it with the second clause. **faxo** Future. See note on 162 and cf. 910. In later Latin a substantive *ut* clause would be expected to follow this verb, although here we simply have a future indicative. **calcem ciuerit** *calx* (see 907) as the object of the verb *cieō, ciēre, cīuī, citus* means "to slide a game-piece," and thus "to make a move" in a game like chess.

909 **faxint** is a perfect (optative) subjunctive here.

910 **conlibertus** Unassimilated form of *collībertus, -ī* (m) "fellow freedman"—cf. *conseruus, -ī* (m) "fellow slave." Unfortunately, neither Milphio nor Collybiscus are seen to receive any rewards for the help they extend to Agorastocles, since Milphio's promise depends on Agorastocles freeing the two of them after Lycus' family has been granted to Agorastocles by the praetor as punishment for his theft—but that's not what happens (see 1398-1422). Cf. the disappearance of Saturio and Virgo in *Persa* (Richlin 2005 266).

912   **sit** In archaic Latin the optative subjunctive can be introduced by *ut* (A&G 442a).

914   **dum calet** Syncerastus is right to urge that the sisters be rescued as soon as possible, since, as Henderson points out, taking the pimp to court on the following day (as planned) would not necessarily prevent them from becoming prostitutes. See note on 807.

915   **materies . . . fabrum** Plautus sets up a pun whereby *faber, fabrī* (m) "craftsman, worker" limits the meaning of *māteriēs, -ēi* (f) "matter, material; cause, opportunity" to its literal sense. **data est** The phrase undergoes prodelision, then the second syllable experiences iambic shortening.

916   **Potin** Contraction of *potis* + *ne.*

917–22   Lines 917–22 and 923–29 are doublets with several similarities: *dī immortālēs* at 917 and 923, *ībō intrō* at 920 in contrast to *intrō ībō* at 929. One doublet may be a post-Plautine addition to the script (Barsby 2004 105), or both could be Plautine and the repetition has resulted from the larger rearrangement of the text or from Plautus' adaptation process (Lowe 2004 258–59). See note on 817–20. Regardless, Milphio makes the consequences of the pimp's illegal possession of the sisters very clear to himself and the audience in this monologue. Cf. *Cas.* 504–14, where the same discovery also occurs (Fraenkel 2007 200).

917–18   **seruatum . . . disperditum** Supply *esse* with both. **exiti** Partitive genitive of *exitium, -ī/-iī* (n) "destruction, ruin" with *tantum* "so much."

919   Milphio employs military imagery, which probably derives from Plautus. Cf. 201; *Bac.* 709–11; *Pseud.* 524, 584 (Fraenkel 2007 47).

920–22   Plautus emphasizes that the actors are performing for the sake of the audience (*audīuistis*) here and at 1224. Cf. 550–52; *Pseud.* 387–89, 720–21 (Petrone 1983 25–27; Moore 1998 205n22). Similar phrases nullifying any obligation to repeat pertinent plot information, thus saving the audience from boredom, also appear at Men. *Dys.* 820–22; Soph. *Ant.* 1180–91. Contrast *Epit.* 883–93, where Menander exploits the repetition (Arnott 2004 81).

921   **iterem** From the frequentative verb *iterō* (1-tr.) "to do [something] a second time, repeat." **inscitia** *inscītia, -ae* (f) is "ignorance, stupidity."

922 **[ero] . . . ero** The first is the dative of *erus*, the second is the future tense of *esse*. **odio** Dative of purpose.

923–29 See note on 917–22. This passage seems to be a post-Plautine interpolation, given that Agorastocles is not in the forum—he entered his house at 807 (Barsby 2004 105). Lowe (1990 290) observes, however, that Plautus himself "is notoriously prone both to repetition and to inconsistency."

924 **sed ego nunc est** Understand a repetition of *calamitās* from the previous line. The sense is *sed nunc calamitās est ego quom mē commoror*. **quom** Archaic spelling of *cum* "when."

928 **qui . . . det** Likely just a relative clause with a verb attracted into the subjunctive rather than a relative clause of characteristic (A&G 535).

929 **dum . . . adueniat** See note on 786.

930–1073 These lines are generally joyful and busy, filled with "a wall-to-wall procession of greetings and best wishes, congratulations and thanksgivings, distributed between the lost and found family members and through them addressed to the beneficent deities responsible" (Henderson 1994 37).

930–60 This speech, part Punic and part Latin, serves as an entrance monologue for Hanno. Even though the Carthaginian was introduced in the prologue (at 121–22), he still has to be joined appropriately to the ongoing action with the other characters we already know (Zwierlein 1990 178). Note too that Hanno stops the music when he enters at 930 and delivers what is essentially the play's second prologue (Moore 2004 147). Moore (2004 149–50) also notes that Hanno sings less than the younger characters, "in keeping with his general seriousness," so only 27 percent of his verses are accompanied through line 1331 (which omits the two spurious endings as well as 1398–1422, which Moore [2004 157] is not certain are Plautine).

However, what appears as a long monologue in the text is actually quite repetitious, since 930–39 and 940–49 are doublets of a single Punic speech and 950–60 (with the exception of the interpolated 954) seem to represent a Latin version of the speech with roughly the same sense. These long Punic speeches are prose, whereas later short phrases in Punic are incorporated into the iambic senarii (de Melo 2012 189–90). Lines 940–49 (from Manuscript A) represent the "genuine version, already desperately corrupt in the early Empire," while 930–39 (from the P family of manuscripts) is a "scholar's

repair, made up independently, but with reference to text II [lines 940–49],
in the contemporary Neo-Punic and Roman orthography of his time"—i.e.,
after the mid-first century BCE (Gratwick 1971 37; Gratwick 1972 228n1).
Finally, it is not clear how much of Plautus' audience would have understood
the Punic elements in this play. Adams (2003 205) and de Melo (2012 7) think
that most of the spectators would have had no idea what these lines actually
said, whereas Röllig (1980 288), Palmer (1997 12), and Richlin (2005 190)
are more sanguine about the possibility of a Roman audience understanding
some Punic. (Röllig points to Roman soldiers' contact with Punic in Africa
and Italy, whereas Palmer points to the long-standing trade agreements with
Carthage that were likely to introduce at least a few Punic words and phrases
into the lexicon of the Romans with whom Carthaginian merchants came in
contact. Richlin focuses on the seizure of many Carthaginian slaves during the
Punic Wars, so any enslaved Carthaginians in attendance at the performance
of the *Poenulus* would have recognized the language as well.) Adams (2003
210–12) does discuss a trilingual (Latin, Greek, Punic) inscription from
Sardinia dating to 180–150 BCE, but Sardinia is a special case—it had been
controlled by Carthage since approximately 500 BCE before Rome seized
control of the island in 238/7 BCE.

Because the Latin speech duplicates material in the two Punic versions,
Gratwick (1972 229n1) argues that it was simply a gloss on the lines for the
actors and was never performed. Lines 950–60 present the audience with
Hanno's identity, his purpose (that Plautus does so via a prayer is clever
because it maintains the dramatic pretense and demonstrates his piety),
and his immediate plans, but much of this information could be presented
via the Punic version of the speech too, since "gesture, tone of voice, mime,
and props" can reveal many important details (Gratwick 1971 32–33). In
fact, Gratwick posits that the audience might be pleased with themselves for
deciphering the gist of the Punic speech, which would be a clever ploy by the
poet who chose to incorporate such a long passage in a foreign language into
his comedy (Gratwick 1971 34). The poet in question could be either Plautus
or Alexis, who was born in southern Italy, close to the Carthaginian sphere
of influence. On the other hand, the Punic speech may have alienated at least
part of the Roman audience. It may also have been difficult for a non-Punic
actor to perform, and therefore perhaps even less intelligible to the audience.

There are, in fact, several good reasons to believe that Hanno delivered
the same speech in both Punic and Latin. First, that 950–60 are written
in iambic senarii does suggest that they were performed. (The Punic text,
remember, is written in prose.) Second, Plautus is often repetitive, and it is
necessary for the audience to understand exactly who Hanno is, given that he
was last mentioned in the prologue. Third, the Latin version affirms patterns

of trickster behavior on Hanno's part that are established in that prologue: the Latin translation "gives a nod to metatheatricality; for it may be asked, for whom does Hanno translate his prayer? Obviously it is not for his own benefit, nor for the benefit of his own Carthaginian slaves. At this point, nobody else is onstage with him. Thus, Hanno must translate his words for the benefit of the spectators watching the play, demonstrating an awareness of the audience, and his own role as actor" (Maurice 2004 280). (Maurice [2004 280] does overreach, however, when describing Hanno's prayer as insincere, "hilariously incongruous posturing, as this sneaky *Poenulus* acts out the part of the pious traveller arriving in the city, and offering prayers of supplication to the gods." Rather, Hanno often resembles other old men in Roman comedy who find their kidnapped children: Hegio in *Captiui*, Periphanes in *Epidicus*, and Daemones in *Rudens*.) Likewise, Henderson (1994 52) believes that this introduction to Hanno is meant to display his formidable linguistic abilities: "No-one will ever upstage *Poenulus*, whose grip over the language of his play is as absolute as any *imperator Historicus* in the Annols of Rome." See the rest of Maurice 2004 for more on Hanno as the "winner" of this comedy, and especially on his metatheatrical skills and acting abilities.

Finally, this commentary employs Leo's text. Interested readers are urged to consult de Melo's 2012 Loeb edition (pages 173–220), where he proposes a new Punic text and some possible translations thereof based on the most recent scholarship on that language. (Sznycer 1967, Krahmalkov 1970 and 1988, and Gratwick 1971 have all attempted reconstructions of the text, but de Melo's is the most up-to-date.)

951   **quod** "In that."

952   **fratris** Short for *frātris pātruēlis* "cousin, a father's brother's son."

953   **siritis** Archaic form of the perfect subjunctive of *sinō, sinere, sīuī/siī, situs* "to allow" (A&G 181b). **di uostram fidem** "For heaven's sake!" See note at 830 above.

956   **sibi quod faciundum fuit** I.e., Antidamas has died. Translate *sibi* as *eī*, since "Plautus uses the reflexive *sibi* as if the relative clause were still part of what people are talking about" (de Melo 2010 92). *faciundum* is simply the archaic spelling of the gerundive *faciendum*.

958   **tesseram** A *tessera, -ae* (f) is a small square or cube with markings (such as a die). The use of a *tessera hospitālis* "token of guest/host friendship" (known as σύμβολον in Greek, thus also *symbolum* in Latin) developed in

Greece. First, a "knucklebone (ἀστράγαλος), coin, tablet or similar object" was split into two pieces. A guest and host would then each take one of the pieces, and they—or their descendants—could therefore "confirm identities even after long separations by the fact that the two pieces exactly fitted together." For σύμβολα in Greek literature see, e.g., Eur. *Med.* 613; Hdt. 6.86. β1; Plato *Symp.* 191d, 193a; Eub. fr. 70 K-A; Arist. *Eth. Eud.* 7.5.6 1239b31. References to σύμβολα and *tesserae hospitālēs* in Roman comedy—e.g., *Bac.* 263–66; *Pseud.* 55–56, 1092—probably derive from the Greek predecessors if the item is integral to the plot, but we cannot be certain because the identification tools were already in wide use in Rome by Plautus' time (Arnott 2004 82).

961–89 Lowe describes why these lines are probably mostly Plautine invention: a) the delay between the entrance of Agorastocles/Milphio and their first words with Hanno; b) the *"liberalis causa* motif" at 963b–66 and 971–74; c) the reference to speaking in Punic at 982–87; d) the dependence of 988–89 on 985–87 "illogically anticipat[es]" the eventual recognition—why doesn't Hanno follow up sooner?; e) the Plautine "style and length" of the aside at 967–70; f) additional illogical anticipation of the eventual recognition at 962–63—why doesn't Hanno follow up sooner?; g) the "typically Plautine" words and style of Milphio's remarks about Carthaginians at 975–81. The delay referenced in item a) above is unlikely to have occurred in Alexis' play (Lowe 2004 260–61). Furthermore, the "passage forms a prelude to the dramatically crucial meeting between Agorastocles and Hanno in 1039ff.; it delays that meeting and is clearly designed for comic effect" because of Milphio's perpetual misunderstanding of Hanno's Punic speech. It's unrealistic that Hanno should continue to use Punic for so long when Milphio clearly doesn't understand it. Additionally, the use of Punic would have been far more topical in Rome than in Athens. So 990–1038 are probably "entirely Plautine," as are most of 961–89 (Lowe 2004 259–60).

961 **Ain** Contraction of *āis* + *ne*. According to Lewis and Short, the question in colloquial contexts often takes on a tone of surprise or wonder: "do you really mean so? indeed? really? is it possible?" and even just "what?" **dixe** Contraction of *dīxisse*.

964 **liberali . . . adseres causa manu** See note on line 905.

965–66 A nod to the slaves in the audience and their experiences. Cf. *Curc.* 300, 607; *Per.* 549–672 (Richlin 2005 267).

969–70 **creta est ... ut mi apsterserunt omnem sorditudinem** The *ut* is exclamatory ("how"). *sorditūdo, sorditūdinis* (f), a Plautine invention meaning "filthitude, defilence," is a pun built from the root of *sordes, sordis* (f) "dirt, squalor" on the unattested form *surditūdo "deafitude, deafness." And the pun is based on a "folk etymology" found in Isidore of Seville: deafness from blocked-up, dirty ears (Fontaine 2010 47–48, 233). The pun is possible because "the syllables [ur] and [or] were homophones in Plautine Latin" (Gratwick 1972 230). *crēta* is also a pun: it may either be "chalk, fuller's earth" from *crēta, -ae* (f), or "understood" from *cernō, cernere, crēuī, crētus*. Since fuller's earth was used to clean clothes (*Aul.* 719), Hanno is saying "in tones reminiscent of tragedy" that the speech removes his filth and removes his lack of understanding (Maurice 2004 280). The joke relies on a metaphor common to Greek and Roman comedy: cf. Ar. *Nub.* 923–24; *Vesp.* 462, 1367; *Pax* 1116; fr. 158 K-A; Plaut. *Asin.* 649; *Aul.* 537; *Cist.* 720; *Most.* 1063 (Arnott 2004 82–83). Because *sordes, sordis* (f) can also be used to refer to "dark clothes worn during mourning," the pun would gain an extra layer of meaning if Hanno were dressed in dark clothing to signify his grief at the loss of his daughters (Richlin 2005 267). Finally, these lines demonstrate how Plautus tends to describe things in a "concretizing fashion." Speech is first heard, then transformed into chalk, and then destroyed (Fraenkel 2007 150).

971–74 There is irony in the fact that witness best able to prove the sisters' free birth is eavesdropping. "This is dramatically brilliant and superbly economical" because Hanno now has a reason to approach the strangers right away (Gratwick 1971 29), and perhaps the titular Carthaginian of Alexis' *Karchedonios* did approach immediately to ask if the two girls are sisters (Gratwick 1972 229). He fails to do so in the *Poenulus* because the Plautine stage is not an entirely logical place.

971–72 **testis** Accusative plural. Ideas of witnesses and witnessing are repeated at 531, 565, 582, 681–82, 723, 764, 765, 786. Thus Milphio can joke about it in response to Agorastocles at 972: "Witnesses? What do you mean?" (Arnott 2004 65). Alternatively, there may be another pun on *testis, testis* (m) "testicle" here (Richlin 2005 267). **quin** "Why not?"

973 **adiutrix** *adiūtrix, adiūtrīcis* is the feminine form of *adiūtōr, adiūtōris* "helper, assistant."

974–1038 The play's dramatic momentum pauses here. These sixty lines of jokes likely are Plautus' invention; they are typical of him, though possible for Alexis. Furthermore, all of the Latin puns are likely Plautus' additions since they would require much adaptation from the Greek (Franko 1996 433). Milphio and Agorastocles mock Hanno by drawing attention to his Otherness (in clothing, speech, and behavior), which may have served to unite Plautus' Roman audience against him (Henderson 1994 52). On the other hand, he shares some of the characteristics of the clever slave and the helpful old man (cf. Periplectomenus in the *Miles Gloriosus*), so allies himself with the winning side of the comedy—he's no blocking figure as so many other Plautine *senēs* are.

974   **multo** Ablative of degree of difference (A&G 414).

975   **cum tunicis** The *tunica, -ae* (f) "tunic" was a unisex undergarment for Romans but is "normal Carthaginian dress," according to Ennius (quoted at Gell. *NA* 6.12.7) and Servius (on Verg. *Aen.* 8.724) (Gratwick 1972 231). Cf. 1008, 1121, 1298. For a Roman citizen to wear a tunic without a *pallium* ("cloak") was considered effeminate and immoral, while an unbelted tunic was considered similarly shameful (Franko 1996 432).

976   **numnam** Like *num* it asks a question anticipating a negative answer, but also indicates "anxious and surprised inquiry," say Lewis and Short. **balineis** Alternative spelling of *balneum, -ī* (n) "bath, bath complex." **circumductust** Prodelision. Colloquially, *circumdūcō, circumdūcere, circumdūxī, circumductus* means "to cheat, deceive" someone in the accusative out of something in the ablative.

977   **facies** In Plautus' time *facies, -ēi* (f) means "form, shape, appearance" more often than it means "face, visage." We do not know whether the actor playing Hanno wore a special mask that marked him as specifically Carthaginian, but certainly Hanno's appearance as otherwise described (975, 1008, 1121) declares his origin (Franko 1996 432, Starks 2000 171n27). **Gugga** The meaning is unknown. The Punic near-equivalent to *gugga*, "GG is attested as the name of a profession in a Punic inscription; since the inscription leaves it unclear what that profession is, and since Hanno has clearly traveled," de Melo (2012 122n53) translates *gugga* as "tradesman." Other suggestions for the meaning of *gugga* seem to be guesses based on the immediate context of the word. These include "barbarian, foreigner, scum, slacker" (Schmidt 1960 382) and something "appropriate to a Carthaginian whose slaves are mere shadows of their youth" (Palmer 1997 35, interpreting line 978 as proof of Hanno's *gugga* status). Given that comedy is rather fond of the *nōn sequitur*, such assumptions are not always safe. The attribution of this entire phrase is also unclear: Leo assigns it to Milphio, but Lindsay and de Melo assign all of 977 to Agorastocles.

978   ueteres antiquosque One of Hanno's slaves is Giddenis' son, and therefore it is unlikely that all of the slaves are aged. They may simply be young men bent over by the weight of their baggage, but this line helps to promote the alternative meaning of *sarcinātōs* in 979 (de Melo 2012 123n54).

979   Qui "How," here and on 986—see note on 169. **sarcinatos** *sarcinātus, -a, -um* means "laden/having luggage," but could also be a pun meaning "patched" since a *sarcinātor* is "a patcher of old garments" (cf. Gratwick 1972 233). Although the number of attendants is unstated, that *sarcinātōs* is plural means that there are at least five characters onstage simultaneously from 1120–54 (Marshall 2006 110n88).

980–81   anulatis *ānulātus, -a, -um* means "wearing or adorned with a ring." Another classic Plautine joke—cf. 1145–46 (Schmidt 1960 323). See Petron. *Sat.* 102.14 and Juv. 1.104–5 for earrings as "a suspicious, exotic accessory of male foreigners from the Orient" (Richlin 2005 267).

987   qui illim ... perierim *quī* here = *cum ego*, introducing a causal clause requiring a subjunctive (A&G 549). For *illim* see 455.

988–89   ad Lewis and Short note that "[w]ith words denoting measure, weight, manner, model, rule, etc." this preposition means "according to, after." **plurumi ... periere pueri liberi Carthagine** Carthaginians were known as slave traders whose captives had been kidnapped by pirates or had been lured into slavery (at least this last is true of the Phoenicians—cf. Hom. *Od.*15.415–84; Hdt. 1.1). Even Carthaginian children could be kidnapped and sold as slaves too, so Romans could have bought Carthaginian slaves from the Carthaginians or other traders (Palmer 1997 25–26).

990–1028   Here begins the *Poenulus'* splendid (mis)translation scene, which features a lot of wordplay from Milphio as he claims to translate Hanno's Punic remarks for Agorastocles. In actuality, Milphio utters a series of Latin puns based on the sound of Hanno's Punic that show him in competition with the Carthaginian for supremacy in deception. They aren't necessarily good puns either—Fontaine (2010 128) notes that with the bilingual wordplay here Plautus "allows himself a little more freedom with his phonemes in making a pun than he usually does," and Milphio's punning translations into Latin are "intelligible, but increasingly absurd in the context." See especially the notes on 998, 1002–3, 1017–18. Indeed, Milphio's mistranslations can be interpreted as aggressive puns intended to increase his own on-stage status—see Johnstone 1979 on "status transactions" in general, and Marshall 1993 and 2006 170–71 on status transactions in Aristophanic and Roman comedy, respectively. Milphio has in fact already shown himself especially adept at retrojecting ambiguity onto his interlocutors' lines with aggressive puns earlier in the play—cf. 295, 313, 327, 427, and 871–72. Henderson (1994 45–46) astutely wonders how the spectators are supposed to understand Hanno when Milphio, the trickiest character, can't do it. Milphio's tricksteresque role and much of this entire scene—even as far as 1038—is probably a Plautine addition, as is 961–89 (Lowe 2004 259–61).

991   **Poenus Poenior** Sound play, similar to *ipsus . . . ipsissumus* at 846, 1177; *Asin.* 267–68; *Pseud.* 669–70 (Mendelsohn 1907 35); *Trin.* 988 (Brinkhoff 1935 8). The comparative of *Poenus* is also similar to the superlative title of one of Aristophanes' (fragmentary) comedies: *Danaōtatos* (Schmidt 1960 261). One anonymous reviewer notes that Milphio is only *Poenus* in this scene in the sense that he is deceitful (a stereotypically Carthaginian trait), especially in regard to his claim to know Punic. Thus Milphio plays metatheatrically with the difference between Agorastocles' and the spectators' understanding of *Poenus*.

993   **quoiatis** An interrogative pronoun (*quōiātis, -is*) that is identical to the archaic genitive form of *cūiās, cūiātis* "whence originating? of what country/town?" (cf. 109). Its meaning is far narrower than that of *unde*. **parseris** From the rare perfect stem of *parcō, parcere, pepercī/parsī, parsūrus* "to spare; abstain (from), stop."

994   **Auo** A greeting. *Aue*, used as a salutation in Latin, may have been borrowed from this Punic verb but employs a Latin-style -*e* as its ending. Such a borrowing would not require the Romans to actually understand the Punic at all, since the word's meaning becomes clear in context (Adams 2003 205).

995-1001   **Anno byn mytthymballe udradait annech** Milphio's translation of Hanno's Punic seems accurate at 996–97 and 1001, and it's possible that he uses a Punic term correctly at 1152 as well. The audience might even believe—if only briefly—that he actually does know Punic.

998   **Auo . . . Donni** A greeting. Milphio "interprets Punic *donni* (= '*dn* 'lord, master') as Latin *doni* 'gift'" (Fontaine 2010 128).

999   **audin** Crasis of *audīs ne*.

1002-3   **Me har bocca** Milphio interprets the phrase as Latin *misera bucca* "aching cheek" where *bucca* is a vulgar term for *ōs* "face" (Fontaine 2010 128).

1008 **zonam** Romans inferred a man's character from the manner in which he belted his tunic. An ungirt tunic was the mark of a dissolute, even effeminate, man (Richlin 2005 268). Cf. 975, 1121, 1298, 1303.

1011–18 Here Milphio implies that Hanno is a merchant (*mercātōr*, 1016), which carries a pejorative connotation. Merchants were not respected in Rome, where farming was esteemed more highly as a means of acquiring wealth.

1011–12 **mures . . . aedilibus** Milphio employs the stereotypes of Exotic Africa and The Carathaginian Merchant to guess at the meaning of Hanno's Punic speech (Richlin 2005 268). Aediles were Roman officials who organized many of the *lūdī* at which comedies and other forms of entertainment were offered, but they were also in charge of public buildings and markets. Palmer (1997 39, 44, 43) hypothesizes that the reference to African mice may be a joke about all the animals imported from Africa for the parades that occurred before religious games in Rome, or for the wild beast hunts that likely occurred in Rome before the Punic Wars, and that the mention of African mice may even allude to the fear of such creatures shown by elephants, which had terrorized Italy in the Second Punic War (Plin. *HN* 8.29).

1014 **ligulas** *ligula, -ae* (f) "shoestrap," is a diminutive of *lingua* "tongue." **canalis** Accusative plural of *canālis, -is* (m) "pipe." **nuces** From *nux, nucis* (f) "nut." Pliny, quoting the Carthaginian Mago at *HN* 17.63, reports that almonds were the only nuts grown in North Africa in Plautus' time (Palmer 1997 45).

1016 **credo** Parenthetical. **Aruinam** From *aruīna, -ae* (f) "grease, suet, lard." Playing a game of associations, Milphio responds to Hanno's *assam* with a mention of lard because *assam* means "roasted" in Latin and lard is a useful fat for roasting something (cf. Agorastocles' pun with the same word on 279). On the other hand, Palmer (1997 40–41) argues that Milphio's interpretation of Hanno's Punic as items commonly traded by Carthaginian merchants (or in the case of lard/bacon fat likely NOT traded by them due to the Carthaginians' abstinence from pork) would be quite humorous for audience members aware of standard Carthaginian merchandise, although some spectators might also "understand the bilingual wordplay."

1017–18 **palas uendundas . . . mergas datas** Understand *esse* with both participles. A *pāla, -ae* (f) is a "spade," while *mergae, -ārum* (f pl) means "pitchfork." The Romans seem to have availed themselves of Carthaginian agricultural products and agricultural knowledge, and perhaps also of their tools (Palmer 1997 47—and see section 2bi of the introduction).

1018-20   Like Rome, Carthage was actually resurrecting itself after the Second Punic War. These lines, where Hanno is growing and harvesting grain, may allude to that fact. Carthage even had enough money in 191 BCE to offer Rome's army free grain and some ships to help fight King Antiochus, as well as multiple payments of their indemnity (Starks 2000 182–83).

1019   **messim** Archaic spelling of the accusative singular of the i-stem noun *messis, -is* (f) "harvest." **tu** The prosodic hiatus following *tŭ* emphasizes that word (Maurach 1988 148).

1023   **caue** *caueō, cauēre, cauī, cautus* "to be on guard, take care" can introduce substantive *ut/nē* clauses, but without introductory words it can also introduce the simple subjunctive with the sense "be careful not to X, don't Y" (A&G 450). **sis** See note on 225.

1024   **ait** The meter in this line depends on *ait* being monosyllabic (which only occurs in archaic and colloquial Latin, according to A&G 206).

1025   **cratim** The archaic accusative singular of the i-stem noun *crātis, -is* (f) "wicker-work." **supponi** "To be placed under a wicker crate" refers to a mode of execution practiced by the Romans: heavy things (perhaps stones) were placed atop a wicker frame in order to crush (and kill) the victim beneath that frame. See Livy 4.50.4 (Richlin 2005 268). **ut iubeas** Understand another *ōrat* (line 1024) with this construction.

1027   **gunebbal samem** Part of the line refers to the god Ba'al. "Ba'al Shamem, Lord of Skies" was worshipped on Sardinia (which Carthage controlled from roughly 500–238/7 BCE) and came to be known many centuries later in Syria as Jupiter Caelestis or Zeus Ouranios. His Roman near-equivalent, *Tempestātēs*, both looked after Roman naval fleets and after Roman merchants, as we learn from *Sti.* 403–6 (Palmer 1997 55).

1030-34   Metatheatrical language from Hanno and Milphio.

1030   **et nequam et malum** As Maurice (2004 281) observes, this line implies that Milphio ought to be *nēquam* (cf. 159) and *malum*, given his role as clever slave, but that he is failing in his role.

1032 **et sycophantam et subdolum** Understand *esse oportet* again (cf. 1030). Milphio responds to Hanno by saying that skill with words isn't enough (*subdolus* and *sȳcophantam* are often applied to clever slaves): Hanno needs to be a good actor to win their *poenior* competition. *sȳcophantam* may possess a "xenophobic overtone" because of its Greek origin—it's a common term used for tricksters in Plautus (cf. line 376) (Franko 1996 434n15). For the root of *subdolus, -a, -um* see the note on 1110. While Milphio's use of *sȳcophanta* here carries negative connotations, he later uses the same phrase *et subdolum* to praise Hanno's skill at 1108 (Henderson 1994 45). Indeed, as Maurice (2004 283) notes, Hanno will not only adopt multiple roles at the end of the play but will also replace Milphio as the *seruus callidus*.

1033 **migdilix** A term of abuse, though the exact meaning is not certain. It probably means something like "one who confuses, distorts, mixes up," combining the Greek μίγδα ("confusedly") and the Latin *-lix* ("tongue") (Starks 2000 173n30, de Melo 2012 129n58).

1034 **bisulci lingua** "With a forked tongue," i.e., "deceptive," but also "bilingual." A student notes that Hanno's bilingualism makes him the ultimate eavesdropper, one who can listen in on the conversation of others without hiding. See note on 684.

1035–36 **face** Archaic singular imperative of *facere*. Like *caue* above (1023), *facere* can introduce substantive *ut/nē* clauses but can also introduce the simple subjunctive without any introductory words. For similar warnings cf. *Aul.* 401; *Men.* 121; *Mil.* 476; *Most.* 1173; *Per.* 797; *Rud.* 1398–99 (McCarthy 2000 156n91).

1039–85 Although *populāris* (1039) and *populāritātis causā* (1041) are Plautine additions, Lowe (2004 261) argues that Plautus probably followed Alexis' play closely in the rest of the scene, except for adding Milphio's lines at 1078–85—the contents of which could have been "more tactfully introduced by Agorastocles or Hanno" in the *Karchedonios*. Finally, it's worth considering what Milphio does during this recognition scene between Agorastocles and Hanno (the slave is silent from 1035–78).

1042 **Antidamae** Here we finally learn the name of Agorastocles' adoptive father and Hanno's guest-friend: Āntĭdămăs, which is declined like Aeneas (cf. 1058).

1044   **ecquem** According to Lewis and Short, *ecquis, ecquid* introduces more passionate questions than *quis, quid*: i.e., "Is there anyone who? Any?" Cf. line 1062. Here the first syllable scans short (*ĕcquem*) and the second elides with *adulescentem* (Maurach 1988 150).

1045   **Siquidem** undergoes enclisis and is thus scanned *sĭquĭdem*. **Antidamai** is genitive singular.

1047   **tesseram** See note on 958.

1049   **Agedum** Cf. 866, 1063.

1050–51   **pater / patritus** Polyptoton (Schmidt 1960 83). *patrītus, -a, -um* means "of one's father/forefathers."

1058   **illim** See 455.

1062   **tuom** An alternative genitive plural form.

1065   **Ampsigura** Agorastocles' mother, Hanno's cousin. Her name, like her husband's, is a necessary element in Agorastocles' recognition. Her name may mean "Servant of ŠGR" (a fertility goddess) or, better, "Mother of the Guest" (Faller 2004 176–77). **Iahon** Hanno's cousin, Agorastocles' father. Like "Hanno," it may be another name formed by shortening "Hannibal," a name that already carried meaning for the Roman audience (Faller 2004 175–76).

1066   **uiuerent** The main verb of a substantive clause serving as the direct object of *uellem* (A&G 565). **uellem** The imperfect tense of the (optative) subjunctive is used to express a wish that's unaccompished in the present (A&G 441, 442b).

1070   **suom** Just as on 860, it undergoes synizesis, then elides with the following word (Maurach 1988 136).

1072–75   Scars as recognition signs in Greek literature appear at Hom. *Od.* 19.388–466, 21.217–24, 24.331–46; Soph. *OT* 1031–38; Eur. *El.* 572–75; Arist. *Poet.* 16.1454b25–30; Heliod. *Aeth.* 5.5 (Arnott 2004 83). The *Poenulus'* monkey-bite scar is, appropriately enough, decidedly less heroic. Scars are actually rarely used as proof of identity in recognition scenes in Roman comedy and Greek New Comedy. More traditional forms of identification for exposed children are the so-called birth tokens left with them (cf. *Cist., Rud.*), but even children kidnapped when they're older (cf. *Curc.*) will sometimes have a ring or other item to prove their identity. Sometimes a name alone is sufficient (cf. Ter. *And.*).

1074   **ludenti puero** Attracted into the dative case from the accusative because of *tibi* in 1073. **memordit** Archaic spelling of the third principal part of *mordeō, mordēre, momordī, morsus* "to bite (into)."

1075   The text of this line is uncertain, but this reconstruction makes sense and fits the meter. **si audes** The uncontracted form of *sōdēs* "please"—cf. 757. **adest** Agorastocles' scar is the subject.

1076–1136   Agorastocles is silent here (though Leo thinks he might have delivered 1077). He's probably confused the entire time though, since Milphio, who's usually much brighter, is now "for the first time the most ill-informed person onstage"—other than Agorastocles, presumably (Starks 2000 174).

1076–85   Hanno is portrayed positively here, with few of the usual "exaggerated" characteristics of other old men in comedies; he's simply a caring father who's stopped at nothing to search for his lost daughters, sparing neither money nor effort. He's also clearly fond of his recently discovered nephew and agrees to return Agorastocles' inheritance (1080–85). This is certainly not the *pūnica fidēs* "Punic trustworthiness" (i.e., "perfidy") that became stereotypical in the later second century BCE (Blume 2004 211). Nevertheless, line 108 may taint his image from the start.

1078–81   Milphio breaks his silence by attempting to regain control of the play (and perhaps his relationship with Agorastocles). One can read the scene as a contest over *calliditās* between Hanno and Milphio (Maurice 2004 282). Cf. 1086, 1089.

1078   **istam . . . euenisse** Maurach (1988 152) notes the shortening of the inital syllables of both words: *ĭstam* and *ĕuenisse*.

1079   **neuis** Archaic form of *nōn uīs* (A&G 199).

1083   **suam** Emphatic *suus* instead of *eius*—see note at 848. **illo** "To that place."

1085   **quid me fuat** *fuat* is an archaic present subjunctive of *esse* that is thought to represent the last vestiges of the Indo-European aorist subjunctive since it's built off the perfect stem (Sihler 1995 552). Here *esse* means "befall, occur."

1086–1110   Another scene in which Plautus has modified the titular Carthaginian of Alexis' play to portray Hanno as a trickster similar to Milphio (Lowe 2004 260). This second trick of the *Poenulus* (and these lines in particular) must have been added by Plautus since the *liberālis causa* theme "is clearly based on Roman law but is inconsistent with the dramatic situation," in which the young women are Carthaginian but live in Calydon (Lowe 2004 257). Typical of Plautus' more relaxed approach to dramatic consistency, the characterization here is rather unrealistic: "the worthy Hanno agrees to take part in the trick (1089f.) . . . [and] Agorastocles' silence throughout the passage is unrealistic; he is suddenly thrust into the background while Milphio holds the stage with Hanno as a compliant stooge" (Lowe 2004 257). Nor does Milphio ever reveal that the sisters are Carthaginian or that he has already successfully entrapped Lycus. "All this is in line with Plautine techniques of composition, which value individual scenes more highly than the coherence of the play as a whole, but not with Greek New Comedy, where consistency is more important than the humor of individual scenes" (de Melo 2012 11).

1087   **Tua opus est opera** The line plays *operā* off of *opus est*, as do *Curc.* 468; *Mil.* 766, 878–80; *Trin.* 365; Ter. *Haut.* 73; *Phor.* 760 (Brinkhoff 1935 122).

1088   **uteris** In preclassical Latin, especially Plautus and Terence, *ūtor, ūtī, ūsus sum* "to use" commonly takes an accusative object.

1089   **subdolus** Milphio's question here is rhetorical, because he'd already declared him *subdolus* at 1032 (Starks 2000 173). Cf. 1108.

1090   Hanno's refusal to trick friends "introduc[es] for the first time in the play a connection between truth and play-acting, that will be emphasized as the trick plays itself out." Cf. 1104–5 (Maurice 2004 282). There is irony too in a Carthaginian declaring before a Roman audience that it's not wise to trick a friend (Starks 2000 173).

1091   **male faxim** *faxim* is a present subjunctive of *facere*. (See note on 909.) When used with the adverb *malē*, *facere* can mean "to hurt, injure."

1092–98   Plautus emphasizes Milphio's role as a trickster here: "Milphio's explanation of the situation in 1092–1098 echoes phrases from the beginning of the play (95f., 98, 153f., 161) and conspicuously ignores subsequent developments, especially in referring to the girls as *meretrices servolae*" (Lowe 2004 257). Alternatively, Milphio may refer to Adelphasium as a prostitute out of spite (cf. 392–99).

1092 **Amat ab lenone** "Loves someone from the pimp's establishment."

1097 **ludificatur** From *lūdificor* (1-tr.) "to mock, make sport of; deceive." **quaestum** It's possible that *quaestus, -ūs* (m) "gain, advantage; business, occupation" may occasionally have the metatheatrical sense "role."

1099–1173 These lines closely parallel Men. *Sik.* 343–76, wherein "a parasite named Theron similarly tries to persuade the newly arrived Kichesias to impersonate the father of a girl named Philoumene, whose true parent by an identical irony he turns out to be" (Arnott 2004 68). Plautus seems to have incorporated allusions to Greek models besides the *Karchedonios* into the second half of the *Poenulus*—cf. 1296–1318. Despite the parallel, the specific details of Milphio's plot reveal Plautine workmanship since Hanno "is treated as a Roman in Rome: in 189 BC a treaty of friendship was established between Rome and Carthage, which would allow him to appeal to the authorities against the pimp, but he would still need a patron to represent him: Plautus presents him as able to appeal by himself (ll. 1102–3), which he could not do as a foreigner" (de Melo 2012 10–11).

1100 **ut** Introduces a substantive *ut* clause (A&G 561) in apposition to the *consilium/fābricam* from the previous line. **allegemus** From *allegō* (1-tr.) "to commission; to incite someone to an act of deceit."

1102 Cf. 906; *Curc.* 620; *Per.* 163, 474–75 (Richlin 2005 268). **manu** undergoes iambic shortening here.

1106–10 Milphio has relayed his master plan of deception to Hanno, who is supposed to pretend that his daughters were stolen from him. Additional humor arises from the dramatic irony of the trickster Milphio "unwittingly proposing as fiction what is in fact true and therefore misconstruing Hanno's sorrowful comments as the inspired play-acting of a fellow trickster." Cf. 1124–26 (Lowe 2004 257). Here the "actors play metatheatrically on their stage personas, especially with Milphio's reference to an actor's gesture and the Carthaginian's replacement of his role as supreme trickster, complete with all the right Plautine vocabulary (*catus, malus, callidus, subdolus*)" (Starks

2000 174). Note the use of *architecton, architectonis* (m) too, a word often associated with clever slave characters—see note on 1110. While the clever slave character is known for his mental agility (cf. Moodie 2009), here Milphio surprisingly loses his ability to interpret situations and devise successful solutions since he "is so convinced that Hanno is the stereotyped Punic he appears to be that the slave cannot conceive that Hanno is actually being honest here" (Maurice 2004 283). Note that if 1169–71 is an interpolation then the text never clarifies how long it takes for Milphio finally to realize that Hanno isn't acting.

1106   in principio "Already at the beginning."

1107–8   catum, / malum crudumque, et callidum et subdolum The Palatine manuscripts contain the impossible phrasing *malum crūdumque, est ollidum et subdolum. et callidum* was proposed by Pylades. Gratwick's emendation also fixes 1107–8 but seems overly complex: MIL: *eu hercle mortālem malum, / <senem> catum crūdumque, Aeolidam subdolum! Aeolidam* "the son of Aeolus" is suitable, he argues, because Aeolus' son Sisyphus is "most crafty of men" at Hom. *Il.* 6.153–54 (Gratwick 1982 99, 103n1).

1110   dolis *dolus, -ī* (m) refers to "either abstract guile, or a concrete means of guile. Its application, like that of *fallacia*, is as broad as is the range of contrivances of the plotter" (Brotherton 1926 14). Its compound *subdolus* appears earlier in the play at 1032, 1089, 1108. For *dolī* cf. *Asin.* 312; *Bac.* 643, 950, 952, 1070; *Capt.* 222; *Epid.* 88, 375; *Mil.* 147, 198, 773, 1154; *Most.* 716; *Per.* 480; *Pseud.* 580, 614, 672, 705a, 927, 932 (Moore 1998 191, 228n35). **architectonem** Creative skill is linked to the clever slave character (Sharrock 2009 16–17). While *architectōn, -onis* (m) doesn't appear elsewhere in Plautine comedy, cf. *architectus* at *Amph.* 45; *Mil.* 901, 902, 915, 919, 1139 (Moore 1998 112, 218n15). Milphio is impressed with Hanno's ability to cry and announces that Hanno is outperforming him in deception—a "prophetic" remark (Franko 1996 436).

1111–73   Lowe (2004 261) argues that Plautus likely invented Milphio's entire role in this scene, much as in 961–1110, since a) Agorastocles would have sent for Giddenis "more appropriately" than Milphio at 1112–21; b) lines 1124–26 and 1169–71 "presuppose" the play's second—Plautine—trick (or 1169–71 are part of a later interpolation); c) all of Milphio's other lines are dispensable, e.g., 1135, 1149–50, or clearly Plautine in vocabulary/style, e.g., 1152–54, 1167b–68.

1111   Franko (1996 436–37n17) observes that Hanno's assumption that the sisters have a nurse reveals that the *Poenulus* either has dramaturgical problems or has a major lacuna and we're missing the lines that first reveal her existence: why otherwise would he assume that these young women are his daughters? We can also see the characterization here as unrealistic: to ask about the nurse represents an "abrupt change of subject" for Hanno. She must have already been mentioned in the *Karchedonios* (Lowe 2004 257).

1112–13   **aquilo est** *aquilus, -a, -um* means "dark colored, swarthy." It is likely that the actor playing Giddenis the nurse wore a mask with dark features and dark hair—cf. the Ethiopian *ancilla* in Terence's *Eunuchus* (Marshall 2006 148). Giddenis could have played a role in Alexis' *Karchedonios*, although it would have been a smaller one. She would have to exit soon enough that the same actor could play her and Milphio, e.g. (Barsby 2004 106).

1113–14   Giddenis may be somewhat old (and likely ugly, as many comic characters are—see notes on 1145–46, 1416), so Milphio is mocking her appearance here: "he makes a cruel joke by describing her as a pimp would describe a desirable piece of merchandise. Hanno then joins in the role-playing, agreeing . . . knowing full well that she is anything but *venusta*" (Franko 1996 436n17).

1120–73   The size of an acting troupe can be deduced from the scenes with the most characters in them. Six characters appear in several scenes of the *Poenulus*; here the six include Hanno, Milphio, Agorastocles, Giddenis, *puer*, and at least one other slave (Marshall 2006 109, 110n88). In a sign of how much Plautus has modified Alexis' comedy, four of these characters have speaking roles, five if we include Giddenis' son's single line (Lowe 2004 256).

1120   **proxumust** Prodelision with *proxumus*, the archaic spelling of *proximus*. The adjective *proximus, -a, -um* "nearest (to)" occasionally takes an object in the accusative case.

1123   **alumnarum** See Joshel 1986 on relations between ancient wet nurses and the children they reared (Richlin 2005 268).

1124   **Hanno Carthaginiensis** Note that Giddenis immediately knows Hanno's name and city of origin, but Milphio still doesn't believe that Hanno is the father of the two young women.

1125   **praestrigiator** *praest(r)igiātor, -ōris* (m) means "prestidigitator, magician" and is used by Plautus "for tricksters when their means of deceit cannot be discerned"—see *Amph.* 782, 830; *Aul.* 630; *Cist.* 297; *Truc.* 134 (Franko 1996 437n17).

1130   **Giddenenem ancillam** Maurach (1988 156) notes that it is fitting to have a hiatus between the first recognition—Giddenis' name—and the second—her relation to Hanno.

1135   Here Plautus contrasts the adverb *hīc* with the pronoun *hĭc* (Brinkhoff 1935 103). Milphio may finally begin to understand the truth of Hanno's relationship with the sisters here.

1139-40   **mutarentur nomina** Plautus occasionally plays with the concept of a person's transformation into an object or different person, followed by the assumption of that object or person's role or fate. Cf. *Amph.* 814; *Asin.* 374; *Aul.* 585; *Bac.* 361; *Pseud.* 191; *Sti.* 239 (Fraenkel 2007 22–23). **genere** Ablative of respect/specification (A&G 418). **corpore** Ablative of means.

1141-42   **Auamma illi** The *puer* greets (cf. *auo* on 998, 1001) his mother. **Hauon bane silli in mustine** Another greeting. The term *puer* can refer to a child, young man, or slave, and this *puer* either accompanied the *hominēs sarcinātōs* of 979 or is one of them. Regardless, he is the only member of Hanno's servants to speak. It's impossible to tell how much of the Giddenis recognition scene is Alexis' or Plautus' work, but the Punic lines and 1145–46 are usually thought to have been added by Plautus (Lowe 2004 261; cf. Arnott 2004 68) since the only line spoken by the Carthaginian *puer* is expendable— cf. the *ancilla* at 332. The actor(s) playing both roles probably doubled in at least one other part (Marshall 2006 100, 96).

1145-46   **muliebri supellectili . . . Clarus clamor** See note on 862–63 for the type of joke. *supellex, supellectilis* (f) means "stuff, apparatus, furniture." Dutsch 2004 argues convincingly that the phrase *supellex muliebris* refers to Giddenis' large breasts. This element of the costume would be appropriate both because she's worked as a wet-nurse and because—according to the Peripatetics—women scream with their breasts. *Clārus clāmor* is thus a surprising joke from Hanno—the audience would be expecting him to mention her bosom (Dutsch 2004 628–29). Hanno's complaint about the loud cries of Giddenis is also funny because the character is actually being played by a man so both breasts and voice are—perhaps obviously—fake (Dutsch

2008 151n4). Hanno's joke is consistent with other comic representations of women as immoderate. In contrast, while many men in comedy "lack self-control, their immoderation is never portrayed as essential to their virility" (Dutsch 2008 151). The joke about Giddenis' noise is more appropriate for the half of Hanno's character that is more like the stock *senex lepidus* and is the play's new comic star (having replaced Milphio) than it is for the stock *pater pius* he appears to be at 930–60 and 1136–40 (Starks 2000 175, who observes an alternation between these two roles; see the notes on 1190–92—piety, 1198a–1200—jokes about Adelphasium, 1211–50—trickiness followed by sincerity, 1276—piety). **Sine modo** Either a preposition (*sine*) and its object (*modus, -ī*) "without limit," or an imperative (from *sinere*) and adverb (*modo*) "but allow [her]." It depends on how we interpret Agorastocles' behavior here—does he support Hanno's interpretation of Giddenis' loud cries or does he understand her joy at being reunited with her son?

1152–53 Milphio threatens Hanno's slaves with a list of punishments. **detrudam** From *dētrūdō, dētrūdere, dētrūsī, dētrūsus* "to drive away, push down." **molas** *mola, -ae* (f) means "mill-stone" in the singular, "mill" in the plural. **puteum** From *puteus, -ī* (m) "pit, well." **robustum** *rōbustus, -a, -um* "of oak-wood; strong, solid." **codicem** A more recent spelling of the older term *caudex, caudicis* (m) "block of wood [to which people are tied as a punishment]."

1156–57 Agorastocles and Hanno use "Roman legal terminology" here, despite the Calydonian setting (Franko 1996 448n33). Agorastocles' emphasis on marrying Adelphasium (cf. the entire plot of the *Trinummus*) betrays a deep anxiety on the part of the Romans for settling young citizen women— even Carthaginian ones, apparently—safely in marriage. Indeed, in Roman comedy the fate of the young woman, whose life can be ruined by a single sex act, is nearly as important as the fate of the *adulescens amāns*. Roman comedy betrays a greater concern for the safety of citizen women than Menander's Greek New Comedy does, as evidenced by the *fābula palliāta*'s more frequent focus on the recognition of young women as citizens (James forthcoming).

1158 Hanno has replaced Milphio as Agorastocles' ally and will maintain his position for the rest of the play—he serves in the *seruus callidus* role and even talks to the young man about the sisters as Milphio had (Maurice 2004 283–84).

1165 **fore** Here the alternative form of *futūrōs esse*.

1168   The text of this line has been much debated. Leo's proposal for this line is best because it follows the typical Plautine joke format by explaining the preceding line(s) and because it breaks the dramatic pretense (Schmidt 1960 329). (Lindsay 1905 prefers *Thraecae sunt: in celonem sustolli solent*— where *cēlōn, -ōnis* (m) derives from the Greek *kēlōn, kēlōnos* (m) "stallion" or *kēlōn, kēlōnos* (m) "swing beam for raising water.") **calones** From *cālō, cālōnis* (m), derived from the Greek *kālon* (n) "timber, wood," and hence meaning "soldier's servant; drudge" (because of such people's proverbial stupidity) and "platform shoe worn by a tragic actor" because the platforms of the boots were made from willow, according to Isid. *Etym.* 19.34 and Festus (Müller 1839 46). Thus Leo's proposal also permits a metatheatrical joke here: Why can Hanno hardly recognize his daughters? They're so tall because they're in *costume*! (cf. Henderson 1994 46).

1169–73   Because Milphio is expected to go inside after 1147–54, these lines are often considered an interpolation, though some see Plautus merely continuing the humor derived from "clever" Milphio being unable to recognize the truth in Hanno's statements. Maurice (2004 283) takes these lines as proof that Milphio doesn't figure out the truth of Hanno's relationship with the sisters until this moment, although it is also possible that Milphio is jealous of Hanno, who has replaced him in all of the scheming, and these lines are Milphio's final and unsuccessful attempt to say something important onstage and regain his role as trickster and tactitian. In either case, these lines reproduce the pattern of delayed and drawn-out exits seen elsewhere in the play (see Henderson 1994 47–48).

1173   **praestolabimur** From *praestōlor* (1-tr.) "to stand ready for, wait for."

1174–1210   Hanno and Agorastocles spy and eavesdrop on Adelphasium and Anterastilis here just as Milphio and Agorastocles had done at 210–330. There are further parallels too: both of the sisters' entrances are with the play's only true *cantica*, each scene shows a clash between male and female characters, and the eavesdropping Agorastocles is rebuked both times for his "lover's inanity" (Moore 2004 147). Franko (1996 439) observes that the "staging [of both scenes] must be nearly identical," which would highlight the repetition.

1174–86   Adelphasium and Anterastilis start up the music again with their entrance: *cantica multīs modīs* from 1174–86, then 1187–1303 are in multiple accompanied meters too (Moore 2004 146). While their first entrance *canticum* at 210–31 started in slow bacchiacs, here Adelphasium and Anterastilis enter to "jauntier anapests," because they're happy about successfully propitiating Venus (Moore 2004 155). Furthermore, just before her recognition as freeborn and her adoption of a new Carthaginian identity, Adelphasium is still "dominated by the values of their future profession": she apparently enjoyed the Aphrodisia (1178–79), and Anterastilis is also proud of how they surpassed the others (1182–83, cf. her boasts about their beauty at 1192–93). But at least Adelphasium says it was their high birth that gave them their good character (1186, cf. 1201–4). This conversation is probably Plautus' work (Fantham 2004 247–48).

1174 **operae pretium** "Reward for trouble," hence "worthwhile." **quoiuis** *cui uīs*. See note on 437. **qui . . . adiceret** Relative clause of characteristic (A&G 535).

1175 **uisere** *uīsō, uīsere, uīsī, uīsus* "to look at attentively, to go to see" is a frequentative verb built off of *uidēre*. The infinitive is occasionally used to show purpose in preclassical Latin (A&G 460c).

1176–78 Adelphasium associates *Venus* with *uenustus, -a, -um* and *uenustās, -tātis* too. Cf. 1180–81 and notes on 278, 623–24, 845–46. The cretics on 1177 "bring some extra dignity" to Adelphasium's reference to Venus (Moore 2004 155).

1176 **illi** The old form of *illīc* "there, in that place."

1178 **in suo quique loco sita** "Each in its own place." *quīque* doesn't match the feminine participle *sita* because it is an archaic ablative form with *suō locō* (de Melo 2010 90n29).

1179 **aras tus** From *āra, -ae* (f) "altar" and *tūs, tūris* (n) "incense." The manuscripts read *ārabius* and *āra(bus)*, but *complēbat* in 1179a requires a direct object. Most editors print *ārās tūs*, as proposed by Leo.

1181 **uenerant Venerem** Sound play. Cf. 278; *Pseud.* 585, 1205–6; *Rud.* 308 (Schmidt 1960 256).

1182a **pacisque potentes** With a genitive, *potēns, potentis* means "partaking of, having attained."

1183–84 **inridiculo / habitae** The phrase *inrīdiculō habēre* means "to make a laughingstock of"; *inrīdiculō* is an unassimilated dative of purpose from *irrīdiculum, -ī* (n) "laughing-stock."

1186   Anapests with a big string of spondees emphasize "the importance of *castitas*" along with the rest of Adelphasium's words (Moore 2004 155).

1187–90   Anapestic octonarii show Hanno's excitement. His speech even starts with eight short syllables in a row. "[S]ober spondees" in 1190, on the other hand, match up with his prayer for the sisters' freedom (Moore 2004 155).

1187   **ueiuimus ueitalem** Archaic spelling of *uīuimus uītālem*.

1188   **penes** Preposition + accusative: "with, in the power of."

1190–92   Hanno asks Jupiter to show him a reward for his piety, and Agorastocles mocks Hanno's appeal, boasting that Jupiter is under his control. Such a boast stands in stark contrast to the very strict religious beliefs in Plautus' time. Agorastocles' impiety is probably Plautus' innovation, rather than a part of Alexis' script (Segal 1968 30–31). For Moore (1998 109) the speech demonstrates the "difference between modern and ancient notions of piety, blasphemy, and reverence" because even though Agorastocles says something blasphemous, the play was probably performed at a religious festival as so many comedies were.

1190   **is** An archaic form of the dative *eīs/iīs*. **inuictae . . . pietati** Purpose clause: understand the word order *ut praemium inuictae pietātī esse sciam*. *inuictus, -a, -um* "could mean 'unconquerable' or 'unconquered' or, more strongly, 'unsurpassed, matchless, peerless' (as the *OLD* takes it)" (Franko 1996 438n19).

1191–2000   Moore (2004 155–56) describes how the meter here fits the context: anapestic lines and two cola reizana "bring closure to Agorastocles and Hanno's brief dialogue" on 1191–92. Next, plenty of dactyls in Anterastilis' iambic octonarii at 1192a–93 help the transition from the anapests into one iambic senarius at 1195 (perhaps the music stopped for this line as well, to show the end of her argument with her sister). Agorastocles responds favorably to her lecture in a heavily resolved iambic quaternarius (1196). Hanno then replies in another iambic senarius at 1196a (during which the *tibicen* could stop playing in order to emphasize a father-daughter parallel with 1195). Next, Hanno and Agorastocles display their excitement with many short syllables in their anapests and iambs at 1197–8a. At 1199 Agorastocles employs an iambic septenarius, "foreshadowing the meter of the reunion," before finishing with an anapestic quaternarius and a colon reizanum at 1200.

1191 **faxo** See note on 162.

1192a **uolup** Adverb: "agreeably," here used as a predicate. **cluet uictoria** *uictōriā* is ablative of cause (A&G 404) with *clueō, cluēre*, —, — "to be esteemed."

1195 **illi** An archaic form of the adverb *illic* "there, in that place." **os oblitum est** *oblinō, oblinere, oblēuī, oblitus* means "to smear on, dirty." Adelphasium seems to be saying that they were simply cleaner than the other prostitutes at the temple. But cf. *Curc.* 589, where the same phrase means "blinded, deceived" (Richlin 2005 269).

1197a **patruissume** Superlative adjective formed from the noun *patruus, -ī* (m) "father's brother," and thus meaning "uncliest." See note at 115.

1198 **Est . . . sapit** Adelphasium is the subject of both.

1198a–1200 After delivering the speech of a very Roman *pater pius* at 1187–90, Hanno next behaves much like a *senex lepidus* (or even a *seruus callidus*) by making comedic remarks about Adelphasium's intelligence here. Cf. the contrast between 1211–24 and 1255 (Starks 2000 175). This prevents the recognition scene from becoming too "sappy" (Franko 1996 438; cf. note on 1216–47).

1199 **Quae res?** "What business is this?" **abusa est** From *abūtor, abūtī, abūsus sum* "to use up, consume."

1201 **prognatae** *prōgnātus, -a, -um* "begotten, born, descended" is archaic even in Plautus' day. It carries tragic resonances here, though it can be used jokingly (de Melo 2011 340). The transition to trochaic septenarii here is fitting for a scene that moves the play toward its climactic recognition (Moore 2004 156).

1205 **uoluptati** Dative of purpose with iambic shortening in the second syllable: *uŏlŭptātī*.

1206 **ambabus** Feminine ablative plural form of *ambō, ambae, ambō* "both."

1207 **fore** Alternative form of *futūrās esse*, appearing here in an indirect statement dependent on *dīxerit* in the previous line.

1208   **faxint** Probably future indicative here (see notes on 162, 909). **qui** "How." The word order in this line should read *haud sciō quī ego spērem id, nisi dī aut parentēs faxint.*

1211–50   Hanno, overly tricky, acts as a potential benefactor to his daughters at 1211–24, a routine he finally drops (after charging the daughters with kidnapping from 1225–50) at 1255 (Starks 2000 175). "The testing of loved ones by those with concealed identity is a common literary motif, which is perhaps being parodied here" (Maurice 2004 285). Starks (2000 176) offers the following comparanda of cruel recognition scenes: Hom. *Od.* 24.280ff.; Soph. *El.* 1118ff.; Genesis 43–45.

1212–15   When Agorastocles presents the young women to their father, he uses suggestive language three times: *bene . . . facere* at 1212, *amīcus* at 1213, *amīcitia* at 1215. Adelphasium is thus completely convinced that Hanno is a client: see *malum* at 1214, *uoluptātī* at 1217 (Maurice 2004 285). Adelphasium also plays with *malus* and *malim* at 1214 (Brinkhoff 1935 137).

1213   **Qui** A connective relative setting up the optative subjunctive *siet*.

1215   **Hau precor** Understand *id* or *illud* as the direct object.

1216–47   Hanno and Agorastocles "play the buffoon" by withholding the good news from Adelphasium and Anterastilis. As Fantham (2004 248–49) observes, several aspects of this scene must also be Plautine inventions intended to bring humor to an otherwise "boring and predictable" recognition scene. First, although Agorastocles presents Hanno to the sisters as a "would-be benefactor" or customer, and Adelphasium's response is that of a *merētrix*, Agorastocles, astonishingly, is amazed at her modesty at 1219–21! Second, Hanno declares that he's suing the young women for kidnapping. Third, "the action passes rapidly beyond the moment of recognition to joking that the girls' fervent embrace will suffocate Hanno before he can pronounce the betrothal (1266–1268)" (Fantham 2004 248–49). The misunderstandings will only continue with Antamynides' entrance.

Alexis' *Karchedonios*, if it contained a conventional recognition, could not have featured four speakers onstage at once: Anterastilis may have been silent or Agorastocles may not have been involved, and Alexis only needed to include a short speech about successful omens (and maybe a prayer for a quick rescue from slavery) from one of the sisters before Hanno arrived to identify everyone properly. Fantham thus suspects that Hanno's trickery derives from Plautus and the sisters probably "behaved like self-respecting maidens" in Alexis' version.

Plautus thus enhanced "both the conventional and the disreputable elements in the girls' dialogue"; he could then appeal to older and/or female spectators with the moralizing elements and use the "voyeuristic exchanges" to appeal to the male spectators "for whom any callgirl of class would be a life-long inaccessible fantasy" (Fantham 2004 249).

1217–18   Though Leo athetized these lines, Franko (1996 439n20) argues that "their flirtatious and incestuous overtones [are] consistent with other parts of the play." He further notes that these lines require some sort of physical contact between the actors.

1219–20   More impiety from Agorastocles. See note on 1190–92.

1221–22   For the language of chastity cf. *Curc.* 698, 700; *Capt.* 992 (McCarthy 2000 200n69). Richlin (2005 269) notes that the string of virtues Agorastocles sees in Adelphasium "bears little resemblance to the ideas she expresses in her song."

1224–47   Hanno's threat of legal action for stealing his daughters depends upon Roman law, and therefore can't have been part of Alexis' play (Gratwick 1982 99–100). Plautus likely added this scene because it a) increases the audience's anticipation of the inevitable recognition scene, b) shows "more of Hanno's crafty nature," and c) shows how much Hanno knows about (Roman) law and what might happen at the end of the play (Franko 1996 440).

1224   Agorastocles acts like a director here, giving metatheatrical stage directions to Hanno (Maurice 2004 285). Concern about the audience's well-being recurs in Plautus (Slater 1985 90n37), but the preoccupation with excessively lengthening a play is an argument sometimes invoked in a play's final scene in order to unify the audience in consensus and prepare them for the rushed and/or arbitrary conclusion. Cf. *Cas.* 1006; *Merc.* 1007–8 (Petrone 1983 27–28). This line also helps to prove that at least a portion of the Roman audience sat while watching plays (Marshall 2006 78n218).

1226–73   Here the trochaic septenarii of the women and eavesdroppers ends, with one iambic octonarius before the meter switches to iambic septenarii, which continue through the reunion of Hanno and his daughters. Plautus often uses iambic septenarii during significant moments of his plays, perhaps because the meter slows down the play's pace without stopping it at each line as iambic senarii do (Moore 2004 156–57).

1229   **antestare** Singular present imperative of *antestor* (1-tr.) "to call as witness." From Hor. *Sat.* 1.9.77 and elsewhere we know that it was necessary to touch a person's ear to call them as a witness. Such an action probably occurs before 1231. **duce** Archaic spelling of the singular present imperative of *dūcere*.

1233   **illi** The old form of *illīc* "there."

1234-35   **adludiato ... dato ... obicito** A series of singular future imperatives. *adlūdiō, adlūdiāre, —, —* "to play, jest with" (later assimilated to *allūdiō*) is, according to Lewis and Short, a "less emphatic form" of *allūdō, allūdere, allūsī, allūsus. ōbiciō, ōbicere, ōbiēcī, ōbiectus* means "to throw to/ before; offer." **pro** should be understood as "instead of" here.

1236   **hanc canem** *canis, -is* (m/f) means "dog," but is also used metaphorically as "an angry to shameless person." Agorastocles is referring to Adelphasium here. **tibi** refers to Hanno.

1237   **ite si itis** The pairing of a second-person indicative with an imperative of the same verb is colloquial (Kay 2010 327). Cf. *Epid.* 196, *Per.* 659.

1239-40   Hanno, doing just what Milphio had described, uses a Roman procedure—*uindicātio aliēnae lībertātis*—to claim his daughters from slavery. See notes on 892 and 1244. Cf. the betrothal of a Carthaginian to an adopted Calydonian with "Roman legal terminology" at 1156-57 (Franko 1996 448n33).

1239   **filias meas celauistis ... me** *cēlō* (1-tr.) can take a single direct object: "to hide/conceal something," or with two accusatives can mean "to hide X from Y."

1241-42   **reperies ... perieres** The two verbs contain the same letters in a different order—they're anagrams (Brinkhoff 1935 147). **in** means "towards, for" here.

1244   Hanno, as a foreigner, can't act for himself legally, so needs Agorastocles as a *pātrōnus*. This should mean that Hanno can't prosecute Lycus himself (and thus Milphio's second trick is "impracticable"), but "Plautus subordinates the rules of Roman law to the demands of the drama and allows Hanno to act as if a Roman jurisconsult"—cf. 1225 (Franko 1996 447).

1251-56   As Franko (1996 440) notes, Hanno's *pietas* is emphasized here (there are four references to the gods in four lines) and at 1137 (by Giddenis), at 1187–90 (Hanno's own speech), and at 1277 (by Adelphasium, though likely a non-Plautine interpolation). The word *pietas* appears twenty-two times in Plautus (cf. *Asin.* 506, 509, 831; *Bac.* 1177; *Cas.* 383, 418; *Curc.* 639; *Pseud.* 122, 268, 291, 292, 293; *Rud.* 11, 29, 190, 1176; *Sti.* 8a; *Trin.* 281) but is applied to Hanno four times in just 140 lines in *Poenulus,* so is an important aspect of his character. Indeed, while Palaestra in *Rudens* and Alcumena in *Amphitruo* are similarly pious, Hanno shows more piety than any Greek male character (Franko 1996 441). For example, Hanno's prayers at 1163–64, 1187–90, 1274–76 are addressed to the Greco-Roman Jupiter; his prayers at 950–54, 1251–56, and 1274–76 are to nonspecific *dī* and *deae*—not Phoenician deities; and his first words in Latin are references to gods at 967 and 988 (Franko 1996 441n23). Even the *Menaechmi,* Plautus' other play about a long search for a lost relative, doesn't contain the terms *pietas* or *pius* (Franko 1996 442).

1253   **danunt** An archaic form of *dant.* **matri** The only mention of Hanno's wife in the play (Richlin 2005 269).

1256   **meae** undergoes synizesis, then the long syllable elides with *estis.* Cf. 860, 1070. **filiae et** Though not metrically necessary, a hiatus between these two words, especially if accompanied by a pause in the music, would emphasize "the moment when Hanno reveals the truth to his daughters" in this line (Moore 2004 157).

1257   **huiusce** Hanno is referring to himself. Cf. 1271.

1262-79   This reunion scene is "constantly undercut by Agorastocles' extravagant protestations of love, and his attempts to kiss his beloved, which detract from the potential seriousness of a reunion scene that is surely more farcical and funny than emotionally charged." Line 1279 in particular undercuts both Agorastocles' claims to passion and his feelings for Hanno, although it is usually considered an interpolation (Maurice 2004 285–86).

1264   **qui** The old ablative of *qui, quae, quod* again, fossilized as an adverb meaning "whereby, how." Understand the word order as *dīcam quī magis crēdātis,* where the initial verb introduces an indirect question.

1265   **prima** The MSS read *prīmum*, but Bentley proposed this emendation, which has been widely adopted.

1268   **desponderit** Hanno has agreed to betroth Adelphasium to Agorastocles already, at 1157, so presumably Agorastocles refers here to a formal ceremony making the engagement official.

1269   **neruom bracchialem** There's a weak pun in the juxtaposition of *bracchiālis, -e* "of the arm," and *neruus, -ī* (m), which normally means "sinew," but here adopts the less common meaning "fetter, prison" (Schmidt 1960 185). Thus Plautus only slightly clarifies the meaning of the noun. Furthermore, this "high-flown and bombastic language" is rather ridiculous (Maurice 2004 285).

1271–73   Agorastocles' overview of the reunion closes the section of iambic septenarii (Moore 2004 157). **O Apella, o Zeuxis** Apelles and Zeuxis were two famous Greek painters of the fourth and fifth centuries BCE and considered "classic" during Plautus's time (Richlin 2005 269). Cf. *Epid.* 626 (Fraenkel 2007 12–13). **numero** is used adverbially: "too soon," which sets up the result clause *hōc exemplō ut [nōn] pingerētis?* **nil moror** See note at 492.

1274–79   The change to trochaic septenarii here emphasizes the completion of the recognition and indicates that the next plot developments can now proceed. Trochaic septenarii continue until 1304, when Antamynides stops the musical accompaniment by crossing the stage to address the other characters (Moore 2004 157).

1276   As at 1137–40, Hanno's piety is emphasized here. It seems genuine, even if the timing of his prayers (and his transitions to them) is rather exaggerated or funny (Starks 2000 176).

1277–79   1277 is usually thought to be non-Plautine because it repeats 1137. 1278–79 are usually thought to be non-Plautine because Hanno had not yet promised any dowry for Adelphasium (Maurach 1988 169–70).

1279   **dotis** Partitive genitive of *dōs, dōtis* (f) "dowry, gift" with *quid*. *prōmīseris* is perfect subjunctive by attraction after *habeās*—a change in construction after Agorastocles' earlier indirect statement from 1278–79.

1280–1422   It is difficult to imagine the final scenes of the play with only three speakers (as would be required by any Greek New Comedy), so Plautus has probably adapted the *Karchedonios* considerably (Barsby 2004 107).

Perhaps Anterastilis left early or didn't speak in Alexis' version, but it's quite probable that Plautus added the entire scene with Agorastocles, both sisters, Hanno, and Antamynides simultaneously appearing onstage and speaking (1280–1337) (Barsby 2004 108).

1280 **ultus fuero** Alternate form of *ultus erō*, from *ulciscor, ulciscī, ultus sum* "to take vengeance on, punish."

1281 **habento** Third-person plural future active imperative. Plautus employs several different phrases that mean "to make fun of" or something similar: *lūdere aliquem, lūdificāre/ī aliquem, lūdōs facere aliquem, lūdībriō/ lūdificātuī habēre aliquem* (Schmidt 1960 395). Cf. 1183–83a. **scurrae** seems to mean merely "jesters, parasites" here, but see the note at 611–12. **ludificatui** is a dative of purpose.

1283 **pro atriensi** *prō* here means "in the place of." An *ātriensis, ātriensis* (m) was a "steward," like a head butler.

1284 **edim** See note on 867.

1286 **aere militari** *aes, aeris* (n) is "bronze" and therefore "wages, pay." *mīlitāris, -e* "of a soldier" is used here to indicate the source of the wages. **tetigero** The phrase *tangere aliquem aliquā rē* means "to cheat someone out of something." Cf. *Per.* 634; *Pseud.* 1308–8a (Schmidt 1960 397). See Brotherton (1926 78–81) on the development of deceptive connotations for *tangere*. **lenunculum** Accusative singular diminutive of *lēno*. Cf. 471.

1287 **nanctus est** From *nanciscor, nanciscī, nanctus sum* "to obtain." The subject is the pimp. **mina** A *mina, -ae* (f) was the weight of one hundred Attic drachmas in silver, and represented 1/60 of a talent. A drachma was worth six obols. The payment for service as a juror in Athens or for attendance at the Athenian assembly was three obols (Ar. *Vesp.* 684), while the daily wage for soldiers and sailors in Athens seems to have been one drachma in the fourth century BCE (Loomis 1998 48–49, 54). The current federal minimum wage ($7.25/hour) nets modern employees $58 each day before taxes, while the lowest-ranking soldiers in the United States military earn roughly $51 each day (http://www.dfas.mil/dam/jcr:7061e0ca-a436-42f9-aa30-1a93b6454aa3/2015MilitaryPayChart.pdf). If one drachma is the wage equivalent of $55, then one *mina* is approximately $550.

1288   **irato** It is not clear why Antamynides would wish to punish Anterastilis, unless he connects her failure to return to Lycus' house before lunch to Lycus' failure to feed him. While his violent reaction seems reprehensible to the modern reader, violence was a frequent theme on the comic stage and would not have been out of character for a mercenary. Cf. *Capt.* 195–200a, 658–59; *Truc.* 775–840; Ter. *Eun.* 771–816. On the other hand, Antamynides is also inconsistent: he threatens to punish Hanno, not Anterastilis, at 1302.

1289–91   These lines are Plautine additions, since Plautus often describes slave punishments in great detail and it was the Romans who used *Aegyptīnī* as slaves at their games. See also *Epid.* 18; *Pseud.* 145, 545 (Fraenkel 2007 13). **merulea** *meruleus, -a, um* "blue-black" is formed from *merula, -ae* (f) "blackbird." **Aegyptini** According to Festus (Müller 1839 28), the term actually refers to Ethiopians, who were probably acquired from Carthaginian slave traders (Gsell 1924 140, cited at Palmer 1997 42n58). **cortinam** A *cortīna, -ae* (f) is a large cauldron, either filled with water for the racehorses (de Melo 2012 157n65) or used as the prize for the victor of the chariot race. **ludis** Perhaps a nod to the performance context of the *lūdī Apollinārēs*—see section 1ci of the the introduction for more on those games. **circum** From *circus, -ī* (m) "circus, Circus Maximus" an oval track for racing horses.

1292   **arte** Adverb meaning "closely, tightly" from *artus, -a, -um.* **uoluptas** Anterastilis addresses Hanno with a term of endearment previously used on 385 to express Agorastocles' feelings toward his beloved Adelphasium (cf. its use at *Truc.* 353 by a prostitute toward a client). It is a reminder of the sensualist-Carthaginian and incest themes established in the prologue—cf. 108.

1295   **hoc** The preceding hiatus emphasizes this ablative of means, which refers to the *pignus* from 1285. We can also guess some of the stage directions: the hiatus probably also preceded—and thus emphasized—Antamynides' display of or gesture toward the *pignus* (Maurach 1988 171).

1296–1318   These lines closely parallel Men. *Mis.* 210–29. In Menander's comedy "Demeas meets and embraces his newly found daughter, whereupon the slave of the girl's lover enters, sees them clasped together, and similarly concludes that this 'grey-haired old man of sixty' (620) is misbehaving" (Arnott 2004 68–69). Cf. note on 1099–1173.

1297   **conduplicationis . . . congeminatio** Partitive genitive of the very rare term *condūplicātio, condūplicātiōnis* (f) "doubling," a synonym of the (also rare) *congeminātio, congeminātiōnis* (f).

1298–1318   The character of the confused soldier provides Plautus with the opportunity to include some racist abuse in his comedy, despite the generally positive portrayal of Hanno. The soldier's insults "are among the most savage in all Plautus," and the focus on Hanno's appearance is racist— most pimps or slaves are instead mocked for their profession or status (Franko 1996 445). Similarly, Antamynides mentions race or country of origin at 1303, 1304, 1314, 1410, and perhaps 1290–91 (Franko 1996 445). Hanno only baits Antamynides in response (see note on 1308–9), instead of answering straightforwardly, thus deceptively contributing to the humor of the play. On the other hand, by refusing to be provoked by the insults Hanno (and Plautus) upends the expectations of any spectators anticipating a caricature of a Carthaginian in the play. Thus Plautus stresses Hanno's aristocratic birth in line 60, and Hanno responds mildly to Antamynides here and to Milphio's bad "translating" at 990–1028 (Blume 2004 210–11).

1298   **puer cauponius** The phrase means "waiter, slave at an inn." Richlin (2005 270) observes, "there is a hint here of sexual use" since "[i]nns were disreputable places to work; waitresses at inns were, in law, the equivalent of prostitutes."

1301   **puellam** The *ue* undergoes synizesis (Maurach 1988 171). **baiolum** Alternate spelling of *bāiulus, -ī* (m) "porter." Hanno "is called a baggage carrier as a general insult to his status and because both girls cling to him like pieces of luggage" (de Melo 2012 158n66).

1302   **carnufici** Cf. 369; *Per.* 547 (Richlin 2005 270).

1303   **mulierosum** The adjective *mulierōsus, -a, -um* means something like "fond of women," but given the connection elsewhere in Latin literature between effeminacy and unbelted tunics (cf. 1008, *dēmissīciīs* later on 1303) it could pick up a hint of "effeminate" as well, especially since Antamynides later implies that Hanno is not very masculine (1311). **demissiciis** *dēmissīcius, -a, -um* means "long, flowing."

1304–97   Unaccompanied iambic senarii here: the music stops at 1304, after Antamynides has entered, delivered two speeches, and decided to address the other characters onstage (Moore 2004 149). The soldier, like the

pimp, is "dissociated from music" in general, since music starts after his exit
at 503 as well, but it is unusual for Plautus to stop and start the music at 1304
and 1398 without any character's entrance or exit (Moore 2004 149, 151).
Every other Plautine comedy ends with an accompanied meter, and all but
the *Pseudolus* and *Stichus* also end in trochaic septenarii, which is a strong
argument that lines 1338–71 are not Plautus' work (Moore 2012 265–66).

1304-6   **hanc amatricem Africam** An *amātrix, amātrīcis* (f) is a "lover,
sweetheart, mistress," although the word often carries a negative connotation.
Richlin (2005 270) and Starks (2000 178) read Hanno, not Anterastilis, as
both the *amātrīcem* of 1304 and the *mulier* of 1305 due to Hanno's effeminate,
unbelted garb. However, there is no reason to assume that lines 1304–5 must
be directed to Hanno just because 1306 clearly is. Both *amātrīcem* and *mulier*
could refer to Anterastilis (or to both father and daughter), and Antamynides
could (re)focus his anger on Hanno between 1305 and 1306.

1308-9   Just as Hanno withholds his identity from his daughters in
order to tease them, here he provokes Antamynides into a tirade by failing
to explain his reasons for hugging Anterastilis. As a student notes, it's good
comedy, but can also contribute to Hanno's portrayal as deceitful.

1308   **hanc** acts as the direct object of the noun *tactio, -ōnis* (f) "touching,
touch."

1309-14   The blustery Antamynides pours forth a flood of epithets here,
none of which appear elsewhere in Latin literature (Schmidt 1960 372).
As such, the meaning of some phrases is still debated. However, the use of
asyndeton as at 1312–14 is common in later Greek comedy: cf. Alexis frr. 96
K-A, 113 K-A (Arnott 2004 83). The insults hurled at Hanno by Antamynides
include the following: **ligula** See note on 1014. As a diminutive it carried a
pejorative sense, although its precise meaning here is uncertain. The tongue's
association with speech suggests "verbose, talkative" here (Schmidt 1960
373), but there's also a possibility that the soldier is inferring that Hanno
performs what the Romans considered "the demeaningly unmasculine act
of *cunnilingus*" (Starks 2000 178–79). Cf. note at 63, and other references to
tongues at 112, 984, 1014, 1034, 1035 (Fontaine 2010 204–5). **hallex** Either
hallex, hallicis (m) "big toe," following Isidore of Seville, or *hāllex, hāllēcis*
(m/f) the "sediment/dregs of fish sauce (*garum*)." Both *hāllex* and *garum*
were popular with the Romans as condiments, and *hāllex* apparently "had
culinary uses different from the upper portion"; cf. *Per.* 107; Plin. *HN* 31.95
(Palmer 1997 37). It is possible that the term derives from Greek while the

sauce itself came to Rome from the Phoenicians, who produced a lot of fish sauce at Gades, in Spain (Palmer 1997 39). **uiri** Appositive genitive with *hāllex/hallex*. **contrectare** See note on 698. **mares** Nominative plural from *mās, maris* (m) "male, masculine." Used in contrast to the effeminacy implied by *tunicīs dēmissīciīs* on 1303 and *cinaedum* on 1318. **deglupta mena**. The *mēna/maena, -ae* (f) is a "sprat," a small fish, like an anchovy or sardine, often eaten by the poor. *dēglūbō, dēglūbere, dēglūpsī, dēglūptus* means "to strip the skin off, flay," though it has sexual connotations as well. The phrase continues the "previous suggestion of fishy odor [from *hāllex*] and insignificance, but more importantly serves as an obscene allusion to Phoenician/Carthaginian circumcision, which was viewed as perverted by many Greeks and Romans" (Starks 2000 179—cf. Plin. *HN* 31.95 on Jewish circumcision). In addition, the fish may also be mentioned as acceptable food for Carthaginians, or as the basis of their *hāllex* (Palmer 1997 37). **sarrapis sementium** This phrase—and even whether the words are related—is unclear. We can take the *sarrapis* as "a Persian cloak, with purple stripes" (Starks 2000 179). The term may pun on *Sarrānus, -a, -um* "of Sarra (Tyre)" the term used for Tyrian Phoenicians and Carthaginians, and especially their purple dye. *sēmentium* on the other hand may be the genitive plural of *sēmentis, sēmentis* (f) "a seeding, sowing; seed-time." The term suggests "lowness and dirtiness" to Starks (2000 179). De Melo (2012 159n70) translates the term as the vocative of "mantle," given that it appears between two other references to clothing. Alternatively, Palmer (1997 37) reads *sēmentium* as a *hapax legomenon*, a neuter noun meaning "seed bed," or something similar—cf. *sēmentis* at Cato *Agr.* 17.2, 27. He notes that if the phrase is meant to be insulting, then *sarrapis* could be a reference to *serapias, serapiadis*, "an orchid with double bulb 'testicles' made into a beverage and then diluted with goat's milk and drunk in order to induce lust. In a word, an aphrodisiac." **manstruca** The *manstruc(t)a, -ae* (f) is the "fleece of a Sardinian (and Corsican) wild goat-like sheep. Sards wore it as a fleece and so made it synonymous with primitive garb. Whether or not the word is of Phoenician origin, *manstrucae* would have been a natural article in trade for Carthaginian cargoes because the Carthaginians controlled Sardinia for centuries down to 238 and had probably traded pelts" (Palmer 1997 37–38). As a result of Carthaginian control of Sardinia, the Romans considered the island's inhabitants to be ethnically Punic, so the reference therefore implies that "Hanno may look fancy and exotic, but to Antamynides he's just a cheap, smelly farmer's coat" (Starks 2000 179). **halagora, sampsa** The manuscripts read *halagorasampsa* here, but the interpretation of the letters is much debated. Palmer and de Melo read *halagora* "salt market," and *sampsa* "olive pulp conserve." It seems best to adopt this reading here, given that it does make sense in context: the salt is related to the conservation of fish in *garum/hāllex* form (Palmer 1997 37–38). Alternatively, Starks (2000 179–80) reads *halagorasama* and interprets it as a *hapax legomenon* for "sea-going merchandise" or "imported goods." Such, he says, would be appropriate for the stereotyped connection between Carthaginians and the sea trade.

plenior / ali ulpicique quam Romani remiges *ālium, -(i)ī* (n) is "garlic," while *ulpicum, -ī* (n) is a "leek" or "Phoenician garlic," a larger variety—cf. Columella *Rust.* 11.3.20 (de Melo 2012 159n71). Gowers (1993 62) labels garlic a food for the poor. Here "the Greek soldier connects Carthaginians and Romans, with the Carthaginian being only just worse. Plautus proves with this line that he is playing on ethnic and class stereotyping by taking a little jab at Rome from the 'Greek' stage" (Starks 2000 180). The reference to Roman rowers is a bold idea—undoubtedly from Plautus—that's funny because of its newness and improbability (Schmidt 1960 373). It's the only place Plautus uses the adjective *Rōmānus, -a, -um* rather than *barbarus, -a, -um*.

1317   tympanum The "hand drum" that Cybele's castrated priests played. It thus suggests sexual passivity—cf. 1318 (Richlin 2005 270).

1318   te cinaedum esse arbitror The only line from Plautus' play with a clear precedent in a fragment certainly known to be from Alexis' *Karchedonios*: βάκηλος εἶ "you are womanish"—fr. 105 K-A (Arnott 2004 62). The term *cinaedus, -ī* (m) starts out with the meaning "lascivious dancer," and by Plautus' time (cf. *Asin.* 627–28) has developed the sense "effeminate male" or "one who plays the passive role in sex" because "a *cinaedus* is a man who fails to live up to traditional standards of masculine comportment" (Williams 2010 193). It is certainly meant as an insulting term from Antamynides, who represents Roman masculinity (Williams 2010 194, 385n84).

1319–21   fustis Accusative plural of *fustis, fustis* (m) "cudgel." It is likely that the club-wielding slaves called by Agorastocles never appear. As Marshall (2006 112–13) observes, there are already six actors onstage, so additional slaves would create a scene larger than any other in Plautus. Furthermore, Antamynides hastily explains away his insults.

1322–25   Here the soldier's "arguments about everyone else's effeminacy are returned on him, when he is ultimately cowed by the girl he wanted and begs pardon from Hanno" (Starks 2000 180). Indeed, nobody utters another ethnic slur about any Carthaginian for the remainder of the play—the worst epithet uttered is Antamynides' reference to Hanno as *Poenus* at 1410. The embarrassment and downfall of the pimp and the soldier thus suggest to the audience that their stereotypes about the Carthaginian characters are wrong;

Hanno in particular is portrayed more positively than the soldier and the pimp (Starks 2000 181).

1325 **fratris** Again, short for *frātris pātruēlis*—see 952.

1326 **uolup** Adverb: "agreeably, satisfactorily."

1328 **uirtute** Does Antamynides use this word sincerely or ironically? He was just verbally abusing Hanno and Anterastilis, while threatening physical violence to Anterastilis as well. On the other hand, Anterastilis accepts Antamynides' apology immediately, so perhaps his anger arose out of jealousy that a new customer (Hanno) has embraced Anterastilis while the soldier himself never managed to do so.

1330 **eccum** See the note on 203. Here the first syllable must scan as short: *ĕccum* (Angelo Mercado *per litterās*).

1332 **commodus** A very common adjective in the *Poenulus, commodus, -a, -um* means "proper; opportune." Here it's used to make a metatheatrical remark on the convenient timing of a character's entrance. Cf. 401; *Mil.* 1198; *Trin.* 400; Ter. *And.* 475, 844, 977a.

1333–35 Identical to 1382–84. Their appearance here is generally thought to be an interpolation carried back from the ending. **Vtrumuis** A compound of *uter, utra, utrum* "which of two" and *uīs* "you wish." See note on 831.

1337 The meaning of this line is unclear, but the grammar seems to be as follows: **iniuriarum** Partitive genitive with *satius est.* **multo** Ablative of degree of difference. **induci** Present passive infinitive; Lycus is the unstated subject. *indūcō, indūcere, indūxī, inductus* can mean "to bring to court," so perhaps the joke is just one of degree: instead of snatching him off to court, as Agorastocles suggests (if we omit lines 1333–35), Hanno says it's quite enough that he be led there, i.e., taken more gently. At lines 1342 and 1343 Hanno and Agorastocles do call Lycus to court.

1342–43 **eamus in ius … In ius te uoco** These lines echo the *ius* threatened at the end of the first trick, while lines 1344–46 employ "language deliberately reminiscent of Milphio's earlier instructions to Hanno" at 1100–1 (Maurice 2004 287). Agorastocles' hortatory command for the pimp

to accompany him to court at 1342 seems to contradict his deferral of his first
suit against Lycus at 800 and 807. Since it is still the Aphrodisia and the courts
are still closed, these reminders of the pimp's legal obligations (and those of
Antamynides at 1349) should be taken as promises of future lawsuits, not
demands for the pimp's immediate presence in court.

1347   **miratus fui** See note on line 40.

1350   **prandio** Lycus deliberately misinterprets *iūs* as "sauce, broth," not
"law," when speaking with Antamynides. Cf. note at 586 (Mendelsohn 1907
131).

1351–53   **Duplum** The phrase *opus est* "there is need of" can also take the
nominative for the needed item. That Lycus must pay twice Collybiscus' value
as a penalty for theft is a remnant of the Alexis' comedy and the Athenian
law code underlying it: a double-value fine was the normal punishment for
any theft in Athenian court—cf. Dem. 24.105, 24.114; Din. 1.60; [Arist.] *Pr.*
29.14 (Arnott 2004 78–79). Roman law, on the other hand, made the thief a
debt slave (*addīctus*) to his victim (cf. 564). **Sume hinc quid lubet** Plautus
especially likes to use repetition in *cantica* passages like this one. Here the
repetition shows Lycus' resignation after losing both the sisters and all of his
possessions (Schmidt 1960 53).

1352   **suppliciis multis** Understand *prō* with these ablatives, just as with
prō furtō in 1351. *Opus est* must also be supplied (as in 1351 as well).

1354   **collo** Lycus may continue the joke about hanging (at 1341), or he
may keep his money in a pouch around his neck (cf. *Per.* 312) and be pointing
to his neck here (Richlin 2005 270).

1355–1422   The end of the *Poenulus* is, frankly, a mess. The manuscripts
provide us with at least two possible endings and other interpolated lines, so
making sense of the end of the play requires some drastic cutting. (Zwierlein
[1990 59] summarizes nineteenth- and early twentieth-century judgments
regarding the end of the *Poenulus*.) First, nearly all scholars agree that 1355–
71 cannot be Plautus' original ending (even though it's easiest to imagine
as Alexis' version thereof—Barsby 2004 109) because it employs iambic
senarii, and every other Roman comedy ends with trochaic septenarii or
"polymetric celebration" in the case of *Pseudolus* and *Stichus* (Moore 2012
265). Lines 1355–71, perhaps written for a later revival production, seem to
shorten the real ending (1398–1422) since the pimp releases the sisters and
repays the soldier (de Melo 2012 9), and the "moral universe of this ending

is simple: the pimp is a villain who gets his just deserts," which is why he says no praetor is necessary at 1361 (Slater 1992 144). Maurach (1988 175, 213) conjectures that neither 1338–71 nor 1372–97 is Plautine, while 1398–1422 might be the original ending of both the *Karchedonios* and the *Poenulus*. Zwierlein (1990 224–25) marks 1322–37, 1342–71, 1385–86, 1398–1401, and 1406 as spurious, which does create a workable script, even if his solution is more complex than those accepting or rejecting entire scenes. Richlin (2005 247) notes that lines 1372–1422 work as a whole to end the play, but require omitting all of 1322–71. Such an approach would require Lycus to wander onstage without being noticed—an unparalleled event for a pimp in Roman comedy (Lowe 1990 287). The best solution is that of de Melo (2012 9), who brackets both 1355–71 and 1372–97 as non-Plautine. Omitting lines 1355–97 results in Antamynides repeating his demand for a *mina* of silver from Lycus, but the repetition can be explained by the soldier's addition of a threat of shackles after the pimp seems to joke in response to his first demand for money.

1355–71   These lines are considered spurious for metrical reasons (see note on 1355–1422 above).

1358   **ausim** Archaic, sigmatic present subjunctive of *audeō, audēre, ausus sum* "to dare."

1359   **arrabonem hoc** *arrabo* is the alternate spelling of *arrhabo, arrhabōnis* (m) "security, pledge." *hoc*, in apposition to *arrabōnem*, refers to something purloined from the house that the soldier must be showing to Lycus at that moment.

1360   **haud multo post** Agorastocles plays with the tense of the common exclamation *periī*.

1362   **simplum** From *simplum, -ī* (n) "the simple sum" (as opposed to double or triple an amount).

1363   **conradi** An unassimilated form of the colloquial verb *corrādō, corrādere, corrāsī, corrāsus* "to scrape together" (Reinhardt 2010 219).

1365   **lignea in custodia** According to early Roman law, debtors could be given as slaves to their creditors. *ligneus, -a, um* "wooden," refers to the *cōdex, cōdicis* (m) "tree stump" to which slaves were chained to prevent them from escaping—cf. 1153 (Richlin 2005 271).

1367   **malo et nostro bono** Datives of purpose.

1368–71   Although they're spurious, these lines nod to the importance of pimps in Plautine comedy—cf. *Per.* 858 (Marshall 2006 140).

1370   **condimentum** See Gowers (1993 65) on food metaphors in Plautus. **fabulae** Perhaps the same pun on *fābula* "story, play" and *fabālis* "beany" as in line 8 (Brinkhoff 1935 81).

1372–97   In atypical iambic senarii (see note on 1355–1422), the content of these lines "overlaps" with 1398–1422 (de Melo 2012 9) so these should be therefore considered spurious as well.

1376–81   **perii . . . perierunt . . . perditus . . . periere . . . periisti** Punning with forms of *perīre* and *perdere* in these lines: the pimp is portrayed as a "(morally) lost" man (Brinkhoff 1935 110).

1381   **qui** Archaic form of the ablative (here ablative of means), singular for plural. **tute** *tū* with the emphatic suffix *-te* is another feature of colloquial Latin.

1386   **norunt** A syncopated form of *nōuērunt* from *noscō, noscere, nōuī, nōtus* "to learn."

1387   **per . . . tua . . . genua** Beseeching someone while touching their knees was a long-standing tradition in the ancient Mediterranean world. Examples can be found in Homer (e.g., *Il.* 24.477; *Od.* 7.139), and even the Romans set their prayers, inscribed on wax tablets, on the knees of the statues of the gods from whom they sought help—cf. Juv. 10.55 (Miller 2005 308).

1393   **meae <eae> . . . non sunt** Giddenis' fate is not clear. She entered Agorastocles' house at 1266, but he may have no legal right to her, depending on whether or not she is free-born. Since Carthaginians were well-known as slave traders, it is likely that she and her son are slaves rather than free-born servants. **prosum** Alternate spelling of *prorsum* "straight forward; absolutely."

1398–1422   Trochaic septenarii begin at 1398, which suggests that the lines are Plautus' work (de Melo 2012 9). Because "the main business of the play is finished, and all that remains are the play's last decisions," the trochaic septenarii are both expected and "especially appropriate, as the play rushes to its conclusion in an unusually rapid, almost incoherent, manner" (Moore

2004 146, 157). Six actors—likely the entire troupe—are onstage here, which allows the play's final scene to serve as a kind of "curtain call," as so often in Plautus (Marshall 2006 112). Regardless of its authorship, Slater (1992 145) believes this ending is more palatable to modern readers (and perhaps to many Romans too). Here Hanno, Antamynides, and Agorastocles all forgive Lycus. Hanno realizes he'll be "at a disadvantage as a foreigner" if he tries to get revenge through the courts (1403–4), and thus the "play ends in a spirit of reconciliation" because of the recognition and impending marriage. This parallels the movement in the prologue from a Saturnalian or inverted world to normal morality, and in the play from the first trick to the recognition (Slater 1992 145).

1398   **inter negotium** *inter* can mean "during, in the midst of." If the last truly Plautine line was 1354, then Lycus may be miming hanging himself—that's his current "business." Cf. *Sti.* 638–40.

1400   **faxint** Present subjunctive in an optative use. See note at 909.

1401   **tris** Accusative plural of *trēs, tria.*

1403   **litis** Accusative plural of *līs, lītis* (m) "quarrel; lawsuit."

1408   **experiar** *experior, experīrī, expertus sum* means "to try, experience," and in legal contexts "to test by law, go to court." Here Hanno removes the threat of a lawsuit regarding his daughters.

1409   **ex nervo . . . in carcerem** A surprise joke from Agorastocles, who replaces one form of imprisonment with another instead of declaring the pimp free (Schmidt 1960 312). **compingare** Second-person singular present passive subjunctive of *compingō, compingere, compēgī, compactus* "to lock up" in the apodosis of a future less vivid condition.

1415–17   Anterastilis' fate is not specified. Since the differing social positions of Anterastilis and Antamynides meant they couldn't have married at the end of Alexis' play, perhaps Alexis' comedy ended with the Carthaginian promising to betroth his younger daughter to someone from an important Carthaginian family, similar to the announcement at Men. *Pk.* 1024–26. Minor characters' love stories are not always explicitly wrapped up (with weddings or betrothals) in Menander either—cf. *Sam., Epit.* (Arnott 2004 84–85).

1415   **nil moror** See note at 492. **tibicinam** A *tībīcina, -ae* (f) is a "piper girl." These musicians, often joined by prostitutes, attended drinking parties (Richlin 2005 271). The joke about the *tībīcina* here may represent a "subtle acknowledgement of the restricted role of music in this play" (Moore 2004 157).

1416   Antamynides does not want a *tībīcina* because he does not know which is bigger, her chest or cheeks. This joke suggests that both large cheeks and breasts are unattractive, which in turn suggests that female characters in Roman comedy would have large breasts (Marshall 2006 65). Cf. *Aul.* 332 for an overweight piper (Marshall 2006 214n48) and Ter. *Haut.* 1061–62 for the rejection of a potential wife on aesthetic grounds (Fraenkel 2007 369n117).

1419-20   Thus all of the Carthaginian characters will leave Calydon and return to Carthage. This is a happy turn of events for them, but a student notes that this departure also represents the removal of these foreign elements from Calydon, which as the site of the play's performance serves as a stand-in for Rome. The ending may therefore set the Roman spectators' minds at ease.

1420   **Vbi** Iambic shortening occurs.

1421   **auctionem facio** "I hold an auction." According to Lewis and Short, "[a]uctions were held either in an open place, or in particular rooms or halls, called atria auctionaria (v. auctionarius), or simply atria (Juv. 7, 7). There was a spear (hasta) set up therein, as the legal sign of the sale, like our red flag; the price was called out by a crier (praeco), and the article sold was adjudged to the highest bidder by the magistrate who was present. A money-broker (argentarius) was also present to note down the price and receive the money or security for it." Plautus' *Menaechmi* also ends with plans for an auction, as another long-lost relative decides to give up his current life and return to his birthplace.

1422   **plaudite** signifies the end of the play. Plautus ends every comedy with a request for applause, sometimes from the troupe as a whole (*grex, caterua*) and sometimes from an individual character, who may have removed his mask to mark the end of the stage world and parallel the prologue's form and function (Marshall 2006 196). Moore notes that at least one manuscript contains a symbol before *plaudite* that may indicate a change of speaker here. He also believes that we are missing the original ending to the play (Moore 2012 74n21, 265n18). The imperative plural of *plaudere* appears also at *Amph.*

1146; *Curc.* 729; *Epid.* 733; *Men.* 1162; *Mil.* 1437; *Per.* 858; *Sti.* 775; *Trin.* 1189; *Truc.* 968. Plautus' three longest plays, however, feature the shortest requests for applause and the quickest transition out of character: *Poen.* 1422—*plaudīte*; *Mil.* 1437—*plaudīte*; *Rud.* 1423—*plausum date* (Marshall 2006 196).

Works Cited

Editions

de Melo, W., ed. and trans. 2012. *Plautus: The Little Carthaginian, Pseudolus, The Rope.* Cambridge, MA: Harvard UP.

Kassel, R. and Austin, C., eds. 1983–2001. *Poetae Comici Graeci.* 8 vols. Berlin: De Gruyter.

Leo, F., ed. 1906. *Plauti Comoediae.* 2 vols. Berlin: Weidmann.

Lindsay, W., ed. 1903. *Nonii Marcelli De Compendiosa Doctrina Libros XX.* Vol. 1. Leipzig: Teubner.

Lindsay, W., ed. 1904–5. *T. Macci Plauti Comoediae.* 2 vols. Oxford: Oxford UP.

Mariotti, S. 1966. *Il Bellum Poenicum e l'arte di Nevio. Saggio con edizione dei frammenti del Bellum Poenicum.* 2nd ed. Rome: Signorelli.

Müller, K., ed. 1839. *Sexti Pompei Festi De Verborum Significatione Quae Supersunt, Cum Pauli Epitome.* Leipzig: Weidmann.

Questa, C., ed. 1995. *Titi Macci Plauti Cantica.* Ludus Philologiae 5. Urbino: QuattroVenti.

Ribbeck, O., ed. 1898. *Scaenicae Romanorum Poesis Fragmenta.* 2 vols. Leipzig: Teubner.

Ritschl, F. 1879. *Opuscula Philologica.* Vol. 5. Leipzig: Teubner.

Ritschl, F. et al., eds. 1881. *T. Macci Plauti Comoediae.* Vol. 2. Fasc. 5. Leipzig: Teubner.

Sandbach, F. 1990. *Menandri Reliquiae Selectae.* Oxford: Oxford UP.

Zwierlein, O. 1990. *Zur Kritik und Exegese des Plautus. I: Poenulus und Curculio.* Stuttgart: Steiner.

Secondary Scholarship

Abel, L. 1963. *Metatheatre: A New View of Dramatic Form.* New York: Hill and Wang.

Adams, J. 1983. "Words for 'Prostitute' in Latin." *Rheinisches Museum* 126: 321–58.

Adams, J. 1984. "Female Speech in Latin Comedy." *Antichthon* 18: 43–77.

Adams, J. 2003. *Bilingualism and the Latin Language*. Cambridge: Cambridge UP.

Allen, W. and Greenough, J. 2006. *New Latin Grammar*. Mineola, NY: Dover. Unabridged reprint of 1903 edition, Boston: Ginn and Company.

Arnott, W. G. 2004. "Alexis, Greek New Comedy and Plautus' *Poenulus*." In T. Baier, ed. *Studien zu Plautus' Poenulus*. ScriptOralia 127. Tübingen: Gunter Narr. 61–91.

Augoustakis, A., ed. 2009. *Plautus: Mercator*. Bryn Mawr, PA: Bryn Mawr Commentaries.

Babič, M. 2003. "Fremdsprachliches in Plautus' *Poenulus*." In R. Oniga, ed. *Il pluralinguismo nella tradizione letteraria latina*. Roma: Il Calamo. 18–30.

Barsby, J., ed. 1999. *Terence: Eunuchus*. Cambridge: Cambridge UP.

Barsby, J. 2001. "Improvvisazione, Metateatro, Deconstruzione: Approcci alle *Bacchidi* di Plauto." In R. Raffaelli and A. Tontini, eds. *Bacchides (Sarsina, 9 settembre 2000)*. Urbino: QuattroVenti. 51–70.

Barsby, J. 2004. "Actors and Act-Divisions in *Poenulus* and its Greek Original." In T. Baier, ed. *Studien zu Plautus'* Poenulus. ScriptOralia 127. Tübingen: Gunter Narr. 93–111.

Beacham, R. 1991. *The Roman Theatre and Its Audience*. Cambridge, MA: Harvard UP.

Beare, W. 1964. *The Roman Stage: A Short History of Latin Drama in the Time of the Republic*. 3rd ed. London: Methuen.

Bernstein, F. 2011. "Complex Rituals: Games and Processions in Republican Rome." In J. Rupke, ed. *A Companion to Roman Religion*. Hoboken, NJ: Wiley-Blackwell. 222–34.

Blume, H. 2004. "Hanno und das Punische Personal im *Poenulus*." In T. Baier, ed. *Studien zu Plautus'* Poenulus. ScriptOralia 127. Tübingen: Gunter Narr. 203–14.

Brinkhoff, J. 1935. *Woordspeling bij Plautus*. Nijmegen: Berkhout.

Brotherton, B. 1926. *The Vocabulary of Intrigue in Roman Comedy*. Menasha, WI: George Banta Publishing Company.

Brown, P. 2002. "Actors and Actor-Managers at Rome in the time of Plautus and Terence." In P. Easterling and E. Hall, eds. *Greek and Roman Actors: Aspects of an Ancient Profession*. Cambridge: Cambridge UP. 225–37.

Capozza, M. 1966. *Movimenti servili nel mondo romano in età repubblicana, I Dall 501 al 184 a.Cr.* Rome: L'Erma.

Chahoud, A. 2010. "Idiom(s) and Literariness in Classical Literary Criticism." In E. Dickey and A. Chahoud, eds. *Colloquial and Literary Latin*. Cambridge: Cambridge UP. 42–64.

Christenson, D., ed. 2000. *Plautus: Amphitruo*. Cambridge: Cambridge UP.

Christenson, D., trans. 2008. *Plautus. Four Plays: Casina, Amphitryon, Captivi, Pseudolus*. Newburyport, MA: Focus.

Clackson, J. 2011. "The Social Dialects of Latin." In J. Clackson, ed. *A Companion to the Latin Language*. Oxford: Wiley-Blackwell. 503–26.

Coarelli, F. 1985. *Il foro Romano II: Periodo repubblicano e augusteo*. Rome: Quasar.

Cohee, P. 1994. "Instauratio Sacrorum." *Hermes* 122: 451–68.

Damen, M. 1992. "Translating Scenes: Plautus' Adaptation of Menander's *Dis Exapaton*." *Phoenix* 46: 205–31.

de Melo, W. 2007. *The Early Latin Verb System: Archaic Forms in Plautus, Terence, and Beyond*. Oxford: Oxford UP.

de Melo, W. 2010. "Possessive Pronouns in Plautus." In E. Dickey and A. Chahoud, eds. *Colloquial and Literary Latin*. Cambridge: Cambridge UP. 71–99.

de Melo, W. 2011. "The Language of Roman Comedy." In J. Clackson, ed. *A Companion to the Latin Language*. Oxford: Wiley-Blackwell. 321–43.

Dobrov, G. 2001. *Figures of Play: Greek Drama and Metafictional Poetics*. Oxford: Oxford UP.

Dodwell, C. 2000. *Anglo-Saxon Gesture and the Roman Stage*. Cambridge: Cambridge UP.

Dover, K. 1972. *Aristophanic Comedy*. Berkeley, CA: U of California P.

Duckworth, G. 1994. *The Nature of Roman Comedy: A Study in Popular Entertainment*. 2nd ed. Norman, OK: U of Oklahoma P.

Dutsch, D. 2004. "Female Furniture: A Reading of Plautus' *Poenulus* 1141–6." *Classical Quarterly* 54.2: 625–29.

Dutsch, D. 2007. "Gestures in the Manuscripts of Terence and Late Revivals of Literary Drama." *Gesture* 7: 39–71.

Dutsch, D. 2008. *Feminine Discourse in Roman Comedy: On Echoes and Voices*. Oxford: Oxford UP.

Faller, S. 2004. "Punisches im *Poenulus*." In T. Baier, ed. *Studien zu Plautus' Poenulus*. ScriptOralia 127. Tübingen: Gunter Narr. 163–202.

Fantham, E. 2004. "Maidens in Other-Land or Broads Abroad: Plautus' *Poenulae*." In T. Baier, ed. *Studien zu Plautus' Poenulus*. ScriptOralia 127. Tübingen: Gunter Narr. 235–51.

Fontaine, M. 2010. *Funny Words in Plautine Comedy*. Oxford: Oxford UP.

Fortson, B. IV. 2008. *Language and Rhythm in Plautus: Synchronic and Diachronic Studies*. Berlin: de Gruyter.

Fraenkel, E. 2007. *Plautine Elements in Plautus*. Trans. T. Drevikovsky and F. Muecke. Oxford: Oxford UP.

Franko, G. 1994. "The Use of *Poenus* and *Carthaginiensis* in Early Latin Literature." *Classical Philology* 89.2: 153–58.

Franko, G. 1995. "Incest and Ridicule in the *Poenulus* of Plautus." *Classical Quarterly* 45.1: 250–52.

Franko, G. 1996. "The Characterization of Hanno in Plautus' *Poenulus*." *American Journal of Philology* 117.3: 425–52.

Gaertner, J. 2010. "The Style of the *Bellum Hispaniense* and the Evolution of Roman Historiography." In E. Dickey and A. Chahoud, eds. *Colloquial and Literary Latin*. Cambridge: Cambridge UP. 243–54.

Glare, P. G. W., ed. 2006. *Oxford Latin Dictionary.* Rev. ed. Oxford: Clarendon P.

Goldberg, S. 1998. "Plautus on the Palatine." *Journal of Roman Studies* 88: 1–20.

Goldberg, S. 2005. *Constructing Literature in the Roman Republic: Poetry and its Reception.* Cambridge: Cambridge UP.

Goldberg, S., ed. 2013. *Terence: Hecyra.* Cambridge: Cambridge UP.

Goldsworthy, A. 2000. *The Punic Wars.* London: Cassell.

González Vázquez, C. 2001. "El léxico del 'engaño' en la comedia plautina." In C. Moussy, ed. *De lingua latina novae quaestiones: actes du Xe colloque international de linguistique latine. Paris, Sèvres, 19–23 avril 1999.* Louvain: Peeters. 801–13.

Gowers, E. 1993. *The Loaded Table: Representations of Food in Roman Literature.* Oxford: Clarendon Press.

Gratwick, A. 1971. "Hanno's Punic Speech in the *Poenulus* of Plautus." *Hermes* 99: 25–45.

Gratwick, A. 1972. "Plautus, *Poenulus* 967–981: Some Notes." *Glotta* 50: 228–33.

Gratwick, A. 1982. "Light Drama." In E. Kenney, ed. *Latin Literature: Cambridge History of Classical Literature.* Vol. 2. Cambridge: Cambridge UP. 93–127.

Gratwick, A., ed. 1993. *Plautus: Menaechmi.* Cambridge: Cambridge UP.

Gruen, E. 1992. *Culture and National Identity in Republican Rome.* Ithaca, NY: Cornell UP.

Gruen, E. 2011. *Rethinking the Other in Antiquity.* Princeton, NJ: Princeton UP.

Gsell, S. 1924. *Histoire ancienne de l'Afrique du Nord.* Vol. 2. 3rd ed. Paris: Librarie Hachette.

Hall, E. 1989. *Inventing the Barbarian: Greek Self-Definition through Tragedy.* Oxford: Clarendon P.

Halla-aho, H. and Kruschwitz, P. 2010. "Colloquial and Literary Language in Early Roman Tragedy." In E. Dickey and A. Chahoud, eds. *Colloquial and Literary Latin.* Cambridge: Cambridge UP. 127–53.

Halporn, J., Ostwald, M., and Rosenmeyer, T. 1994. *The Meters of Greek and Latin Poetry.* Indianapolis: Hackett.

Hammond, M., Mack, A., and Moskalew, W., eds. 1963. *Plautus: Miles Gloriosus.* Rev. ed. Cambridge, MA: Harvard UP.

Handley, E. 1968. *Menander and Plautus: A Study in Comparison.* London: H. K. Lewis.

Handley, E. 1997. "Menander, *Dis Exapaton.*" In E. Handley and U. Wartenburg, eds. *The Oxyrhynchus Papyri.* Vol. 64. London: Egypt Exploration Society. 14–42.

Harrison, S. 2010. "*Sermones deorum*: Divine Discourse in Virgil's *Aeneid.*" In E. Dickey and A. Chahoud, eds. *Colloquial and Literary Latin.* Cambridge: Cambridge UP. 266–78.

Henderson, J. 1994. "Hanno's Punic Heirs: Der Poenulusneid des Plautus." *Ramus* 23: 24–54.

Hoyos, D., ed. 2011. *A Companion to the Punic Wars*. Malden, MA: Wiley-Blackwell.

Hurka, F. 2013. "Plautus und die Erschaffung des Zuschauers: Publikumsnormierung und narrative Perspectivensteuerung im Prolog des *Poenulus*." In T. Moore and W. Polleichtner, eds. *Form und Bedeutung im lateinischen Drama/Form and Meaning in Latin Drama. Bochumer altertumswissenschaftliches Colloquium* 95. Trier: Wissenschaftlicher Verlag Trier.

James, S. Forthcoming. *Women in New Comedy*.

Jeppesen, S. 2013. "Performing Religious Parody in Plautine Comedy." Ph.D. Thesis. Santa Barbara: U of California at Santa Barbara.

Jocelyn, H. 1990. "Plautus, *Poenulus* 200–202 and the *ballistarium*." *Liverpool Classical Monthly* 15: 5–8.

Johnston, P. 1980. "*Poenulus* I, 2 and Roman Women." *Transactions of the American Philological Association* 110: 143–59.

Johnstone, K. 1979. *Impro: Improvisation and the Theatre*. London: Faber and Faber.

Jones, L. and Morey, C. 1930–31. *The Miniatures of the Manuscripts of Terence Prior to the Thirteenth Century*. Princeton, NJ: Princeton UP.

Joshel, S. 1986. "Nurturing the Master's Child: Slavery and the Roman Child-Nurse." *Signs* 12: 3–22.

Karakasis, E. 2005. *Terence and the Language of Roman Comedy*. Cambridge: Cambridge UP.

Kay, N. 2010. "Colloquial Latin in Martial's Epigrams." In E. Dickey and A. Chahoud, eds. *Colloquial and Literary Latin*. Cambridge: Cambridge UP. 318–30.

Krahmalkov, C. 1970. "The Punic Speech of Hanno." *Orientalia* 39: 52–74.

Krahmalkov, C. 1988. "Observations on the Punic Monologue of Hanno in the *Poenulus*." *Orientalia* 57: 55–66.

Lancel, S. 1999. *Hannibal*. Malden, MA: Blackwell.

Lefevre, E. 2004. "Plautus' *Poenulus* zwischen *Néa* und Stegreifspiel." In T. Baier, ed. *Studien zu Plautus' Poenulus*. ScriptOralia 127. Tübingen: Gunter Narr. 9–59.

Lefkowitz, M. 2012. *The Lives of the Greek Poets*. 2nd ed. Baltimore: Johns Hopkins UP.

Leigh, Matthew. 2004. *Comedy and the Rise of Rome*. Oxford: Oxford UP.

Lewis, C. and Short, C., eds. 1879. *A Latin Dictionary Founded on Andrews' Edition of Freund's Latin Dictionary*. Oxford: Clarendon P.

Lindsay, W. 2010. *The Latin Language: An Historical Account of Latin Sounds, Stems and Flexions*. Cambridge: Cambridge UP. Digital reprint of 1894 edition published by the Clarendon Press.

Loomis, W. 1998. *Wages, Welfare Costs, and Inflation in Classical Athens*. Ann Arbor, MI: U of Michigan P.

Lowe, J. 1988. "Plautus *Poenulus* I 2." *Bulletin of the Institute of Classical Studies* 35: 101–10.

Lowe, J. 1990. "Plautus' Choruses." *Rheinisches Museum* 133: 274–97.

Lowe, J. 2004. "Plautus' Expansion of Milphio's Rôle." In T. Baier, ed. *Studien zu Plautus' Poenulus.* ScriptOralia 127. Tübingen: Gunter Narr. 253–65.

Lowe, N. 2007. *Comedy. Greece & Rome* New Surveys in the Classics 37. Cambridge: Cambridge UP.

Maltby, R. 1979. "Linguistic Characterization of Old Men in Terence." *Classical Philology* 74: 136–47.

Maltby, R. 1995. "The Distribution of Greek Loan-words in Plautus." *Papers of the Leeds International Seminar* 8: 31–69.

Manuwald, G. 2004. "Die ungleichen Schwestern in Plautus' *Poenulus.*" In T. Baier, ed. *Studien zu Plautus' Poenulus.* ScriptOralia 127. Tübingen: Gunter Narr. 215–33.

Manuwald, G. 2011. *Roman Republican Theatre.* Cambridge: Cambridge UP.

Marshall, C. 1993. "Status Transactions in Aristophanes' *Frogs.*" *Text and Presentation: Journal of the Comparative Drama Conference* 14: 57–61.

Marshall, C. 2006. *The Stagecraft and Performance of Roman Comedy.* Cambridge: Cambridge UP.

Marshall, C. 2011. "Livy's Census Data and Death in the Hannibalic War: A Note on Plautine Audiences." Lecture. Annual Meeting of the American Philological Association. San Antonio, TX. January 9.

Maurach, G. 1988. *Der Poenulus des Plautus.* Heidelberg: Carl Winter.

Maurice, L. 2004. "The Punic, the Crafty Slave and the Actor: Deception and Metatheatricality in the *Poenulus.*" In T. Baier, ed. *Studien zu Plautus' Poenulus.* ScriptOralia 127. Tübingen: Gunter Narr. 267–90.

McCarthy, K. 2000. *Slaves, Masters, and the Art of Authority in Plautine Comedy.* Princeton, NJ: Princeton UP.

McGinn, T. 2004. *The Economy of Prostitution in the Roman World: A Study of Social History and the Brothel.* Ann Arbor, MI: U of Michigan P.

Mendelsohn, C. 1907. *Studies in the Word-Play in Plautus.* Philadelphia: U of Pennsylvania P.

Miller, P., ed. 2005. *Latin Verse Satire: An Anthology and Critical Reader.* London: Routledge.

Moodie, E. 2009. "Old Men and Metatheatre in Terence: Terence's Dramatic Competition." *Ramus* 38.2: 145–73.

Moore, T. 1988. *The Theater of Plautus: Playing to the Audience.* Austin: U of Texas P.

Moore, T. 2004. "Music in a Quiet Play." In T. Baier, ed. *Studien zu Plautus' Poenulus.* ScriptOralia 127. Tübingen: Gunter Narr. 139–61.

Moore, T. 2012. *Music in Roman Comedy.* Cambridge: Cambridge UP.

Muecke, F. 1986. "Plautus and the Theater of Disguise." *Classical Antiquity* 5: 216–29.

Palmer, R. 1997. *Rome and Carthage at Peace*. Historia Einzelschriften 113. Stuttgart: Franz Steiner.

Parker, H. 1989. "Crucially Funny or Tranio on the Couch." *Transactions of the American Philological Association* 119: 233–46.

Petrone, G. 1983. *Teatro Antico e Inganno: Finzioni Plautine*. Palermo: Palumbo.

Poccetti, P. 2010. "Greeting and Farewell Expressions as Evidence for Colloquial Language: Between Literary and Epigraphical Texts." In E. Dickey and A. Chahoud, eds. *Colloquial and Literary Latin*. Cambridge: Cambridge UP. 100–26.

Prag, J. 2006. "Poenus Plane Est—But Who Were the 'Punickes'?" *Papers of the British School at Rome* 74: 1–37.

Questa, C. 1967. *Introduzione alla Metrica di Plauto*. Bologna: Ricardo Pàtron.

Questa, C. 2007. *La Metrica de Plauto e di Terenzio*. Urbino: QuattroVenti.

Rawson, E. 1993. "Freedmen in Roman Comedy." In R. Scodel, ed. *Theater and Society in the Classical World*. Ann Arbor, MI: U of Michigan P. 215–33.

Reinhardt, T. 2010. "Syntactic Colloquialism in Lucretius." In E. Dickey and A. Chahoud, eds. *Colloquial and Literary Latin*. Cambridge: Cambridge UP. 203–28.

Richlin, A. 1995. "Making Up a Woman: The Face of Roman Gender." In H. Eilberg-Schwartz and W. Doniger, eds. *Off With Her Head! The Denial of Women's Identity in Myth, Religion, and Culture*. Berkeley: U of California P. 185–213.

Richlin, A. 2005. *Rome and the Mysterious Orient*. Berkeley: U of California P.

Richlin, A. 2006. "Roman Comedy and the Near East: Geopolitics and Cultural Work." The Thirty-Seventh Annual Gail A. Burnett Lecture in Classics. San Diego: San Diego State U Department of Classics and Humanities.

Richlin, A. 2014. "Talking to Slaves in the Plautine Audience." *Classical Antiquity* 33.1: 174–226.

Röllig, W. 1980. "Das Punische im Römische Reich." In G. Neumann and J. Untermann, eds. *Die Sprachen im Römischen Reich der Kaiserzeit*. Köln: Rheinland-Verlag. 285–99.

Rosivach, V. 1983. "The *Aduocati* in the *Poenulus* and the *Piscatores* in the *Rudens*." *Maia* 35: 83–93.

Saunders, C. 1909. *Costume in Roman Comedy*. New York: Columbia UP.

Scafuro, A. 1997. *The Forensic Stage: Settling Disputes in Graeco-Roman New Comedy*. Cambridge: Cambridge UP.

Schmidt, W. 1960. "Die sprachlichen Mittel des Komischen bei Plautus." (Microform) Ph.D. Thesis. Tübingen: Eberhard Karls Universität.

Segal, E. 1968. *Roman Laughter: The Comedy of Plautus*. Cambridge, MA: Harvard UP.

Sharrock, A. 2009. *Reading Roman Comedy: Poetics and Playfulness in Plautus and Terence*. Cambridge: Cambridge UP.

Sihler, A. 1995. *New Comparative Grammar of Greek and Latin.* Oxford: Oxford UP.

Slater, N. 1985. *Plautus in Performance: The Theatre of the Mind.* Princeton, NJ: Princeton UP.

Slater, N. 1990. "*Amphitruo, Bacchae* and Metatheatre." *Lexis* 6: 101–25.

Slater, N. 1992. "Plautine Negotiations: The *Poenulus* Prologue Unpacked." *Yale Classical Studies* 29: 131–46.

Slater, N. 2002. *Spectator Politics: Metatheatre and Performance in Aristophanes.* Philadelphia: U of Pennsylvania P.

Slater, N. 2004. "Slavery, Authority, and Loyalty: The Case of Syncerastus." In T. Baier, ed. *Studien zu Plautus' Poenulus.* ScriptOralia 127. Tübingen: Gunter Narr. 291–98.

Smith, M., ed. 1975. *Petronii Arbitri Cena Trimalchionis.* Oxford: Oxford UP.

Starks, J., Jr. 2000. "*Nullus Me Est Hodie Poenus Poenior*: Balanced Ethnic Humor in Plautus' *Poenulus.*" *Helios* 27.2: 163–86.

Starks, J., Jr. et al. 1997a. *Latin Laughs: A Production of Plautus' Poenulus.* Student Edition. Wauconda, IL: Bolchazy.

Starks, J., Jr. 1997b. *Latin Laughs: A Production of Plautus' Poenulus.* Teacher Edition. Wauconda, IL: Bolchazy.

Steinby, E., ed. 1993. *Lexicon Topographicum Urbis Romae. I: A-C.* Rome: Quasar.

Stewart, R. 2012. *Plautus and Roman Slavery.* Malden, MA: Wiley-Blackwell.

Syed, Y. 2005. "Romans and Others." In S. Harrison, ed. *Companion to Latin Literature.* Oxford: Oxford UP. 360–71.

Sznycer, M. 1967. *Les passages puniques en transcription latine dans le 'Poenulus' de Plaute.* Paris: Klincksieck.

Tarrant, R. 1983. "Plautus." In L. Reynolds et al., eds. *Texts and Transmission: A Survey of the Latin Classics.* Oxford: Clarendon P. 302–7.

Taylor, H., trans. 1995. *The Weevil.* In D. Slavitt and P. Bovie, eds. *Plautus: The Comedies.* Vol. 1. Baltimore: Johns Hopkins UP. 319–73.

Taylor, L. 1937. "Opportunities for Dramatic Performances in the Time of Plautus and Terence." *Transactions and Proceedings of the American Philological Association* 68: 284–304.

Thompson, F. 2003. *The Archaeology of Greek and Roman Slavery.* London: Duckworth.

Traina, A. 1989. "L'ambiguo invito (*As.* 5, *Poen.* 15)." *Poeti latini e neolatini* 3: 71–74.

Wallace-Hadrill, A. 2008. *Rome's Cultural Revolution.* Cambridge: Cambridge UP.

Welsh, J. 2007. "Plautus, *Poenulus* 16." *Hermes* 135: 109–11.

Welsh, J. 2009. "The *Balli(o)starium*: Plautus, *Poenulus* 200–2." *Mnemosyne* 62: 94–99.

Williams, C. 2010. *Roman Homosexuality.* 2nd ed. Oxford: Oxford UP.

Woytek, E. 2004. "Zur Datierung des *Poenulus.*" In T. Baier, ed. *Studien zu Plautus' Poenulus.* ScriptOralia 127. Tübingen: Gunter Narr. 113–37.

Wright, J. 1974. *Dancing in Chains: The Stylistic Unity of the Comoedia Palliata.*
   PMAAR 25. Rome: American Academy in Rome.

Yon, A. 1940. "À propos du latin 'ludus.'" In A. Ernout, ed. *Mélanges de philologie,*
   de littérature et d'histoire anciennes offerts à Alfred Ernout. Paris: Klincksieck.
   389–95.

Zehnacker, H. 2000. "Les intentions de Plaute dans le *Poenulus.*" In E. Stärk and G.
   Vogt-Spira, eds. *Dramatische Wäldchen: Festschrift für Eckard Lefèvre zum 65*
   Geburtstag. Hildesheim: Olms. 415–30.

Zucchelli, B. 1964. *Le denominazioni dell'attore.* Brescia: Paedeia.

Index

Note: The following index covers the introduction and commentary, not the Latin text. All numbers listed are page numbers.

violence, 106–7, 123, 125–27, 134, 139, 151, 158, 194, 199

vocative, 124, 128, 130, 134, 197

women: as comic targets, 113–15, 118, 182–83; language of, 107, 128; spectators, 15, 94–95; worship of Venus, 110. *See also* Adelphasium, Anterastilis, Giddenis, nurse, prostitute

Zeus, 123, 174. *See also* Jupiter